THE WORLD GUIDE TO COOKING WITH
FRUIT & VEGETABLES

THE WORLD GUIDE TO COOKING WITH
FRUIT & VEGETABLES

JOHN GOODE

MACDONALD · LONDON

First published in 1973 by
Macdonald & Co. (Publishers) Ltd,
St Giles House, 49/50 Poland Street, London, W. 1
Copyright © John Goode 1973

ISBN 0 356 04416 5

Designed and photographed by David Hornblow Graphic Design
Recipe photographs by Kevin Gleeson
Set in 10/11 Monotype Times Series 327
Printed and bound in Hong Kong

CONTENTS

Introduction   vi

Metric Conversion   ix

Using Fruits and Vegetables   xi

Preparation of Fruit and Vegetables   xii

Cooking of Fruit and Vegetables   xii

Alphabetical list of Fruit and Vegetables   2

Index of Fruit and Vegetables   185

Index of Recipes   193

INTRODUCTION

W HEN the word 'revolution' has become commonplace
a remarkable change has swept through the fruit and
vegetable markets of the world. Walk through the crate-
stacked streets of London's Covent Garden and you'll see
yams and sweet potatoes, paw-paws and vegetable pears
alongside the traditional cabbages and potatoes, peaches and
cherries: at the other end of the world, in Paddy's Market in
Sydney, you'll now see aubergines and capsicums, fennel and
zucchini which were unknown there a decade ago. It's the
same in France and America and in many other parts of the
world. The fruit and vegetable stalls in downtown New York
or the small shops in the coloured quarter of Paris now
abound with an exciting array of exotic products which it
would have been impossible to find twenty years ago.

How has this happened? Mass emigration, such as West
Indians and Pakistanis to England; Puerto Ricans to the
U.S.A.; Mediterranean peoples to Australia; and Africans
to France—all these people have demanded fruit and
vegetables which the locals had never even heard of before.
And the advent of cheaper air-freight, of new methods of
preserving foods (such as deep-freezing and freeze-drying,
etc.) has made it possible for these new populations to
obtain their former staples and luxuries in their new
homelands.

But for older residents, these strange and wonderful fruits
and vegetables still pose problems. How many people are
game to ask a Jamaican how to use ackee? Or are able to
watch a New Guinea native show them the best way to cook
breadfruit? Or know a Lebanese well enough to learn how
pomegranate may be used in savoury dishes?

I have been fortunate. I've travelled widely, I've the hide of
a rhinoceros and the curiosity of a cat. Wherever I go, if I see
something new, I ask 'What is it? How can it be prepared for
eating? And in what ways can it be used?' The result may be
found in the following pages though not all this information
was obtained first-hand. For example, I had to visit the
Melbourne Herbarium to discover why *Monstera delicosa*
left a nasty after-taste in the mouth; and it was in a
Malaysian cookery book where I discovered how to
eliminate it.

People are now much more adventurous and catholic in their attitudes towards food and this is an attempt to communicate some of the many surprises and the wealth of strange facts which have never ceased to surprise me.

There is the versatility of the basic method of cooking spinach which may be applied to so many other forms of greens. And there are so many different types of dried beans, each with a different name, each likely to be listed in some recipe book as though the reader is supposed to know automatically what it is, and yet, with one exception, each is subject to identical treatment and preparation; and after trying those available, it would be an understatement to describe variations in the taste of these as subtle.

Parts of this book have been designed to answer many questions which, even if never uttered by readers, must have given them cause to wonder. While this book is comprehensive, it cannot be definitive. I have attempted to include most of the well-used or staple fruits and vegetables but a check of any botanical work on plants-used-by-man would show that it was impractical to include every known variety.

Names presented a problem. The 'chayotte' of Mexico is sold in Australia as the 'choko', or the 'chojo' in Jamaica. Only illustrations revealed that it has names ranging from the euphonious 'xuxu' in Portugal to 'vegetable pear' in England, which seemed the most aptly descriptive. Similarly, what is the difference between chicory and endive? A table had to be devised to illustrate the differences in varieties and the terminology in different countries.

Frequently, arbitrary decisions had to be made, and often unrelated to the appearance of the fruit or vegetable concerned. Synonyms are given, but in cases of doubt, readers are advised to make full use of the comprehensive index which includes every synonym listed.

Minor repetition has occurred where plants such as fennel rated a full entry as a vegetable but also warranted inclusion in the section on Herbs and Spices.

In every instance, indication has been given on the ways the fruit or vegetable can be prepared and used. Where possible, traditional recipes have been given for those which, if not uncommon, are still far from popular in many places.

Recipes for quinces came from Persia and mousaka (aubergines) from the Arabs (plus a special quick-to-make version from my old friend Peter Grose); and beans include the Mexican recipe for *chile can carne*.

Beyond identifying and stating briefly how the many fruits and vegetables may be used, the recipes reflect my own tastes for the traditional, the exotic and the unusual. It is hoped that readers don't find them too distant from the forms of cooking they normally practise.

John Goode
Sydney, Australia and London, England

EXPLANATION OF METRIC CONVERSIONS

I have attempted to assist cooks by including both imperial and metric measures. It must be emphasized that the metric measurements given are *not* direct conversions since this would mean including impractical measurements. Instead, I have adopted the approach recommended by the Metric Conversion Board and have used the most practical metric replacement. Thus, while one ounce may convert directly to 28·3 g the metric replacement is 30 g. The following tables give the recommended metric quantities.

Weights

½ oz replaced by	15 g	10 oz replaced by	315 g
1 oz ,, ,,	30 g	11 oz ,, ,,	345 g
2 oz ,, ,,	60 g	12 oz ,, ,,	375 g
3 oz ,, ,,	90 g	13 oz ,, ,,	410 g
4 oz ,, ,,	125 g	14 oz ,, ,,	440 g
5 oz ,, ,,	155 g	15 oz ,, ,,	470 g
6 oz ,, ,,	185 g	1 lb ,, ,,	500 g
7 oz ,, ,,	220 g	1½ lb ,, ,,	750 g
8 oz ,, ,,	250 g	2 lb ,, ,,	1 kg
9 oz ,, ,,	280 g	2½ lb ,, ,,	1·25 kg
		3 lb ,, ,,	1·5 kg

Canned Foods may vary in size following metric conversion. Using the table above, select a can closest to the equivalent metric weight of the can in the imperial units recipe.

Measures

Cups; Simply replace the standard 8 fl. oz cup by the standard metric 250 ml cup.

Spoons; Continue using the standard 20 ml tablespoon and 5 ml teaspoon. Although this gives a slightly reduced proportion of ingredients measured by spoons it should still give a good result.

¼ teaspoon	= 1·25 ml
½ teaspoon	= 2·5 ml
1 teaspoon	= 5 ml
1 tablespoon	= 20 ml

Fluids

	1 fl. oz replaced by			30 ml
	2 fl. oz ,, ,,	¼ metric cup		
	3 fl. oz ,, ,,			100 ml
	4 fl. oz ,, ,,	½ metric cup		
	5 fl. oz ,, ,,			150 ml
	6 fl. oz ,, ,,	¾ metric cup		
	7 fl. oz ,, ,,			200 ml
	8 fl. oz ,, ,,	1 metric cup		
½ pint	10 fl. oz ,, ,,	1¼ metric cups		
	12 fl. oz ,, ,,	1½ metric cups		
	14 fl. oz ,, ,,	1¾ metric cups		
¾ pint	15 fl. oz ,, ,,			475 ml
	16 fl. oz ,, ,,	2 metric cups		
1 pint	20 fl. oz ,, ,,	2½ metric cups		

Using Fruits and Vegetables

Fruits and vegetables can provide all the nutriment, vitamins and basic minerals needed by the human body, but this is no reason for anyone to become a vegetarian. The variety of these foods is endless and treated correctly, they enhance and improve every dish they are served with or the meals they contribute to.

In recent years, considerable research has been devoted to the preparation and cooking of fruit and vegetables so that their maximum vitamin content and flavour can be retained. These methods have been listed in this book and although they may clash with traditions still existing in some parts of the western world, it is worth noting that many of the 'new' methods have been practised for centuries, if not eons in the countries of Asia, notably China and Japan.

Vegetables may be used as part of a main dish, as a course in themselves, or as ingredients in a combination recipe. Often fruit and vegetables can be interchanged and it is difficult to define whether an avocado, for example, is gastronomically a fruit or a vegetable.

Such classification is pedantic. From a cook's viewpoint, the aim is to find the apt combination for every occasion.

In some places, many of the items treated in the text may not be readily available. However, remarkable improvements in food processing have resulted in canned, deep-frozen or quick-dried varieties of many fruits and vegetables becoming known in countries far from the places where they are grown. Traditionalists may object to using dried Chinese mushrooms, canned Jamaican ackee or rapidly dried peas and beans. However I see no objection to this, although obviously the fresh variety is preferable, and if possible, straight from the garden or farm.

Often gourmet and specialist shops (Chinese stores for instance) will have forms of fruit and vegetables unobtainable elsewhere.

An alternative is to grow your own. In places where they are not grown commercially at present, both fruit and vegetable varieties may be obtainable as seed, seedlings and saplings. Often these can be grown in the home garden.

Obvious starting points are the herb garden and planting and training espalier fruit trees.

Any fruit and vegetable picked only minutes before use has a flavour which is always lost in goods sold commercially. Those in shops are usually harvested days before. By the time they reach the table, they possess little of the flavour which was present when they were harvested.

Preparation

Always select fruit and vegetables which are crisp, look fresh and are brightly coloured. Green vegetables bought from shops often need reviving. Soak them in iced water for 30 minutes to attempt to restore some of their freshness. Before soaking, remove outer, damaged and discoloured leaves.

If a tablespoon of vinegar is added to 2 pints of cold water, this will also remove any insects from the inner leaves.

Do not peel root vegetables. Their vitamin content is usually close to the surface and to preserve this, wash under a cold tap to remove surface dirt, if necessary lightly scrubbing with a nail brush to remove soil in cracks. After cooking, they may then be peeled. Similarly, some other vegetables should be cooked whole and only cut afterwards.

When storing vegetables in a refrigerator, place them first in sealed plastic bags or in boxes with tightly fitting lids to prevent them becoming dry.

Cooking

Fruit and vegetables, depending on the variety, may be cooked in every possible way. However in all cases, the following principles should apply:

cook vegetables quickly so that they are crisp when served

water extracts vitamins so use the least amount of water

preferably, cook vegetables in their own juices, or with just a little butter or oil

juices remaining after vegetables have been cooked should be stored in a screw top jar, and kept in the refrigerator.

They may be added to soups, stews or the gravy from the meat.

Many different utensils can be utilized to cook vegetables but three are most important. They are:

1. A heavy saucepan with a thick bottom and a tightly-fitting lid. The thick base allows the whole saucepan to maintain an even heat and it reduces the tendency for the contents to burn. The tightly fitting lid reduces the amount of steam escaping and allows this to help in cooking the vegetables.
2. A heavy frying pan with a thick bottom. The advantages of this are the same as for the saucepan and such an implement is a joy to use compared with the pressed aluminium rubbish so often found in many kitchens today.
3. A suitable fireproof/ovenproof casserole or earthenware crock with a lid which may be used, either on top of the gas flame or electric elements, or within the oven.

Raw Tenderizing

In Asia, daikon (Japanese radishes) and carrots are tenderized only by sprinkling with salt to extract surplus fluids. They are then dried in a cloth or paper towel, quickly rinsed and dried again. Often, the Chinese and Japanese initially cut the vegetables into very small pieces i.e. matchsticks, dice, chips, before tenderizing. Eggplant may also be treated this way before cooking.

Steaming with Butter

A knob of butter is first placed in the bottom of the saucepan, the vegetables should be washed and shaken and placed in the saucepan which is then tightly covered. Cooking can be fairly rapid but the pan must be shaken constantly to prevent sticking or burning. With coarser greens such as cabbage and celery, first place in a collander and pour over boiling water to *scald* or *blanch* them. An alternative to the knob of butter can be a very small quantity of chicken or beef stock, or olive oil.

Stir Frying

In a frying pan, place just enough oil to cover the bottom of the pan when the oil has been heated. Vegetables should be cut into small pieces (matchsticks, etc.), placed in the hot oil and stirred and turned constantly. The hot oil seals the juices inside the vegetables and they become crisp outside and soft within. In this form of cooking, only fry small batches at a time and cook for about 1 minute.

With larger vegetables, such as beans, cauliflower fleurettes, *parboil* for 1–5 minutes before use, depending on their size. Parboiling is to drop the pieces or chunks into rapidly boiling salted water, but only for a minimum time.

Deep Frying

As above, the vegetables may be blanched or parboiled, then drained and dried. They are then deep fried in hot oil until lightly browned. Then drain and place in a saucepan with a little stock, some chopped herbs to suit (see *Herbs and Spices*, p. 72), salt, and a little wine. In this they are braised for 5 minutes, the vegetables are then removed and the liquid is thickened with a little flour and served as a sauce over them.

Pan Shaking

Main ingredients may first be marinated in wine to which has been added minced onion, ginger and salt (or other spices to suit). After marinating, drain then roll in flour and then in beaten egg. Cook in hot oil (or lard) shaking the pan constantly until the whole surface is lightly brown. Lower the heat, sprinkle the vegetables with stock and continue shaking and cooking until the liquid has evaporated.

French Pre-Cooked Vegetables

Prepare and cook vegetables until they are about nearly cooked. Remove from heat, place in a colander and run cold water over them until they are the same temperature as the cold water. Then replace them in the saucepan, cover with cold water and replace the lid. They may stand in this for several hours until they are needed. When required, drain and dry the vegetables, pour boiling water over them and heat until the water begins to simmer. At this point they should be hot enough to serve. If not, simmer for a few minutes until they are hot enough. Drain and place in serving dish with knobs of butter on them.

Types of Vegetables

Vegetables may be grouped as follows. Where possible, try to represent as many different groups in any menu.

Greens: leaf variety or leaves of root vegetables, rich in vitamin C

Roots: Wide range of tuberous roots which are edible. They include potatoes, carrots, parsnips, yams, etc.

Pulses: peas, beans and other 'podded' seeds. When dry, they are rich in protein and vitamin B

Onions: vegetables made up of concentric layers of skin and including leeks and garlic

Fungi: many varieties of which the best known are mushrooms.

Cooking Advice

Shred greens so that they will cook quickly

Cook root vegetables in their skins and peel after cooking

Never use bicarbonate of soda in vegetable cooking

Never boil greens in a lot of water

Never remove peas from their pods until a few minutes before cooking

Never overcook vegetables until they become mushy or soft

Abiu: *Lucuma; Caimito*

Tree of South America with edible fruit in the form of red capsules whose pulp is edible

Use: stewed
     grilled

Acacia: *Wattle Blossoms*

Blossoms of some forms of acacia (known as wattle in Australia) are used to flavour fritters and home-made liqueurs.

WATTLE FRITTERS

bunches of wattle (acacia) blossom	½ teaspoon salt
4 tablespoons rum or brandy	2 tablespoons beer
prepared batter	4 tablespoons water
For batter:	1 tablespoon brandy (optional) or rum
125 g — 4 oz. plain flour	2 egg whites, beaten stiffly
30 g — 1 oz. butter, melted	

To prepare blossoms: Cut off stalks and sprinkle bunches of blossoms with sugar. Pour over rum or brandy and soak for 30 minutes.

To prepare batter: Place flour, salt, and melted butter in a basin and mix thoroughly. Dilute with beer and then add warm water, mixing gently. When ready to use, fold in egg whites and add rum or brandy in which flowers were soaked.
    Dip flowers in batter, fry in deep oil or deep, very hot butter. Drain, sprinkle with sugar and serve on paper napkins.

Accoub

A form of thistle originally from Syria but now widely grown throughout the Mediterranean region. It is almost the perfect vegetable as its roots, shoots and buds are all edible and their flavour is reminiscent of both the globe artichoke and asparagus.
Preparation:

buds—parboil in salted boiling water, toss in butter and season with salt and pepper
shoots—cut when 6 inches long and cook like *asparagus*
roots—prepare and use like *salsify*

Achojcha: *Achojcho*

Edible fruits of a South American forest tree, found mainly in some inland provinces of Argentina.

Ackee: *Akee*

Edible pods of a small tree, related to the maple, originally from West Africa but now extensively grown in the West Indies. When unripe, the flesh is poisonous but when the pods open, they reveal a fleshy centre topped with a large black seed. The butter-yellow flesh is collected and used as a vegetable, its flavour is bland and not unlike the avocado. It may also be obtained canned.

Use: in *vinaigrette*.

Preparation: fresh—remove seed and the pink membraneous veins. Boil 20 minutes in salted water, or until tender.

ACKEE SAWFISH

Traditional Jamaican Dish
Serves: 3–4

250 g 375 g	8 oz. salt cod or ling or similar fish, soaked and flaked	1 × 12 oz. can ackee black pepper, freshly ground baked sweet potatoes
	rashers of bacon	1 avocado
	2 large onions	boiled green banana
	2 tomatoes	

Soak dried salt fish overnight in cold water. Drain and wash under cold tap. Fry bacon and then onions and tomato in fat from bacon and when cooked, add the fish, which should be flaked. Add 1 × 12 oz. can ackee, stir together and heat through. Sprinkle with freshly ground black pepper. Serve with baked sweet potato, a slice of avocado (raw) and boiled green banana (not plantain).

375 g

ACKEE PIES

Time: 50 minutes
Serves: 6 (as entrée)
Temperature: 425°F — 220°C

½ lb. prepared short pastry	6 ackee, cooked or canned	250 g
1 small onion	pepper to taste	
¼ lb. salt fish, washed, cooked and flaked	parsley to garnish oil for frying	125 g

Roll pastry into flat sheet and cut into circles. Fry onion and flaked fish and boiled ackee together in oil, well peppered. Crush ackee and fish to form a paste. Place spoonfuls of this filling into each circle, fold over pastry, seal edges with water and crimp with fork.
Bake in oven at 425°F for 20 minutes, pricking pies to let out air. Garnish with parsley. Serve hot or cold. — 220°C

ACKEE FLOAT

Serves: 4 (as entrée)

| 1 dozen ackee, prepared and cooked or contents 1 × 12 oz. can ackee | pepper to taste ½ pint oil 1 clove of garlic | 1¼ cups 375 g |
| 3 eggs | | |

Empty can and drain or cook ackee until tender, but not mushy. Beat eggs and season with pepper. Heat oil with crushed clove garlic until it is brown. Remove garlic, dip each peg of ackee into the egg and fry in the deep oil. Pour remaining egg in the oil, cook and drain. Serve ackee on the deep fried beaten egg.

Agi

See *Herbs and Spices*, p. 72.

Aguay

See *Berries* p. 24.

Aguncate

Peruvian type of gourd, with green shiny skin. When ripe, skin is easily removed to reveal flesh similar to avocado.

Use: raw, well-salted or like *avocado*.

Alecost

See *Herbs and Spices* p. 72.

Alectryon

Red fruit of New Zealand tree, prized for its delicious acid taste.

Use: raw or to flavour a refreshing cool drink.

Alisander

See *Herbs and Spices* p. 72.

Alliaria

See *Herbs and Spices* p. 72.

Allspice

See *Herbs and Spices* p. 72.

Almond

See *Nuts* p. 114.

Amaranth: *Chinese Amaranth*

Cultivated Italian plant whose tender young leaves are edible when cooked. In China, where it originated, it is known as 'Spinach of the East' and it is widely grown as one of the main green-leaf vegetables in the warmer areas of Asia.

Preparation: as for *spinach*.

Use: as for spinach.

Amazombe

Edible leaves of a weed grown in some countries of southern Africa. They may be eaten fresh or dried for winter use.

Preparation: as for *spinach*.

Ambarella: *Golden Hog* or *Otaheite Apple (or plum)*; *Spondias*; *Yellow Mombin*; *Jungli Amba* (India)

Fruit of Polynesian *Spondias* tree, grown throughout the Pacific and in many tropical areas including the West Indies and India. It is related to the mango but tougher. The flesh is firm, juicy and pale yellow, its pungent, resinous sub-acid flavour is reminiscent of an apple. It is considered inferior to imbas or imbus.

Preparation: remove peel and remove flesh from skinny oval seed.

Use: unripe—in curries and pickles
ripe—eat raw, in jam or preserves, like *mango*

AMBARELLA AND CHICKEN

Serves: 4
220°C Temperature: 425°F

For stewed ambarella

1 kg	6 ambarellas, washed and sliced	2 lb. boned chicken, cut into pieces for frying
	oil for frying	salt to taste
	1 clove garlic	1 teaspoon black pepper
60 g	1 spring onion, chopped	2 oz. butter
250 g	3 onions, sliced	½ lb. stewed ambarella
	fresh breadcrumbs	6 tablespoons honey
30 g 250 g	salt and seasoned pepper	½ lb. potatoes, cooked, mashed and creamed
	1 oz. butter	

Prepare ambarella: fry ambarellas in oil in which crushed garlic has first been fried dark brown. Add spring onion and onions and fry. Drain then place a layer of ambarella, layer of onion and layer of breadcrumbs in a saucepan. Season with salt and pepper, dot with butter, apply tightly fitting lid, and cook gently for 30 minutes.

Season chicken with salt and pepper and brown in butter for 10 minutes using a heavy frying pan. Place stewed ambarellas in bottom of casserole dish. Place chicken pieces on top and brush with honey. Top with creamed potatoes and dot with butter. Bake in hot oven
220°C (425°F) until potato is brown.

Anchovy Pear

See p. 136.

Angelica

See *Herbs and Spices* p. 72.

Anise

See *Herbs and Spices* p. 72.

Apples

Fruit of a widespread botanical group of trees belonging to the genus *Pyrus* varying in size from small, very sour and wild crab apples to highly cultivated varieties noted for their particular qualities. In general, apples are classed into two groups: cooking apples are sharply acid and have a flesh which becomes soft and pulpy when cooked; dessert or eating apples are usually smaller, have darker skins and are sweet and fragrant. However, there are also varieties such as the Granny Smith which are equally good for the table and for cooking. Tastes in apples vary between markets. British people prize dessert apples with a keen aromatic flavour and with a crisp flesh. In the opinion of many, this might be epitomized by Cox's Orange Pippin. American apples usually possess a strong colour and shining skins. They are sweet and fragrant but rarely possess the aromatic qualities sought by the British. American apples have a softer texture and when cooked, retain their shape. Sweet apples become tough and leathery when cooked.

Preparation: eat dessert apples raw with skin. For cooking, peel and core and cut into appropriate pieces.

Use: dessert apples—
raw in fruit salads and jellies
grated in vegetable salads
cooking apples—
baked whole
made into pulp for flans and cake fillings
for compotes
in many other forms of prepared desserts

APPLE AND HORSERADISH SALAD

4 oz. grated horseradish	8 oz. apples	125 g	250 g
1 oz. sugar	1 dessertspoon olive oil	30 g	
4 tablespoons white vinegar	freshly ground black pepper		

Finely grate horseradish and mix with sugar and vinegar. Peel apples and slice them, then sprinkle with oil and pepper. Mix together horseradish and apples and serve with roast beef.

FRIED APPLE RINGS

Time: overnight
Serves: 4

1 lb. apples, peeled, cored	1 teaspoon cinnamon	500 g
and sliced into rings	1 tablespoon flour	
2 tablespoons sugar	2 tablespoons beer	
1 glass of brandy	butter for frying	

Place apple rings in a dish and sprinkle with 1 tablespoon of sugar. Cover with brandy and stand overnight. Mix cinnamon, remaining sugar and flour together and gradually add beer. Coat apples in this mixture, fry in butter and serve straight from the pan.

APPLE AND CREAM CHEESE TART

Serves: 6

9 inch diameter prepared	8 oz. packet cream	22 cm	250 g
and cooked pastry case	cheese		
For filling:	2 oz. sugar		60 g
4 oz. sugar	*For glaze:*	125 g	
juice of half a lemon	2 tablespoons red currant		
½ pint water	(or cranberry) jelly	1¼ cups	
3 cooking apples, peeled,	1 tablespoon lemon juice		
cored and cut in halves	2 teaspoons water		

To make filling: place sugar, lemon juice and water in a saucepan, bring to boil and reduce until a syrup. Reduce heat, add apples and cook until just tender. Remove apples and drain. Cream the cheese and sugar then spread over the bottom of the pastry case. Arrange cooked and drained apple halves, cut side down, on the cheese.

To make glaze: place red currant jelly, lemon juice and water in a saucepan and stir over a gentle heat until it is dissolved. Increase heat and gently reduce until slightly thickened but not too thick. Spoon glaze over apples, cool, then chill in refrigerator and serve.
See recipes for *Red Cabbage and Apples* p. 34., *Baked Parsnips and Apples* p. 132, *Carrots, Apples and Cheese* p. 38, *Sloe and Apple Jelly* p. 169.

Crab Apple

Wild apple, originally from Siberia, northern China and Manchuria, cultivated mainly for its flowers. The small, bitter fruit is suitable only for making jelly or pickling whole as a spiced fruit.

CRAB APPLE JELLY

6 lb. crab apples	juice of 2 lemons,	3 kg
1 lb. sugar to each pint	strained	500 g
of juice		

Wash apples, cut in quarters and remove cores. Place in preserving pan and cover with cold water. Boil for 45 minutes, strain through a muslin bag and measure the juice.

Add 1 lb. sugar to each pint of juice and boil together for another 45 minutes, stirring constantly. Add strained lemon juice just before removing from heat. Test for gel on a cold spoon to determine when sufficiently cooked. Store in sterilized bottles.

500 g

Custard Apple: *Corossol*

Fruit of various forms of the *Anona* tree, originally from South America and the West Indies but now grown in many tropical and sub-tropical countries. The more common varieties are:

Alligator or *Monkey Apple*

An inferior variety, claimed by some to be poisonous. Grown in South America and West Africa.

Bullock's Heart

Tropical American variety, also grown in India and elsewhere. Large somewhat strawberry shaped fruit weighing up to 8–10 lb. with skin covered with light green soft prickles. Flesh has sour quality with an aroma reminiscent of black currants. Used to make refreshing beverage.

4–5 kg

Cherimoya: Peruvian Custard Apple

Grown in Ecuador, Peru and cultivated in West Africa. Fruit grows best in an oceanic climate at altitudes of 1,000 feet. Its flavour and texture are considered the best of the whole group of custard apples. This type is grown commercially in New South Wales, Australia.

334 m

Ilama

Variety of custard apple, grown in Guatemala, resembling the cherimoya in size and flavour and considered particularly delicious.

Monkey Apple

See above.

Soncoya

Variety grown throughout central America from Mexico to Panama, taste reminiscent of the mango and particularly aromatic.

Soursop: Prickly West Indian Custard Apple

Originally from West Indies, this elongated fruit possesses a purple skin marked with small pimples. Its flavour is similar to black currants and it grows to 5 lb. Used to make sherbets and other drinks. Eaten raw or used in tropical fruit salad.

2·5 kg

Sweetsop: Scaly or Sugar Apple; Indian Custard Apple

Egg-shaped fruit with thick segmented rind, and luscious pulp. Used in India to flavour rice puddings.

Skin of all is green or purply green, the flesh white

with black or brown seeds. When ripe, the flesh is juicy and of varying sweetness with a fragrant sour-sweet taste.

Use: remove ripe flesh from skin and seeds and eat raw
crush flesh and mix with five times its volume of water, chill in refrigerator and serve as a summer drink
in fruit salads, with oranges, strawberries, melon and raspberries, nectarine and blueberries
to flavour desserts

Kangaroo Apple

Yellow, egg-shaped fruit of Australian grass, *Solanum aviculare*. It has a mealy texture and sour-sweet flavour.

Love Apple

See *Tomato* p. 175.

Malay Apple: *Ohia; Mountain Apple*

Large fruit, similar to an apple, grown on a variety of myrtle tree in Malaya and the tropical south Pacific area. Fruit varies from white to crimson and is 2–3 inches long. See also *Eugenia* p. 56.

5–8 cm

Use: for desserts

Rose or Brush Apple

Variety of Jambolan grown in Malaya. Large edible berry with a fragrance said to resemble that of a rose.

Star Apple

Fruit of West Indian tree *Chrysophyllum cainito*, about the size of an elongated orange with a soft thick skin which is purple. The flesh is light purple and after eating, leaves a delicious after-taste in the mouth.
Eat: remove skin and eat flesh.

Apricot

Small golden stone fruit with a velvety skin, originally a native of China and first cultivated in Europe in Armenia. Today it is widely grown in Mediterranean and sub-tropical countries and there are both dessert and cooking varieties. Major orchard countries are now Australia, California and South Africa with Spain and France's Loire Valley also being important suppliers to world markets. Available fresh, canned and dried.

Use: raw—when ripe. The skins may be eaten or peeled, according to taste.
    cooked—in compotes, dumplings, pies, ices, puddings and in salads

LAMB CHOPS AND APRICOTS

Serves: 5
Time: 1½ hours

		metric equivalent
2½ lb. forequarter lamb chops	⅔ cup dried apricots	1·25 kg
3 tablespoons oil	2 heaped tablespoons seed raisins	
½ teaspoon salt	2 oz. butter	60 g
pinch pepper	2 tablespoons water	
¼ teaspoon nutmeg	long grained rice, cooked for	
¼ teaspoon cinnamon	8 minutes only, sufficient	
3 tablespoons water	for 5 people	

Clean chops and trim fat. Heat oil and add salt, pepper, nutmeg and cinnamon. Sauté chops in seasoned oil until meat is brown on both sides. Add water and simmer 30 minutes. Cut each apricot in four pieces, and wash together with raisins. Melt 1 oz. butter in another frying pan and sauté fruit for 5 minutes, turning constantly. [30 g] Place 1 oz. melted butter and 2 tablespoons water in [30 g] bottom of fireproof dish. Add rice and arrange chops and fruit in layers above rice. Put lid on dish and cook for 10–15 minutes on top of stove at medium heat. Reduce flame to minimum and simmer a further 40 minutes.

APRICOTS IN BRANDY

Serves: 6–8 as dessert

12 large apricots	1 cup sugar
2 cups water	¼ cup brandy

Peel and stone apricots and cut in halves. Boil water and sugar for 10 minutes, skimming scum from surface.

Reduce to simmer, add fruit carefully and simmer until fruit has absorbed all syrup but is not burned. Sprinkle with brandy and cool. Chill in refrigerator and serve in chilled glasses.

APRICOT PUDDING-CAKE

		metric equivalent
½ loaf stale bread	1 teaspoon cinnamon	
2 oz. suet, finely shredded	6 dried apricots, soaked	60 g
4 oz. mixed fruit	and minced	125 g
½ cup brown sugar	1 egg, lightly beaten	
1 oz. mixed peel		30 g

Break bread into manageable pieces, place in basin and cover with water. Soak 30 minutes then strain and squeeze in a cloth to extract maximum water. Place in a bowl, break any lumps with a fork and mix well with suet, mixed fruit, brown sugar, mixed peel, cinnamon and apricots. Stir in egg and spoon mixture into a 7-inch [18 cm] cake tin. Bake in oven at 350°F for 1 hour or until top is [175°C] golden and a skewer will pierce it without any of the pudding adhering to it when removed. Serve hot with fresh cream. Can also be eaten cold as cake.
See recipe for *Pear and Apricot Flan* p. 136.

Chinese Apricot Plum

See p. 143.

Arachichu

Edible fruit of a South American tree.

Arbute

See *Berries* p. 24.

Arracacha: *Arracacia; Apio*

Edible root of a South American plant, used to make flour or cooked as yams or *sweet potatoes*. Starch extracted from these tubers is similar to arrowroot.

Preparation: as for *yams*.

Use: fried, boiled or baked

Arrowhead

Group of plants, originally from China but now grown in many countries, with leaves shaped like an arrowhead. The roots are edible and starchy.

Artichokes

Globe Artichokes: *True or French Artichokes*

Buds of a perennial plant of the thistle family which have beautiful green and purple shades but less spines than most thistles. They grow wild in southern Europe and North Africa but are now cultivated extensively, particularly in California. The edible parts are the succulent base of the surrounding flower scales and the core of the bud or 'choke'. Select young artichokes with close, fleshy scales, and little or no purple.

Preparation: cut off stem and larger outside scales or leaves. Rub cut with lemon to prevent it blackening. Snip away tip of each leaf with scissors or sharp knife to within two inches of base. If desired, remove inner 'choke' for separate use or tie thread around widest part of the head. Plunge head in fast boiling water to which has been added 1 teaspoon vinegar or lemon and 1 teaspoon of salt. This preserves the colour. Simmer 15–20 minutes, testing with a fork until bottom is tender.

To eat: pull off leaf; dip end into melted butter or mayonnaise. Scrape base of leaf between teeth to skim off edible part, discard rest. When all outer leaves have been pulled, cut out fuzzy centre or 'choke' with spoon or fork and discard. Cut remaining heart into chunks, dip in butter, and eat. Serve 1 artichoke a person.

Use: heads without chokes may be eaten by pulling out scales and eating
  hot with butter or Hollandaise sauce
  cold in vinaigrette
  baked
  fried
  stuffed

30 g

FRIED GLOBE ARTICHOKES

prepared artichokes (1 a serve)	crushed garlic to taste
1 oz. butter	oregano

Place chokes in bottom of wide saucepan with butter, in which garlic has been fried until soft. Fry until crisp underneath. Serve with butter poured over them and sprinkle with oregano.

STUFFED GLOBE ARTICHOKES

Serves: 6 as entrée

6 large artichokes	1½ cups mayonnaise
2 tablespoons vinegar	1 tablespoon chives, finely chopped
3 cups canned crab meat (or frozen shrimp or chicken)	1 tablespoon parsley, finely chopped
1½ cups celery, finely chopped	wedges of cheddar cheese
2 tablespoons green capsicum, finely chopped	

Prepare and cook artichokes as described above, removing chokes and plunging into boiling vinegar water. Simmer for 15–20 minutes. Drain upside down and spread leaves outwards. Mix crab, celery, capsicum, 1 cup mayonnaise, chives and parsley and then spoon this mixture into the artichokes. Top with remaining mayonnaise. Eat leaves first by dipping in mayonnaise and eat remaining stuffing with cheese wedges and artichoke hearts.

Japanese or Chinese Artichokes: *Chorogi; Knotroot*

Perennial plant of Asia cultivated for its edible roots and now grown in Europe and the U.S.A. Roots should be fresh, white and used soon after they are dug up. Otherwise they shrivel and lose flavour very quickly.

Preparation: place tubers with coarse salt into a cloth bag. Shake thoroughly, remove tubers, and wash to remove any remaining skin. Blanch in salted boiling water then sauté in butter but do not allow to brown. May also be boiled after blanching in minimum water for 20 minutes or until soft.

Use: as for *Jerusalem artichokes*
    as a vegetable
    as a garnish with roast beef
    with melted butter
    in white sauce

Jerusalem Artichokes

Delicately flavoured tubers or roots of a plant in the sunflower family. Originally from North America where they were cultivated by American Indians, the tubers were first brought to Europe in the seventeenth century. Most sources suggest the name 'Jerusalem' is a corruption of the Italian *girasole* meaning sunflower. However André Simon suggests that after arriving in France, the tubers were grown in Holland at Ter Neusen and that when they arrived in London, they were called *artischokappeln van Ter Neusen* which became anglicised as Jerusalem artichokes. When buying, choose the largest as there is much waste in the awkwardly shaped small tubers.

Preparation: wash thoroughly then scrub clean. Do not peel or pare. Then steam or boil in just enough water to cover them. This water should be saved as a base for artichoke soup. When cold, it will form a jelly and contains the best flavour of the artichokes. When the tubers are tender, rub off their skin. They take about 30 minutes to cook, longer if they are steamed or large tubers.

Use: with melted butter
    in white sauce (Béchamel)
    roasted or baked
    pickled
    with cheese sauce
    puréed
    in soufflés
    for soup

CURRIED JERUSALEM ARTICHOKES   *metric equivalent*

Time: 1½ hours
Serves: 6

1 large onion, peeled and chopped	10 oz. stock made from chicken stock cube or	1¼ cups
1 oz. cooking oil (olive preferably)	5 oz. stock from artichoke cooking and	30 ml 150 ml
1 dessertspoon plain flour	5 oz. coconut milk	150 ml
2 teaspoons curry powder	2 lb. artichokes, boiled,	1 kg
salt	drained and sliced	
cayenne pepper	1 tablespoon chutney	
	Boiled rice to serve	

Fry onion in oil until soft and golden, remove from heat. Stir in flour, curry powder, salt and cayenne into oil and onions. Add stock (and/or coconut milk) and simmer for 30 minutes. Place artichoke slices in curry sauce and leave over gentle heat for 30 minutes. Add chutney, simmer a few minutes then serve with boiled rice.

Asparagus

A member of the lily family, asparagus grows wild in many parts of Europe and western Asia. It has been cultivated since ancient times in the Middle East, Greece and Rome. There are two main forms obtainable. The French type has white fleshy stems with only the tips showing green. The other has slender green spikes which are cut close to the ground and tied in bundles. Preparation for both is the same.

Preparation: scrape or peel the stalks, wash and tie in modest sized bundles. Cook in plenty of salted boiling water (1½ teaspoons to 2 pints water) for   *5 cups* about 20 minutes with the stalks standing upright and the heads out of the water. Asparagus should not be overcooked as it becomes watery and tasteless. Drain thoroughly and serve as separate course with melted butter or Hollandaise sauce.

Use: hot or cold
    suggested garnishes—
        crumbled pieces of bacon
        toasted slivers of almond

sautéed mushrooms
minced garlic and chopped chives
horseradish
parmesan cheese
chopped hard-boiled egg
diced capsicums
sliced olives
salad dressing

See recipe for *Orange and Asparagus* p. 123, *Potato Salad with Asparagus Tips* p. 147.

Asparagus Bush

West African plant whose shoots are eaten. In the Camerouns and Gabon, natives also eat the leaves.

Preparation:
shoots—as with *asparagus*
leaves—boiled

Use: leaves—cooked, chopped and mixed with boiled rice

Asparagus Pea: *Yardlong Bean; Winged Pea; Catjang*

Plant of southern Europe, usually used for decorative purposes, whose thin green rectangular pods are edible. It has neither shoots like asparagus nor seed like peas. Pods are gathered when 2 inches long. They are tender and tasty but sometimes stringy.

5 cm

Preparation: simmer pods in a minimum of water for 10 minutes only. Serve with melted butter, seasoned with freshly ground black pepper and salt.

Use: as a vegetable to accompany meat, poultry or game as an entrée

Aubergine

See *Eggplant* p. 54

Avocado: *Aguacate; Alligator Pear*

Fruit of a tree originally grown in tropical America but now cultivated in Mexico, West Indies, U.S.A.,

Australia and other warm climates. The flavour is more like a vegetable than a fruit but its size and shape resemble a large pear. The skin is a rich dark green while the rich oily flesh is a much paler delicate green with a smooth bland taste and nutty flavour. Avocados are becoming increasingly popular as a base for an entrée or first-course dish, served on their own, or with other vegetables in salads. Ripe avocados yield to light pressure on skin. Avoid fruit with dark soft sunken spots on the skin. Avocados cannot be preserved.

Preparation: cut in half, remove stone and slit flesh without damaging skin. Often the flesh is removed from the skin and mixed with other ingredients; or served in a vinaigrette.

Use: fresh sprinkled with:
salt only
lime juice
white pepper
lemon juice and sugar

AVOCADO DIP
Mexico's classic Guacamole

1 very ripe avocado
1 tomato, skinned and seeded
pinch oregano
1 bunch spring onions, finely chopped

green chile sauce to taste
lemon juice to taste
salt to taste

Mash avocado flesh with a fork and blend in tomato, oregano, onions and chile sauce to taste. Use lemon juice to provide the right consistency and add plenty of salt.
Pomegranate seeds or fresh chopped coriander may be used as topping.

MALAYSIAN AVOCADO DESSERT
In Malaysia, avocado is used as a dessert
Serves: 2

½ cup

1 avocado, mashed, with skin preserved and halved
2 dessertspoons of sugar
4 oz. cream

Mash the avocado and blend in the sugar and cream. Fill the halved avocado skin with the mixture piled high and place in refrigerator until very cold.

AVOCADO SOUP

Time: 30 minutes
Serves: 6

1½ pints chicken broth	fresh cream	3¾ cups
2 ripe avocados	salt and pepper to taste	
½ pint sour cream	grated nutmeg	1¼ cups

Peel and stone avocados, mash flesh and add to chicken broth. Heat, then stir in sour cream. Sieve the mixture to eliminate any lumps, add salt and pepper and again heat but only so that it hardly simmers. Do not allow it to bubble or boil. Serve hot, top each plate with a spoon of fresh cream and sprinkle with grated nutmeg.

Azarole: *Neopolitan Medlar*

Fruit of a particular hawthorn tree, widely grown in the Mediterranean area. Berries are oval, reddish yellow and have a sweet, acid flavour.

Note: not all hawthorn fruit is edible.

Use: for fruit compote, jam making, to flavour liqueurs.

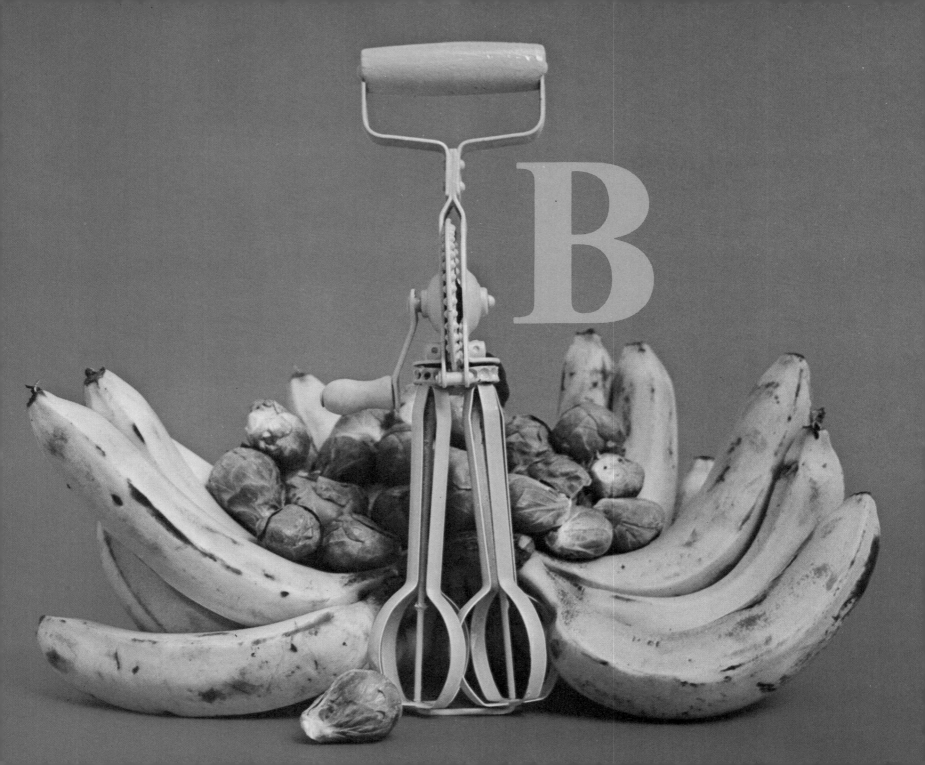

Badian

Edible fruit of an anise tree in China, said to be useful in dispelling flatulence.

Bael: *Bengal Quince*

Fruit of an Indonesian citrus tree, particularly sour.

Use: dried to make preserves or as a flavouring agent.

Balm

See *Herbs and Spices* p. 72.

Bamboo Shoots: *Jook Sun*

Prepared ivory-coloured shoots have a delicate flavour and are often specified for use in curries and in Chinese dishes. Tins of bamboo shoots, either salted or unsalted, may be bought almost everywhere. Indonesian dishes use only the unsalted shoots and they are known there as 'achard' when pickled in vinegar or Japanese saké vinegar. Fresh bamboo shoots are cut just as they appear above the ground. They are covered with very fine but sharp hairs and these must be removed before cooking, otherwise they can lead to an intestinal perforation.

Use: fresh in salads or after simmering (parboiling) for 15 minutes. Prepared fresh shoots should be kept in water in a refrigerator. The water should be changed daily.

BAMBOO SHOOTS BRAISED WITH CHICKEN BREASTS

Time: 30 minutes
Serves: 4

2 chicken breasts, skinned and boned
1 can bamboo shoots
2 tablespoons soya sauce
½ teaspoon sugar
¼ cup chicken stock (made from stock cube)
2 tablespoons sherry or rice wine (saki)
1 teaspoon salt

Thinly slice the chicken breasts across the grain. Sauté canned bamboo shoots (or boil fresh ones for 15 minutes) and add the chicken. Sauté for 1 minute, add the soya sauce, sugar, stock, sherry and salt. Sauté for 2 minutes more but do not overcook the chicken.

Bananas

Yellow skinned and sub-tropical fruit, originally from Africa and now grown in many warm and hot countries. Bananas grow as a bunch on a long stalk and the bunch is composed of 'hands'. Varieties of bananas include the small plump 'lady's fingers' which are sweet and juicy; and the larger Cavendish. They may be purchased green but they ripen quickly. Sometimes available are red or claret bananas with a stronger flavour. See also *Plantains* page 143.

Use: remove skin and eat flesh when it is soft, white and full of flavour
sliced with cream
banana slices eaten with curry reduce the pungency of the hot spices

Cooking suggestions:
baked green in skin
peeled and fried in butter
sliced in fritters
dipped in egg and breadcrumbs
dipped in batter and fried
baked with sugar, rum and butter
boiled green in a little water then mashed in milk with salt and pepper

BANANA BREAD

Time: 1½ hours
Temperature: 350°F

4 oz. butter
1 cup sugar
2 eggs, beaten
½ cup sour milk
1 teaspoon bicarbonate of soda
2 cups plain flour
pinch salt
3 bananas, ripe and crushed

Cream butter and sugar, stir in eggs, mix sour milk and bicarbonate of soda together and add to mixture and fold together. Stir in flour, salt and bananas and mix thoroughly. Pour into a cake tin and bake in oven at 350°F for 1 hour.

metric equivalent

175°C

125 g

175°C

14

BANANA WITH HARICOT BEANS

Serves: 4 for breakfast or snacks

		metric equivalent
4 rashers bacon	1 lb. dried haricot beans,	500 g
2 onions, finely chopped	soaked and cooked	
1 large can tomato purée	salt and pepper to taste	
pinch oregano	1 banana, peeled and sliced	

Cut bacon into squares and lightly brown in a frying pan and drain. Fry onion in bacon fat until transparent, add tomato purée and oregano and simmer until warm. Add bacon and beans to purée, season with salt and pepper. Heat and when thoroughly hot, add banana, mix in well and serve on hot toast.

SCHNITZELS, BANANAS AND CHEESE

Serves: 4

		metric equivalent
4 veal steaks, cut very thin	1 egg, beaten	
salt and pepper	dried breadcrumbs	
4 slices gruyere cheese	2 oz. butter	60 g
2 bananas, sliced		

Flatten steaks and make thinner by pounding. On top of each place a slice of gruyere cheese and slices of banana. Fold steak in half to make a sandwich, secure with a cocktail stick and coat with breadcrumbs. Place in refrigerator to allow flavours to mingle, for at least half an hour. Then fry in butter, turning several times until meat is cooked through.

Bangi

Green orange-sized fruit from a Philippine tree with milky juice.

Bannet

See *Herbs and Spices* p. 72.

Barbarine

See *Marrow* p. 101.

Barberry

See *Berries* p. 24.

Basela, Baselle: *Indian Spinach, Malabar Nightshade*

Tropical plant now grown in Europe whose tender leaves may be eaten as a vegetable. White variety is grown in India and a red variety in China.

Preparation: as for *spinach*.

Basil

See *Herbs and Spices* p. 72.

Bay Leaf

See *Herbs and Spices* p. 72.

Beans

World-wide group of leguminous plants grown for food. Generally they are eaten:

(i) in their unripe state as a green vegetable, either the beans (or seeds alone) or the immature beans and the pods.

(ii) as the dried seed, bean or haricot.

In some places, dried harictos are ground into flour. Botanically, all beans fall into two basic genera. They are the broad beans (*Vicia fabia*) and the kidney beans (*Phaseolus* spp.) which include both the small and tender kidney or French beans, the larger coarser runner beans, and lima beans which are treated like broad beans.

Broad Beans: *Windsor; Horse; Scotch; Flava or Shell*

Originally natives of North Africa and the Near East, they have a thick pod which becomes furry inside and is then inedible. When young (less than 3 inches long) both pods and beans are edible. When very large, the grey skin should be removed from the flat broad seeds. Varieties include some with purple pods and others with white pods marbled with pink.

8 cm

Preparation: smallest may be cooked whole or sliced.
Small beans may be shelled and the beans blanched in boiling water, then served cold with vinaigrette

sauce as an entrée, hors d'oeuvre or salad accompaniment. Large beans should be shelled, blanched by immersing in fast boiling water for two minutes, rubbing or peeling away the bean's outer skin and then cooked.

Use: cook in boiling salted water until tender (15–20 minutes), top with butter and sprinkle with chopped parsley or savory. Broad beans are a classic accompaniment with boiled bacon.

Field Beans (Europe)

Preparation: as for *broad beans*.

Green Lima Beans (*Phaseolus lunatus*)

While generally grown to become dried haricots, in some places green lima beans are sold. Only baby ones should be used and the edible beans should be shelled just before cooking. 2 lb. weight beans in pods is sufficient for 4 people.

1 kg

Preparation and use: as for *broad beans*.

SUCCOTASH

Serves: 2, as vegetable accompaniment

> 1 cup freshly cooked baby green lima beans
> 1 cup freshly cooked sweet corn
> ¼ cup melted butter

Prepare beans and corn, drain, mix together and pour over butter. As a variation, add ½ cup cream and sprinkle with paprika. Beans may also be served in a Mornay or cheese sauce, sprinkled with buttered breadcrumbs and grated parmesan cheese and browned in the oven before serving.

BROAD BEANS WITH BACON

Serves: 4

250 g

½ lb. shelled broad beans	1 dessertspoon plain flour
salt	1 dessertspoon butter
1 onion, sliced	1 teaspoon fresh tarragon
½ lb. bacon rashers, rind removed and cut into small pieces	(or parsley) chopped fine

250 g

Place beans in saucepan, sprinkle with salt and add just enough water to cover them. Add onion and boil until tender (15 minutes or more depending on their age). Fry bacon gently for 3–4 minutes, add flour to pan and cook in bacon fat. Add butter, and blend with flour and bacon, then add 1 tablespoon of liquid from beans and onions. Cook gently, stirring to prevent burning.

Strain beans and add to bacon sauce. Stir in tarragon and heat a minute or two. Serve in a pre-heated dish or tureen.

Hot fried potatoes go well with the beans and bacon.

BROAD BEANS IN POULETTE SAUCE

Serves: 4–6

500 g

1 lb. boiled broad beans, tossed in butter and kept hot	large sprig parsley
	2 cups chicken stock
	salt
For sauce:	4 tablespoons butter
3 mushrooms	3 tablespoons plain flour
1 small onion, sliced	2 egg yolks
¼ bay leaf	juice of ½ lemon
1 carrot, sliced	parsley to garnish

Simmer mushrooms, onion, bay leaf, carrot, and parsley in chicken stock for 10 minutes. Salt to taste and strain.

Blend butter and flour in a double saucepan but do not brown. Add stock slowly, stirring constantly until it thickens. Cook for 5 minutes. Add egg yolks and blend well with wooden spoon or whisk.

Just before serving, add lemon juice and parsley and heat but do not boil. Pour over beans and serve.

Kidney Beans: *Kidney Beans* or *Field Garden Beans* (England); *Snap* or *Green Beans* (U.S.A.)

Very wide range of beans with long, smooth green pods eaten when young ,whole or snapped in half. The beans inside are usually kidney shaped and may be of various colours.

Many varieties of kidney beans are used under different names throughout the world. The following selection are the main varieties likely to be encountered in recipe books.

Preparation: young beans may be left whole, older beans should be topped and tailed then snapped in half. On larger ones, the string or filament binding the two halves of the pod should also be removed and they should then be sliced thinly. Young kidney beans should not be boiled. Wash, then place in a basin with a little butter and steam them. Larger ones should be placed in a saucepan with just enough lightly salted water to cover them and gently boiled with a whole onion until they are tender but still crisp. Depending on the age of the beans, this will take from 12 to 25 minutes. Drain and serve with butter, garnish with crisply fried pieces of bacon.

Adzuki (*P. angularis*)

Bushy bean grown in China, extensively used when freshly picked. Dried mature beans may be crushed and made into a flour which is used in cakes and pastry.

Butter Beans

See *Wax Pod Beans* (this page).

Coco Beans (*P. vulgaris*)

Variety of French beans acclaimed for delicate flavour. Raw pods are purple or blue but change to green when cooked. Before deep freezing, blanche in boiling water until pods change colour.

French Beans (*P. vulgaris*): *Haricots Verts* (France); *String Beans* (U.S.A.); *Snap Beans; Kidney Beans*

Originally a native plant of South America, possibly the most commonly known form of kidney bean.

Goa Beans

Indian trailing plant, grown during the wet season and used like *kidney beans*.

Moth or **Mat Bean** (*P. aconitifolius*)

Bean with edible pods and seeds, widely grown in India.

Rice Beans (*P. calcaratus*)

Variety of kidney beans grown in Asia and closely related to the adzuki.

Sword Beans (*Canavalia ensiformis*): *Sabre, Horse; Jack* or *Snake Beans; Canavalis Gotani* (*S. Rhodesia*)

Beans with long slender grey-green pods, 18–24 inches long, grown extensively in tropical countries. When young they may be cooked like kidney beans. When mature, seeds are roasted to make substitute coffee.

45–65 cm

Tongan: *Poor Man's Beans*

Originally from Tonga and now grown in Australia, these beans are grown only in tropical and sub-tropical areas. Plant is prolific, with tendrils up to 25 feet long and beans have broad flat pods, 2–5 inches long and about 1½ inches wide. Pick and cook when young and treat as for *kidney beans*.

8 m
5–12 cm
3 cm

Wax Pod or *Butter Beans* (England): *Wax Beans* (U.S.A.)

Form of kidney beans with tender waxy golden yellow to yellow-white pods. Pick young and treat as for *kidney beans*.

Dried Haricot Beans

Although the term haricot is used by some cooks to refer to the seed of any bean, in general usage, haricot bean is the term used to refer to dried seeds from beans, usually grown for this purpose. In many parts of the world, such beans, which are rich in proteins, are a staple for most of the population. All are prepared in an identical manner and choice of using one variety or another is mainly a matter of taste. In Europe, haricots of various colours are the ripe seeds of various kinds of dwarf and climbing beans.

Preparation: all haricots except soya beans—soak overnight then simmer in their own water until tender. Bring water to boil slowly and when it begins to boil, remove all surface scum. Add to pan 2 onions stuck with cloves, 2 or 3 carrots, cut in quarters, and a bouquet garni, 1 clove garlic and a stick of celery. Replace lid and simmer until beans are tender.

Use: to make Boston baked beans
served with white or cheese sauce
with boiled bacon
in soup
with tomatoes and grilled baby sausages

Fresh Haricot Beans: *Flageolets*

These are certain varieties of kidney beans, usually grown to produce dried haricots, but which can be eaten as a fresh vegetable, although the pods are usually inedible.

Preparation: young beans as for kidney beans. Fully-grown runner beans are large but neither tough nor old. They should be cooked whole and then cut after cooking. If runner beans are cut before cooking they lose most of their flavour and vitamins in the cooking.

Use: as for *kidney beans*.

Fresh White Haricot Beans (England): *Haricots Blancs Frais* (France)

Preparation: cook in salted water into which has been added a *bouquet garni*, a medium-sized carrot and an onion, both cut into quarters.

Use: tossed in butter

in reduced cream
in Lyonnaise sauce
puréed
cold in a vinaigrette sauce

Pea Bean (England): *Beautiful Beans* (U.S.A.)

Variety of kidney bean grown for its seeds or beans which are round and resemble peas. As a plant it is noted for its bicoloured blossoms. The flavour is reminiscent of Mange-tout peas but is finer. These beans should be cooked as soon as they are picked or they become tough. Cook as for *fresh white haricot beans* (see above).

Runner: *Scarlet Runner Bean; Stick Bean* (*P. multiflorus*)

Originally from Mexico, tall growing beans with brighter darker green pod, growing up to 8–10 inches long, and often with slightly abrasive skin compared to the smooth skin of a kidney bean pod.

Preparation: young beans as for kidney beans. Fully-grown runner beans are large but neither tough nor old. They should be cooked whole and then cut after cooking. If runner beans are cut before cooking they loose most of their flavour and vitamins in the cooking.

Use: as for kidney beans.

Varieties of Dried Haricot Beans

Asparagus Bean (*Vigna catjang, Doliches sesquipedalis, D. unguiculatus*); Cuban bean

Black-Eyed: Bird's Foot Bean

Brown Dutch Bean (Europe)

Butter Beans (Europe)

Large white beans. Also a name used for soya beans.

Cajun: *Congo Beans; Pigeon Peas (Cajanus indicus)*

Tropical shrub with pods which may be eaten green or as ripe seeds.

Chartres Beans (France)

A brown variety.

Chevriers Beans (France)

A green variety.

Dutch Beans (Europe)

A brown variety.

Flageolets (France)

Variety of small green dried beans.

Kotenashi Beans

Small white dried bean, grown in Korea and sometimes canned.

Lablab Bean *(Lablab vulgaris)* (India): *Bonavist; Egyptian; Hyacinth; Tonka*

Widely grown staple in Egypt and Middle East. Beans are brown with a white keel along one edge. They are short, broad, and thick. In some places green pods and leaves may also be used.

Lima Bean (*P. lunatus inc. P. limensis*)

White, flat slightly kidney-shaped beans with one half usually larger than the other, and marked with wrinkles.

Madagascar Butter Bean (England)

Larger white variety of Lima bean, often canned.

Marbled Cape Kidney Bean

Variegated variety of Lima beans.

Mottled Lima Bean

Variegated variety of Lima beans.

Mung Bean (*P. aureus, P. mungo radiatus*): *Golden Gram; Green Gram*

Originally from India, ripe seeds are boiled whole or split, like peas. They may also be ground into a floury meal.

Navy Bean (U.S.A.)

White variety.

Otenashi Beans (*P. vulgaris*) (Japan)

Small white dried beans, similar to Korean Kotenashi beans.

Pea Beans (U.S.A.)

A white vareity with round seeds, resembling peas.

Pinto Beans (U.S.A. and Mexico)

A tawny variety.

Rangoon Beans (England)

Red variety of Lima beans.

Red Kidney Beans (U.S.A.)

A red variety.

Sieva Beans (*P. lunatus*): *Burma* (England); *Civet, Sibby*

Native of South America, a small variety often sold as Lima beans and best known because they are green when dried.

Soya Beans (*Glycine max, soja, G. hispida*): *Soja; Soy; China; Japanese; Javan Haricot*

Originally native to China but now widely grown throughout the world, the soya bean is claimed to be the most nutritive of all dried beans. Varieties include black, green and yellow beans. May also be eaten fresh as with *fresh haricot beans*.

Preparation: soak for 30 minutes before boiling in their own water.

Urd Beans: *Black Gram* (*P. mungo*) *India bean, Chinese bean, Black bean*

Popular bean in Asia, used by some Chinese to grow bean sprouts. In Bombay, urd beans are soaked for 48 hours and then crushed under a stone and dried to prepare *Papad*.

Velvet Bean (*Mucuna nivea; Stizolobium deeringianum*)

Native of Burma and Bengal, this bean is very similar to white haricot beans of Europe.

BITTER-SWEET HARICOT BEANS

Serves: 4

250 g
2½ cups

8 oz. white haricot beans	2 teaspoons golden syrup
1 pint water	1 teaspoon salt
1 teaspoon brown sugar	cinnamon stick
2 tablespoons wine vinegar	

Wash beans, cover with water and soak overnight. Simmer for 30 minutes in the same water. Add other ingredients, and cook slowly, stirring occasionally, for another 30 minutes. Serve hot with freshly fried bacon for breakfast.

CANNED BEAN SALAD

Serves: 6

1 large can kidney or lima beans	¼ cup tomato sauce
2 eggs, hard boiled and sliced	1 teaspoon salt
½ cup celery, chopped	pinch pepper
1 onion, finely chopped	washed lettuce
3 gherkins in brine, chopped	sprigs of parsley
½ cup mayonnaise	

Drain beans, place in a collander and pour boiling water over them. Drain and cool. Mix eggs, celery, onion, gherkins, with beans. Mix mayonnaise and tomato sauce. Add salt and pepper to sauces, pour over the other ingredients and toss well. Place a large spoonful on a large curly lettuce leaf and garnish with a sprig of parsley.

CHILI CON CARNE

Serves: 6

625 g   1 kg
2 cm

1 kg

1¼ lb. dried red kidney beans	2 lb. braising steak, trimmed of fat and cut in 1-inch cubes
2 tablespoons bacon fat	
3 cloves garlic, crushed	2 lb. tomatoes, skinned and chopped with juice retained
2 onions, chopped	
3 teaspoons chili powder (more if desired)	1 teaspoon oregano
2 tablespoons plain flour	1 teaspoon powdered cumin or cumin seed
	2 teaspoons salt

Soak beans overnight and simmer in same water until almost tender. Strain then put to one side. Heat bacon fat in a thick saucepan, crush garlic in it, add onions and cook until soft. Add chili powder and meat, turning meat until evenly browned. Blend in flour then add tomatoes and juice, oregano and cumin and salt and fit with a tight lid. Simmer for 1 hour.

Add beans and salt and cook a further 15 minutes.

To obtain the finest value from the herbs, cook the day before and heat when ready to serve. As an accompaniment, crisp green salad and cold beer.

CANADIAN BAKED BEANS

Time: 1½ days
150°C   Temperature: 300°F
Serves: 8

1 kg

2 lb. small white haricot beans (navy beans)	1 tablespoon brown sugar
3 small chunks salt pork	½ cup vinegar
2 onions, thinly sliced	½ cup molasses
salt and pepper to taste	2 cups water

Wash beans, cover with cold water, then soak overnight. Boil until skin breaks when a bean is touched. Drain. In earthenware casserole dish with lid place 1½ inches of beans, thinly sliced onions, salt and pepper and sprinkling of brown sugar, and a chunk of pork. Repeat these layers until all ingredients are used. Mix vinegar, molasses and water, pour over beans and cover.

    Place in oven at 300°F for 5 hours. Look at beans occasionally, and if they seem dry, add more water.

4 cm

150°C   4½ hrs

BARBECUE BAKED BEANS

Time: 20 minutes
Serves: 4

1 lb. canned baked beans	2 teaspoons brown sugar
2 medium tomatoes	½ teaspoon mustard powder
1 clove garlic, crushed into butter in fry pan	½ teaspoon chili powder (or chili sauce)
1 oz. butter	salt to taste
1 onion, sliced	

500 g

30 g

Pour boiling water on tomatoes, remove skins and chop roughly. Crush garlic in warmed butter, add onion and cook until soft. Add tomatoes, brown sugar, mustard powder, chili powder and salt. Cook for 10 minutes, add baked beans, mix and thoroughly heat through.

RED BEAN SAUCE

Chinese cooking sauce, obtainable prepared, made from mashed red soya beans. It has a strong smell and a distinctive flavour. Is best used with poultry and meat. See recipes for *Banana with Haricot Beans* p. 15, *Yam and Haricots* p. 181.

Bean Sprouts

A classic ingredient for Oriental dishes, bean sprouts are made by placing beans in a saucer of water and allowing them to sprout. The Chinese prefer golden coloured soya bean sprouts which have a stronger flavour and a crunchier texture. The Indonesians use mainly mung or urd beans. Both may be bought canned in temperate climates or sometimes fresh from Chinese and other Oriental shops. Often these stores will supply the beans and the sprouts can be grown at home.
To grow: See *Pea Sprouts* p. 140.

Black Bean: *Australian* or *Moreton Bay Chestnut*

Edible, chestnut-like seeds, three or four to the pod, grown on a native Australian tree (named the Black Bean) highly regarded for furniture manufacture. Preparation: roast and eat like chestnuts.

Locust Bean: *Carob; Caroube; Algaroba*

Long pods from a shrub originally from Asia but now growing wild in many countries bordering the Mediterranean. The pulp of the pods contains numerous seeds and is sweet but tasteless. Carob is also the name of a West Indian tree, renowned for the gum produced from its bark.

Use: roll pulp into balls and roast or fry.

Manioc Beans

See *Yams* p. 181.

Fermented Black Soya Beans

Tiny fermented beans which are washed and crushed to add flavouring to dishes. They are often added to Chinese fish dishes to counteract smell of fish and are a major ingredient in Cantonese lobster.

CANTONESE LOBSTER

Serves: 4–6

1 lb. lobster or crayfish	salt, pepper	500 g
4 oz. lean pork, chopped	1 teaspoon sugar	125 g
2 tablespoons fermented black beans, crushed	sherry or saki	
	8 oz. fish stock	1 cup
1 garlic clove, crushed	cornflour	
2 dessertspoons cooking oil	1 egg, beaten	

Cut lobster into 1 inch pieces and cut claws in half.

2 cm

Sauté pork, black beans and garlic in oil for 2 minutes. Add lobster and season with salt and pepper, sugar and sherry. Add stock, stir then cover and simmer for 5 minutes. Add cornflour to thicken the sauce and simmer for 4 minutes. Remove from heat, add beaten egg and stir in. Serve immediately.

Beetroot (England): *Beet* (U.S.A.)

Root vegetable with rich red flesh, globular or tapered and related to sea-kale (chard) and silver beet. In Russian cookery leaves and roots are used.

Preparation:
> boiled beet—Cut off leaves an inch or two above the beet. Soak beet in cold water and without scrubbing, remove earth with care. Place in saucepan and boil in skins, ensuring that skin is not damaged. If pricked or scratched, they will bleed and lose colour. Boil until tender (soft when pressed with finger) and after draining, remove skins by rubbing away.
> baked beet—Wash and dry and bake in oven. The beet is cooked when finger pressure leaves an indentation. Remove, cool and use as for boiled beetroot.
> boiled beet leaves—Take leaves, wash, tie together and place in half an inch of boiling salted water. Reduce heat and simmer until tender. Drain, chop, add a little butter and warm gently. Serve on buttered toast with knobs of butter or in white sauce.

BEETROOT IN ASPIC

Serves: 6–8

1½ pints chicken stock (made from stock cubes)	6 cloves
¾ oz. gelatine	1 bay leaf
4 oz. celery, chopped fine	spring of parsley
small onion, sliced	sprig of thyme
juice of ½ lemon	salt and pepper
3 tablespoons vinegar (if	white and shell of 1 egg, crushed

available 1 tablespoon each of tarragon, malt, and spiced vinegar) — 1 tablespoon sherry, 1 lb. cooked beetroot, sliced

Strain stock and remove all fat. Dissolve gelatine in 4 oz. hot water. Put stock in clean saucepan and add vegetables, lemon juice, vinegars with spices and herbs tied in a muslin bag. Season with salt and pepper. Whisk in egg white and crushed shell, stir in sherry. Whisk all together over moderate heat until frothy. When just at boil, remove from heat and add dissolved gelatine. Cover and keep just warm for 10 minutes. Strain through cheesecloth into a mould and add beetroot.

The advantage of serving beetroot this way is that it reduces the likelihood of it dripping or spilling and is also much tastier than being served in vinegar alone.

Silver Beet: *Beet Spinach; Perpetual Spinach*

Grown extensively in southern Spain where no spinach is grown, and where it is known as *Acelga*. Silver beet is also widely grown in Australia. It has a much larger, longer and tougher leaf than spinach and a long fleshy stalk. Both leaf and stalk can be used though many people use only the leaf. Silver beet can be used for any dish where spinach is used but this vegetable is much coarser and not so strongly flavoured as true Spinach.

Use: stalks can be chopped off, cut in pieces 1½–2 inches long, boiled until soft and then served in vinaigrette
stalks and leaves can be dipped in eggs and breadcrumbs and fried.

VINAIGRETTE SAUCE FOR SILVER BEET

1 tablespoon lemon juice	salt and pepper to taste
2 tablespoons wine vinegar	6–8 tablespoons olive oil
¼ teaspoon dry mustard (English)	

Mix lemon juice, vinegar and dry mustard, season to taste, then add olive oil and beat with a fork until mixture emulsifies.

SILVER BEET, THE SPANISH WAY

1 bunch silver beet	1 red capsicum, with seeds
1 clove garlic	removed and sliced
1 teaspoon paprika	oil for frying (preferably olive)
2 oz. breadcrumbs	1 dessertspoon vinegar
1 sprig parsley	salt to taste

metric equivalent

60 g

Wash leaves well, place in boiling salted water and simmer for 20 minutes. Remove from water, drain and press water from the leaves. Fry together garlic, paprika, breadcrumbs, parsley and capsicum slices in oil. Then pound together in a mortar. Mix resulting paste with vinegar, add salt and pour over the cooked silver beet. Place above hot water and serve hot.

See recipe for *Chick Pea and Silver Beet Soup* p. 139.

BORSCH

Time: approx. 3 hours
Serves: 6

3 beetroots, with stalks	knuckle of bacon
and leaves, peeled and	1 tablespoon tomato purée
chopped	1 tablespoon lemon juice
4 onions, chopped	1 tablespoon chopped dill
1 stalk celery, chopped	or 1 teaspoon dill seeds
bacon fat for sautéeing	½ small cabbage, shredded
1 tablespoon plain flour	1 raw beetroot, grated
10 oz. can beef consomme	1 teaspoon vinegar
1½ pints water	¼ pint sour cream
2 beef stock cubes	finely chopped parsley,
bay leaf	boiled potatoes or rice
salt and pepper	to serve
1½ lb. stewing steak, cut	
in cubes	

315 g

3¾ cups   150 ml

750 g

Sautée beetroot, onion and celery in bacon fat until soft. Sprinkle in flour, stir and cook for 2 minutes. Add consomme, water, crumbled stock cubes, bay leaf and season with salt and pepper. Boil then simmer 10 minutes, then add beef and bacon. Cook slowly for 2 hours.

Skim fat from top, remove bacon bone, cut any remaining meat into small pieces and return to saucepan. Add tomato purée, lemon juice, dill and cabbage and simmer for 20 minutes.

To improve colour, grate the extra beetroot into a small saucepan, add vinegar and a little stock and simmer for 3 minutes. Add to soup. Bring to boil and serve. Add sour cream to each plate, sprinkle with parsley and add boiled potatoes or boiled rice. This makes a substantial meal.

Bergamot

See *Herbs and Spices* p. 72.

Berries

Berry fruits come in different groups. From the wild and cultivated blackberry have come the bramble hybrids—boysenberry, lawtonberry, loganberry and youngberry. Currants and gooseberries grow from bushes and raspberries from canes. Bilberries and strawberries grow from small plants while the Mulberry grows on large trees. Cape gooseberries (related to the tomato) and Chinese gooseberries (vine fruits) are not true berries (see pp. 62–3).

Aguay	Edible berries from a shrub, a native of South America.	In jams and preserves.
Arbute: *Tree Strawberry*	Scarlet granular berries about ¾ inch wide, from the Strawberry Tree, native of southern Europe and the Killarney district of Eire.	In Italy used to make confectionary. In Spain and France for liqueurs.
Barberry: *Berberry*	Fruit of a group of plants related to the buttercup, growing wild in many parts of the world.	
England	Grows wild, has red berries.	Sauces, tarts and pies; preserved in syrup.
Scandinavia		In cool drinks; to flavour ices; in punch.
Normandy (France)	Seedless variety	Used in preserves and jam.
Himalayan	Particularly large berries.	
Nepal	Purple berries, dried in sun like raisins.	As dessert fruit.
Magellan or *Calafate* of South America	Black berries of good flavour.	
Darwin, from Chile	Has abundance of little berries.	
Blue Barberry from west coast of U.S.A.	Different type of plant.	Refreshing drinks; flavouring ices and preserves
Black Berberry	Low arctic-alpine shrub with edible black berries.	
Bilberry: *Blaeberry*, *Hurt* or *Whortleberry*, *Worts Huckleberry* (U.S.A.), *Whinberry*	Small black fruit of English moorland plant with pleasant flavour.	Stew or make into wine; in fritters; for jam.
Blackberry	Fruit of wild bramble, black with hard seeds. Grows wild and is also cultivated.	Has little pectin and apples usually added to set jam or jelly. To eliminate seeds, purée or make into fool or sauce.
Blackcap	Black raspberry cultivated in New England states of U.S.A.	
Blueberry	See also *Bilberry*. Varieties of this bush grown in Canada and U.S.A.	Mix with maple syrup and cream; with peaches and maple syrup; soak in port for one hour and dust with sugar; blueberry pie.
Boysenberry	Cross between blackberry and raspberry and loganberry with highest quality bramble fruit. Length 1½ inches and round, purple black, with sweet-acid flavour and no hairs or core and few seeds.	As for *raspberries or loganberries*.

2 cm

3 cm

Sea Buckthorn	Orange-red edible berry of silver-leaved seaside shrub found in Asia and Europe.	
Buffalo Berry: *Rabbit Berry; Nebraska Currant*	Red or yellow currant-sized berries of North American bushy tree, used to make sauce to eat with buffalo.	Use: in jams and preserves. With game, like red currant jelly
Camambu	Gooseberry type fruit of a shrub, native to South America.	Use: as *gooseberries*.
Barbados Cherries	Acid berries of a West Indian Malaphigia tree, resembling cherries in shape and size. Very sour.	In pies or tarts with plenty of sugar and some lemon juice.
Cloudberry: *Baked Apple Berry* (Canada); *Yellow Berry*	Low growing plant related to the bramble, found on high ground in various parts of Europe including Scotland and Norway and North America. Orange-red berries have a delightful apple flavour when fully ripe.	As dessert, with thick cream, ice cream or mixed into whipped cream and vanilla. In pies, puddings and jam.
Cornel: *Cornelian Cherry*	Edible, red, olive-shaped berries of a small European tree or shrub, said to be tasteless.	Use: pickled like olives or made into a jelly.
Cranberry: *Mossberry; Cowberry; Foxberry; Partridgeberry; Bog Strawberry*	European and North American wild plant, related to blueberry, found on moorland and hills. Fruit looks like cherries, pink to deep red with acid astringent taste when raw.	Sauce or jelly is traditional accompaniment to duck, turkey and goose. CRANBERRY JELLY: Boil berries 15 minutes, add half their weight of sugar and heat again until syrup thickens. When thick enough, it will form into jelly when cool.
Crowberry: *Crakeberry*	Berry from hardy bush growing wild in mountainous part of Scotland, northern U.S.S.R. and Scandinavia.	Use: like *cranberry*.
Currants	Summer fruit, grown from a bush. *Black Currants:* used mainly for cooking as too sour to eat raw. *Red Currants:* Sweeter variety may be eaten raw with sugar and cream. *White Currants:* less common than other varieties but may be eaten raw. *Indian Currants:* Less common than other varieties but may be eaten raw. *Buffalo, Missouri* or *Golden Currants:* wild native currants of U.S.A. having distinctive aromatic quality. They may be yellow or black and are an acquired taste.	Black currants rich in Vitamin C and valued to make syrup and jam. Rich in pectin and used to make red currant jelly served with meat and game; also syrups for long drinks. Used for jellies, syrups and desserts. In pies and preserves, like *blackberries*.

Dewberry	Fruit of bramble, related to blackberry with bluish, dew-like bloom on fruit.	Use: like *blackberries*.
Elderberry	Berries of European elder plant.	Use: to make wine, syrup and jelly.
Gooseberry	Red, yellow or green globular fruit of prickly shrub, rather hairy. Sweet varieties may be smooth-skinned and eaten raw.	Use: to make sauce traditionally served with European mackerel; gooseberry pie; poached in syrup with elderflower and served chilled with thick cream; also in fools, jam, jelly and wine.
Goumi	Wild Chinese berry, related to the cranberry, now grown in the U.S.A. Berries are orange or red with tiny silver specks. They are too acid to eat raw but are excellent cooked.	In sauces, preserves, tarts and pies.
Riverside Grape	Black sour berry from wild American grape, usually growing on river banks.	Must be cooked, use in tarts, pies, and preserves with plenty of sugar.
Hackberry: *Sugarberry*	Fruit of native plant of north-east U.S.A.	
Huckleberry	See *Blueberry* above. American variety of same plant. Berries may be blue, white or black.	Use: as *blueberries*.
Lawtonberry	Cross between blackberry or dewberry and loganberry, similar to blackberry with small round bright black fruit growing in clusters.	Use: as *blackberries*.
Loganberry	Cross between raspberry and blackberry with bright red fruit but half the size of Boysenberry. Flavour is sweet and acid.	Use: as *blackberries*.
Miraculous Fruit (*Sideroxylon dulcificum*)	Berries of a tree from tropical Africa which have the property of neutralizing acidity of sour drinks without themselves being particularly sweet or flavoured.	
Mulberry	Fruit of Mulberry tree (originally from Persia), similar to a large blackberry but sweet without the blackberry's acidity.	Can be eaten fresh with sugar and cream. Use in apple and melon jam; to make mulberry wine; for mulberry pie; as compote; to make mulberry gin.
Newberry	Bramble type berry, a hybrid derived from the blackberry.	Use: as *blackberries*.

Raspberry: *Black Cap*	Fruit of native European bush usually red, occasionally white or black, renowned for its delicate flavour.	Popular in jams and jellies, and to flavour cordials and liqueurs; raw with sugar and cream, sprinkled with brandy; or in sauternes or champagne.
Salmonberry	Wild raspberry, growing in North America from Alaska southwards with red flowers and large salmon-coloured or wine red conical berries.	Use: raw or cooked as *raspberry*
Service Berry (*Pyrus domestica*); *Juneberry; Shadberry; Sugar or Grape Pear; Whitebeam*	Edible, pear-shaped fruit of the shadbush (wild service tree or white-beam tree) which grows wild in European mountainous areas and is also grown in North America. Berries vary in size from that of a pea to crab apple, colour ranging from dark red to purplish-black, which are acid sweet and juicy, and best when over-ripe. Similar fruit of the mountain ash or rowan tree known as sorb or rowan maybe used in the same manner.	Use: eat raw or with apples and sugar; in jam or jelly.
Strawberry	Fruit of small, ground-growing plant originally wild in Europe.	May be eaten fresh with cream (and sugar if desired); very popular in jam and for making into fruit drinks.
Susumber	Jamaican berry, very acid and not to be confused with similar berry with different leaf which is poisonous.	Used in savoury dishes.
Tangleberry	Variety of huckleberry grown in the U.S.A. with dark blue berries which are sweet and piquant.	Considered the best of all varieties of *blueberries* or *huckleberries* and for recipes using those berries.
Thimbleberry	Wild American flowering raspberry with light red berries having a pleasant flavour.	Use: as *raspberries*.
Red or **True Whortleberry**	Small, reddish, acid-tasting berry of Europe, used to make sweet-sour accompaniment to red meat and game, similar to cranberries.	For compotes to eat with red meat and game.
Wineberry: *Checkerberry*	Red, spicy berry of the wintergreen plant, a low evergreen herb of America.	In pies and pudding; for sauces and stuffings; like *Cranberries*.
Youngberry	Cross between loganberry and dewberry, yielding large purple-black fruit with less flavour than Boysenberry and more seeds and a core.	

BERRY CHEESE

1 pint thick cream
sugar to taste
8 oz. berries

2 tablespoons gelatine dissolved
in 6 oz. hot water

Whip cream with sugar and add berries. Melt gelatine
in hot water then cool and add to cream. Pour into a glass
bowl and decorate with fresh berries. Chill and serve with
sweet wafers or biscuits.

Note: Raspberries, strawberries or cloudberries are
ideal for this recipe.

Bilberry

See *Berries* p. 24.

Bilimbi: *Carambola; Cormandel Gooseberry* (*Averrhoa carambola*)

Erroneously cited in some works as Chinese gooseberry
which is a vine, this is the acid fruit growing in clusters
from two related trees grown in Malaya and India.
Carambolas are yellow.

Use: preserved in sugar as a sweetmeat
     cooked

Bilva: *Mahura*

Fruit of the ugli tree of Indonesia. It is round and about
the size of an orange with a thick hard skin. Its smell is
rather strong but its taste insipid. A jam made from it is
sometimes available in exotic food shops.
Use: bake whole in the coals (or an oven)
     cut open when cooked and eat sprinkled with sugar

Bistort

Edible S-shaped roots of a plant in the dock family, grown
wild in Europe.

Use: roots baked in coals
     leaves of some alpine varieties may be eaten like
          spinach

Blackberry

See *Berries* p. 24.

Blackcap

See *Berries* p. 24.

Blueberry

See *Berries* p. 24.

Borage

See *Herbs and Spices* p. 72.

Bouquet Garni

See *Herbs and Spices* p. 73.

Boysenberry

See *Berries* p. 24.

Braganza

See *Cabbage* p. 35

Breadfruit

Large tropical fruit from a tree related to the mulberry
(*Moracea*) the fig, and the Ceará rubber trees. Fruit is
large, ovoid and green skinned, turning yellowish when
ripe, with a fine spikey surface. Its shape and size may be
likened to a green melon. When fully ripe, the yellowish
flesh has a sweet taste but it will not remain fresh for long.
When immature, the flesh is firm, white and rich in starch.
The jackfruit is related to the breadfruit but has an
inferior flavour. When breadfruit is cooked its taste
resembles freshly baked bread with a slight flavour of
artichokes. Cooked seeds resemble chestnuts in taste and
appearance.

Use: mainly when mature but still green
     ripe—flesh may be eaten raw but is an acquired taste
     cooked—sliced and baked

toasted on hot coals
baked whole in oven until skin turns dark
fried in oil
boiled and used like *marrow*
seeds—roasted in ashes
boiled in water
Serving suggestions:
    with meat and gravy as potato substitute
    with sugar and milk, butter or treacle as a pudding

BREADFRUIT AND BULLS TESTICLES

1 mature but green breadfruit   salt and pepper to taste
1 set bulls testicles (from an
   abattoir)

Cut stem and top by slicing off the breadfruit, put aside
till later. Remove flesh and put aside. Clean testicles,
chop, season to taste, and place inside breadfruit case.
Top with chopped breadfruit flesh and replace stem and
top. Stand overnight and bake in hot ashes or in moderate
oven until breadfruit is tender. The taste of the meat
permeates the breadfruit and the dish, in Jamaica, is
alleged to possess aphrodisiacal qualities.

BREADFRUIT FRITTERS

½ breadfruit, peeled, boiled   oil for deep frying
   and mashed with butter   red and green capsicum
   and milk   sticks
3 eggs, well beaten   chopped parsley
salt and pepper

Season the breadfruit and the beaten eggs, and mix
together. Drop spoonfuls of the breadfruit egg mixture
into the oil and fry until golden. Garnish with capsicum
strips and parsley.

BREADFRUIT AND LIVER

2 lb. lambs liver	1 breadfruit	1 kg
salt and pepper	1 oz. butter	30 g
1 lb. onions	¼ cup cold milk	500 g
2 cloves garlic	grated cheese	
cooking oil		

Cut liver in thin slices, scald by pouring over boiling
water, season with salt and pepper and mince with onions
and garlic. Cook in a little hot oil until onion is
transparent. Peel breadfruit, cut in slices and cook in
salted water until tender. Mash breadfruit and cream with
milk and butter. Line casserole dish with breadfruit, add
cooked minced liver and onions, sprinkle with grated
cheese and bake until brown in oven at 375°F.   190°C

Hairy Brinjal

See pp. 54, 103.

Broccoli: *Asparagus Broccoli; Calabrese*

Plant related to cabbage and cauliflower, native of
southern Europe, long neglected but now coming into
greater use. Select only deep green or greenish purple
'flowers' which have close, tightly packed heads. If heads
have started to open, and flower, broccoli will be tough,
woody and flavourless.

Preparation: cut off lower portion of stalks and scrape
    remaining stalks. Remove any large wilted leaves.
    Divide thick and thin stalks into two bundles to
    allow uniform cooking time.
    To freshen, soak broccoli in a basin of water to
    which has been added 1 teaspoon salt and 1
    teaspoon lemon juice (or white vinegar).

Cooking Methods: Drain broccoli after soaking. Cook in
    minimum amount of salted water for 8–15 minutes,
    keeping heads out of the boiling water. This may be
    achieved by tying stalks in a bunch and standing in
    deep saucepan with a tight lid. It is cooked when
    stalks can be pierced with a fork. Drain, remove
    strings around bundles and use as follows.

Use: dip soaked and dried flowers into fritter batter,
    deep fry in oil until well browned, drain and serve.
    sautéed—drain 1 lb. cooked broccoli flowers,   500 g
      sautée quickly in ¼ cup olive oil in which was first
      sautéed 1 clove garlic
    serve generously sprinkled with grated parmesan

cheese, buttered breadcrumbs and freshly ground
black pepper

vinaigrette—use hot and cooked, in vinaigrette of
3 tablespoons olive oil, 1 tablespoon vinegar,
½ teaspoon salt and pinch of fresh ground black
pepper

cold—cool cooked stalks and flowers and serve with
mayonnaise. Eat like asparagus

with bacon—serve cooked with crisp fried bacon,
brown butter sauce garnished with finely chopped
parsley and chives

BROCCOLI ITALIAN STYLE

Serves: 6

1 kg · 90 g · 125 g

2 lb. cooked broccoli flowers	5 eggs, lightly beaten
4 oz. butter	3 oz. parmesan cheese, grated

Melt butter in a thick frying pan and add broccoli. Mix
beaten eggs and parmesan and pour over broccoli.
Cook over medium heat until eggs are set. Serve hot
immediately.

PURÉED BROCCOLI

Serves: 3–4

500 g · 125 g

1 lb. cooked broccoli, forced through a sieve or minced into a purée	2 tablespoons heavy cream
	1 tablespoon onion, finely chopped
4 oz. butter, melted	salt and pepper to taste

Mix ingredients together and serve hot.

BROCCOLI IN BUTTER SAUCE

Time: 30 minutes
Serves: 6

1 kg

About 2 lb. broccoli
For butter sauce:

125 g

⅔ cup green onions, finely chopped	2 tablespoons lemon juice
	1 teaspoon salt
4 oz. butter	½ teaspoon pepper

Trim large leaves and tough lower stems and slash stems

---

across the base. Wash and drain broccoli and cook until
tender.

To make butter sauce: sauté onions in butter for 5 minutes.
Remove from heat, add lemon juice, salt and pepper,
heat and pour over the broccoli.

Yellow Broome

See *Herbs and Spices* p. 73.

Brussels Sprouts

A relatively young member of the cabbage family first
grown in Belgium about 500 years ago. The plant has
neither heart nor head like a cauliflower but is grown for
the sprouts which are produced in the joints of leaves
along the stem. Small, spoon-shaped leaves are closely
and compactly wrapped around each other to form
'sprouts' and are a valuable winter vegetable. The best are
the tiny, tightly closed sprouts which are small, even sized
and compact. They should be green and fresh.

Preparation: remove outer leaves, cut end and make a
cross cut on bottom of each stalk. Wash well and
cook in a small amount of boiling salted water in a
tightly closed saucepan for about 10 minutes. They
should be crisp when drained.

BRUSSELS SPROUTS AND CHESTNUTS

Serves: 4–6

500 g · 30 g

1 lb. brussels sprouts, cooked as above	¼ teaspoon salt
	pinch black pepper
1 oz. butter	¼ teaspoon basil
1 tablespoon flour	1 cup chestnuts, cooked,
½ cup chicken stock, made from stock cube	peeled and sliced

Make roux sauce with butter, flour and chicken stock.
Season to taste and add basil and cook until thickened.
Place sprouts in dish and mix with chestnuts. Pour over
hot sauce and serve.

Black Bryony

Wild creeper in England with bright heart-shaped leaves and red berries. The only edible parts are the young shoots.

Preparation: soak in salted water for 2 hours, boil in salted water then simmer until tender.

Use: with Hollandaise sauce or vinaigrette like *asparagus*

Buchu: *Bucku*

Fragrant leaves of a South African plant, growing wild in the Cape Town area, used to make an aromatic hot drink which is a diuretic. According to André Simon, its taste is reputed to be considerably improved by liberal addition of brandy.

Sea Buckthorn

See *Berries* p. 25.

Buffalo Berry

See *Berries* p. 25.

Bullace

See *Plump* p. 143

Burdock: *Great Burdock; Gobo* (Japan)

A species of *Xanthium* grown in Japan for its long-tapering and tender edible root which is known there as *gobo*. It is obtainable at Japanese shops preserved or canned. In Europe it grows wild and is considered a troublesome weed. Burdock is claimed to have a finer flavour than salsify.

Preparation: fresh—peel burdock root and soak in 3 cups cold water with 1 tablespoon vinegar or lemon juice added for 30 minutes. Cut into 2-inch lengths and boil in salted water until tender.

5 cm

Beef and Burdock

		metric equivalent	
8 oz. burdock root	⅔ oz. green ginger, sliced thinly	250 g	22 g
⅓ lb. round steak, sliced very thinly	4 tablespoons soya sauce	160 g	
⅓ lb. rump steak, sliced very thinly	2½ tablespoons sugar	160 g	

Peel burdock root and cut into slanted ovals, ¼ inch thick. Soak in water and vinegar for 30 minutes, rinse then boil in 4 cups salted water until tender (about 30 minutes). Add beef, sliced ginger, soya sauce and sugar and simmer for 2 hours. Serve with boiled rice.

1 cm

Burnet

See *Herbs and Spices* p. 73.

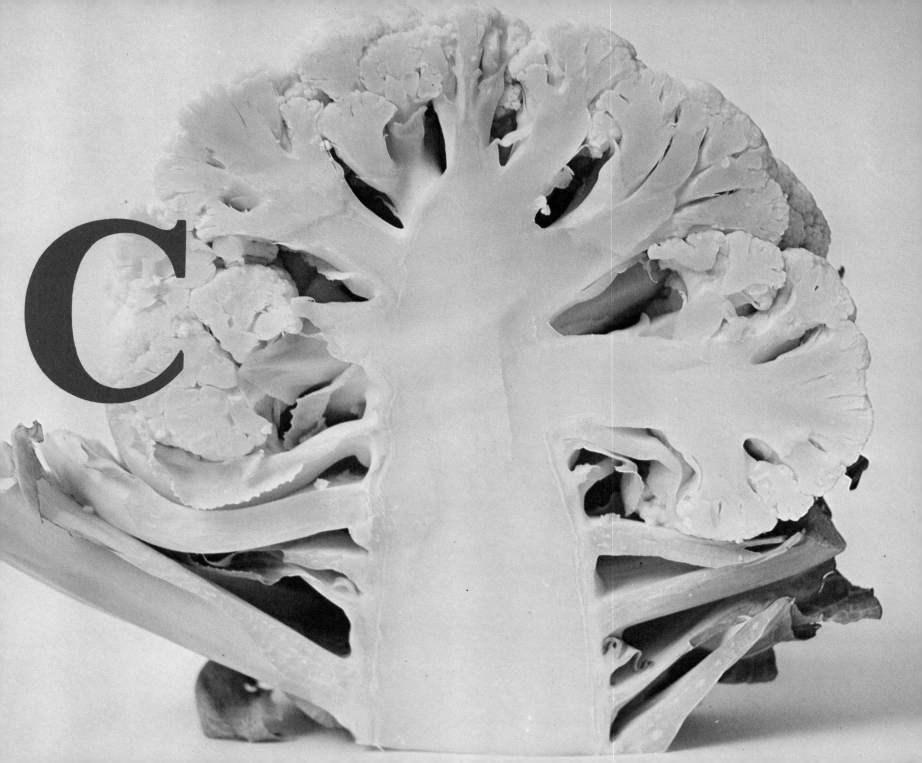

C

Cabbage

Originally from western Asia, the cabbage is one of the most widespread varieties of the *Brassica* family which also includes the kales and cauliflowers. Varieties of cabbage available include:

Savoy or Loose-headed Cabbage

Bright green, crinkled leaves. Especially good braised and served with rolled bacon or broiled whole and served with white sauce.

Hard-headed Cabbage

Drum-head or White Dutch Cabbage

A large white, hard-headed variety used shredded in salads or cooked in butter with a little wine or stock.

Green Cabbage

1 kg

About 2 lb. weight with round firm heart, best in the autumn, winter and spring months.

Red Cabbage

Actually reddish-purple, another hard-headed variety. It is best shredded before cooking and should be blanched in boiling water. Needs longer cooking than drum-head and should have a little vinegar, sugar and salt sprinkled on the stock in which it is cooked slowly (poached) for 1–2 hours. Served with rich meats such as hare and game. Can also be served in a salad or pickled.

Spring Cabbage

Oval pointed heart with outer leaves of bluish-green.

1–2 cm

Preparation: remove coarse outside leaves and any damaged ones. Wash and shake off water. Shred into strips $\frac{1}{2}$–$\frac{3}{4}$ inch wide, place in a colander and blanche by pouring some hot water over the cabbage.

Cook: place knob of butter in a saucepan with a tight lid.

Shake surplus water off cabbage and place in saucepan. If preferred, half an onion, chopped, may be added. Sprinkle with salt and pepper and place lid on tightly. Cook briskly without adding any more water. Shake frequently to prevent any burning. Cooking time about 5 minutes for a young cabbage, no more than 8–10 minutes for mature ones. Drain and place in hot dish.

Cabbage must not be boiled and should always be crisp when served. Bicarbonate of soda should never be added to it or to any other green vegetables.

RED CABBAGE WITH CARAWAY SEEDS AND ALLSPICE

Serves: 6

1 kg	2 lb. red cabbage, outside leaves removed and cut into wedges	1 tablespoon vinegar 2 teaspoons caraway seeds $\frac{1}{4}$ teaspoon allspice
2 cm	$\frac{1}{2}$ inch salted water in bottom of saucepan with tight lid	

Wash cabbage and place in boiling salted water. Pour over vinegar to help preserve colour. Add caraway seeds and allspice to water. Place tight-fitting lid on pan and cook briskly for 8–12 minutes or until just tender, shaking so that it will not burn. Drain and serve with plenty of melted butter.

RED CABBAGE WITH APPLES

1 red cabbage, cut in quarters and finely sliced and chopped	2 cloves 4 cooking apples, peeled, cored and chopped
salt and pepper to taste grated nutmeg 4 tablespoons vinegar	2 teaspoons brown sugar red currant jelly 1 teaspoon vinegar

Place cabbage, seasoning, nutmeg, vinegar and cloves into a greased earthenware crock, cover tightly and cook slowly for 1 hour. Add apples and sugar and leave in slowest oven overnight. In morning, taste and add a little red currant jelly, 1 teaspoon vinegar and more salt and pepper if needed.

SAUERKRAUT

Serves: 6

		metric equivalent
2 lb. cabbage, red, white, or green, washed and finely shredded	12 juniper berries, crushed	1 kg
	12 peppercorns	
handful of coarse salt	1 bayleaf	
juice of ½ lemon or 1 dessertspoon vinegar	1 teaspoon caraway seeds rind of ½ lemon	
1 large onion, finely chopped	2 tablespoons wine vinegar 1 dessertspoon sugar	
1 tablespoon olive oil	8 oz. stock (made from stock cube)	1 cup
1 clove garlic finely chopped		

Place cabbage in large bowl and sprinkle over salt and juice of half a lemon. Mix well together then place small plate over cabbage and weight it down to press the cabbage. Leave 1 hour then squeeze cabbage with your hands, wash under cold tap and squeeze again until cabbage has reduced to half its original bulk.

Fry chopped onion in olive oil until golden. Add cabbage and sauté for 10 minutes. Add garlic, juniper berries, peppercorns, bayleaf, caraway seeds, lemon rind, vinegar, sugar and stock. Sauté together until cabbage is tender. If juice disappears, add more stock to prevent burning. Cooked sauerkraut should be pinky-brown. Serve hot with roast poultry or grills; or cool and serve as salad.

The traditional method for making sauerkraut has not been included as today it is more convenient to make it as above, or buy it ready prepared. Sauerkraut bought from a shop should first have boiling water poured over it in a collander (blanched) and may then be braised, or stewed.

Sauerkraut is ideal to serve with goose, boiled pork, and other rich meats.

COLE SLAW

Serves: 8 as salad

1 cabbage, shredded except for heart	pinch paprika
3 tablespoons olive oil	black pepper, freshly ground
1 tablespoon wine vinegar	salt to taste
½ teaspoon caraway seed, chopped	lettuce

Shred cabbage then soak in iced water for 1 hour. Drain and dry. Mix oil, vinegar, caraway seed and seasoning except for salt and pour over cabbage. Sprinkle with salt so that crystals do not dissolve. Serve on a bed of lettuce leaves.

FRUIT SLAW

Serves: 4–6

4 cups shredded cabbage	2 tablespoons pineapple syrup (from canned pieces)
½ cup mandarine wedges	
½ cup pineapple pieces (canned)	1 tablespoon sugar
½ cup diced apple	3 tablespoons olive oil
¼ teaspoon nutmeg	1 tablespoon lemon juice

Shred and wash cabbage and soak in iced water for 1 hour. Drain then combine with fruit. Mix nutmeg, pineapple syrup and sugar with oil and lemon juice and pour over the cabbage and fruits. Toss, chill in refrigerator and serve.

Braganza: *Portugal Cabbage; Couvé Tronchuda*

Variety of cabbage, originally from Portugal with white ribs cooked in the same way as sea-kale. The head may be used like *cabbage*. There is also a curly leafed variety.

Use: as in *sea-kale*.

Celery Cabbage: *Wong-Nga-Bok (Brassica chinensis)*

Tall yellow-white closely-leaved vegetable, common in the U.S.A., resembling a head of celery but more tightly packed.

Use: raw in salads
sautéed

CREAMED CELERY CABBAGE

Serves: 6

		metric equivalent
1½ lb. celery cabbage	4 tablespoons finely chopped ham	750 g
3 oz. chicken fat		90 g
1 cup milk mixed with 2 tablespoons cornflour and 1 teaspoon monosodium glutamate (optional)	salt and pepper	

Wash cabbage well and cut length ¼ inch wide and then cut strips 2½ inches long. Heat chicken fat and when very hot (smoking) add cabbage. Reduce heat, cover pan and cook no more than 10 minutes, ensuring that cabbage is tender but crisp. Season with salt.

1 cm
7 cm

Add thickening of milk and cornflour and MSG and cook with cabbage for 4 minutes. When properly thickened and cooked, place in a heated serving dish, sprinkle with ham and freshly ground black pepper and serve immediately.

Caribbean Cabbage

Root of arum plant, used in Asia and Africa.

Preparation: see *turnips*.

Chinese or White Cabbages

Two main varieties of Chinese cabbage are available fresh from Chinese shops and a further five varieties of salted mustard greens may be available in some places.

Chinese Cabbage: *Pe-Tsai; Bok Choy* (*Brassica pekiznensis*)

Termed 'white cabbage' in Chinese language, a slender green vegetable with succulent white stems with dark shiny leaves at the top, resembling Swiss chard. Sometimes obtainable whole, or inner hearts only.

Use: raw in salads
 sautéed
 in soup

CABBAGE HEARTS WITH CRAB MEAT SAUCE

Serves: 4

500 g	1 lb. Chinese cabbage hearts	1 teaspoon sherry or saki
¾ cup	4 tablespoons peanut oil	6 oz. chicken stock (made from cube)
	salt and pepper	1 tablespoon cornflour mixed with 3 oz. water
250 g 100 ml	½ lb. crab meat, fresh or tinned	

metric equivalent

Wash cabbage hearts and cut into quarters. Blanche in boiling salted water for 1 minute. Drain well.

Heat 2 tablespoons of oil in pan and sauté cabbage until it is transparent but still crisp. Remove and keep hot. Add remaining oil to pan and sauté crab meat for 1 minute. Add sherry, chicken stock and season. Add cornflour and water and stir for 1 minute. When very hot and thick, pour sauce over cabbage and serve immediately.

CHINESE CABBAGE SOUP

Serves: 4–6

125 g

3 slices green ginger root	¼ lb. raw lean pork, chopped
peanut oil	½ teaspoon sugar
½ teaspoon salt	2 teaspoons soya sauce
1 small head Chinese cabbage, sliced thinly	freshly ground black pepper

Sauté ginger in peanut oil in saucepan for 1 minute. Add hot water and salt. Boil and stir in cabbage. Cover and simmer for 10 minutes. Add pork, sugar and soya sauce. Season with pepper and simmer for 15 minutes more.

Palm Cabbage

See *Palms* p. 131.

Collards

Any sort of cabbage whose green leaves do not form a compact head. See *Kale*.

Cactus

The leaves and fruit of some types of cactus may be eaten. The fruit of the prickly pear or tuna (*Opuntia tuna Ofinesque*) may be eaten raw or stewed. Leaves of the nopal cactus are also edible. They may be obtained fresh or canned. Barbados gooseberries are the smooth, sweetish fruit of a West Indies cactus (*Perskia esculenta*).

Preparation: fresh cactus leaves—handle with gloves or tongs and cut off every spike or prickle. Peel and dice and wash in fresh water.
 canned nopal leaves—drain viscous juice and wash under cold tap.

Use: boiled or fried

SAUTÉED NOPAL LEAVES

1 can nopal leaves, cubed   red chile sauce, to taste
equal quantity of onions,   olive oil
   sliced

Sauté onions until soft and then add nopal leaves. Add chile sauce and simmer until tender.

SCRAMBLED NOPAL LEAVES

1 can nopal leaves, cubed   butter
equal quantity of onions,   3 eggs, beaten and salted
   sliced   1 oz. milk

Sauté nopal leaves and onion in butter, pour over beaten eggs to which milk and salt have been added and scramble together. Serve hot from pan.

Calabash: *Bottle Gourd*

See *Gourd* p. 64.

Calalu: *Malanga; Yauta*

Plant of tropical America including West Indies. Pods are used in the same was as *okra*.

Camambu

See *Berries* p. 25.

Canistel

West Indian tree bearing edible, orange fleshed fruit with exceptionally sweet and cloying flavour.

Use: raw

Capers

See *Herbs and Spices* p. 73.

Capsicum

See *Herbs and Spices* p. 73.

Cardamon

See *Herbs and Spices* p. 73.

Cardoon

Mediterranean plant related to the Globe artichoke cultivated both for its roots and stalks. It looks like sea-kale. The ribs of its inner leaves may be eaten like celery, its leaves may be cooked like *sea kale*, and its thick and fleshy main root has a pleasant flavour.

Preparation:
   stems—discard all outer stems and use only the
      inner leaves. Cut off outside prickles from these
      and also remove the strings running the length of
      the ribs. Cut leaves in lengths from 4–5 inches,   10–12 cm
      rub with half a lemon to prevent blackening, then
      blanch in boiling salted water to which vinegar
      has been added for 10–15 minutes. Drain then
      treat as *celery*
   roots—boil plainly until just tender then serve cold
      dressed with oil and vinegar
   heart—prepare like stems but cook in salted water
      and vinegar until tender (1½–2 hours). Serve with
      melted butter or Hollandaise sauce.

Use: cooked then fried in batter, after marinating in oil,
      lemon juice and parsley
      with vegetable marrow
      with mornay sauce
      cooked and chilled in a salad with oil, vinegar, salt
      and pepper, sprinkled with chopped parsley and
      chervil

Caraway

See *Herbs and Spices* p. 73.

Carrots

Root vegetable, probably of Asian origin, known to have been used for at least 2,000 years. Extremely versatile, it may be used in almost every type of recipe from stews to jam making. Carrots contain a high sugar content and are said to contain a substance helpful to improving night vision. Although most carrots have orange flesh, one Asian variety is reddish purple, like beet, and others are white. Japanese carrots grow to a length of three feet

Preparation: scrub with hard brush and cook within their skin. Vitamins are contained close to surface and carrots should never be peeled and only grated for use in salads. With old carrots, rub skin off after cooking.

To cook: do not boil but steam them, for $\frac{1}{2}$ hour if young, $1\frac{1}{2}$ hours if old and large. For speed, slice carrots in thin circles at right angles to longest axis, cook in very little water in tightly closed saucepan until tender. Then serve with melted butter.

CARROTS, APPLES AND CHEESE

Serves: 4–6

1 lb. medium carrots, scrubbed and sliced	1 teaspoon salt
1 cooking apple, cored, peeled and thinly sliced	1 teaspoon grated lemon rind
	2 tablespoons water
2 tablespoons butter	1 cup shredded Edam cheese chopped parsley

Arrange alternate layers of carrots and apple in saucepan, dot with butter, sprinkle with salt and lemon rind and add water. Cover and cook on low heat for 20 minutes or until tender. Arrange cheese on top, replace lid and steam for 5 minutes. Serve sprinkled with parsley.

CARROT PURÉE WITH RICE

Serves: 4–6

1 lb. carrots, young and sliced	salt
	1 teaspoon sugar
4 oz. long grained rice	4 oz. butter

Cook carrot slices and rice in sufficient salted water to absorb the rice. To the water add sugar and 1 oz. butter. When carrots and rice are tender, drain and save any of cooking liquid. Press through a fine sieve. Heat the

purée and add a little of cooking liquid if it is too thick. Just before serving add 3 oz. butter. Mix well with a fork and serve.

MARINATED CARROTS

Serves: 4–6 as side dish

1 lb. baby carrots	salt and freshly ground black pepper
boiling salted water	
$\frac{1}{2}$ cup white wine	3 tablespoons cooking oil
$\frac{1}{2}$ cup wine vinegar	sprig of parsley, green
1 clove garlic, crushed	salad and cold meat to
1 bayleaf	serve

Scrape carrots, cook 10 minutes and drain. Mix wine, vinegar, garlic, bayleaf and salt and pepper to taste. Pour over carrots and cook gently until tender. Add oil when cooking is almost complete. Serve carrots cold with a little marinade poured over them with parsley, green salad and cold meat.

SAUTÉED CARROTS AND ONIONS

2 oz. butter	$\frac{1}{2}$ teaspoon sugar
12 baby white onions	salt and pepper to taste
8 young carrots, scraped and cut into matchsticks	4 oz. water
	finely chopped parsley

Melt butter in frying pan and add peeled whole onions. Brown them lightly on all sides. Add carrot sticks and then sugar, salt and pepper. When carrots are lightly browned, add water. Simmer for 30 minutes until vegetables are tender and liquid is almost all evaporated. Sprinkle with parsley and serve.

Cashew: *Cashew Pear*

Fruit of tropical tree of which the hard kernel is the cashew nut (see p. 115). Around this there is the cashew pear, which has a pleasant if tart flavour.

Use: ripe—with sugar in preserves
    to make a cool summer drink

Cassava: *Manioc; Yuca; Sagu*

Plants, originally from Brazil with fleshy tubers, now grown widely throughout the tropical regions of the world. There are two types—sweet cassava which can be baked whole and eaten; and bitter cassava which contains hydrocyanic acid. This must be eliminated by fermentation and cooking. Cassava is a staple food for natives in many tropical countries. When boiled, it has a heavy consistency and is tasteless. Juice extracted from it is used to make an alcoholic beverage. When processed industrially, tapioca is also made from it.

Preparation:
   sweet cassava—peel, cut in small pieces, boil until tender and serve with butter on top; bake in oven.
   bitter cassava—boil whole, pulverize flesh, ferment, then dry into a meal or flour (*farinha* of Brazil) or shred and dry.

Use: served with gravy
   with beans
   added to sauces and soups

Catmint

See *Herbs and Spices* p. 73.

Cauliflower

Variety of cabbage, cultivated for its undeveloped flower and not its leaves. Cauliflower is delicately flavoured green vegetable, originally from Asia but used in Europe since the sixteenth century. When buying, ensure that leaves are green and crisp and that the flower is white and close packed. See also *broccoli*.

Preparation: when cooking whole, always leave a few tender leaves around the head as they add to appearance and flavour and prevent breakage of fleurettes while cooking. Wash thoroughly in cold water, remove projecting part of lower end of stalk.

Cook: place cauliflower in a saucepan with a tight fitting lid and with about ¼ inch salted water. Cook in steam until tender (20–45 minutes depending on size).

1 cm

Serve with white or cheese sauce
coat with cheese sauce, sprinkle with grated parmesan and brown in hot oven
sprigs may be coated in batter and fried
serve cold with tartare sauce

FRIED CAULIFLOWER

| small sprigs of cauliflower | beaten egg |
| vinegar with salt and parsley added | oil |

Cut off smallest sprigs of cauliflower and marinate in vinegar, salt, and parsley for ½ hour. Drain well, dip in beaten egg and deep fry in hot olive oil. Drain and serve hot.

CAULIFLOWER AND LETTUCE SOUP

Time: 45 minutes
Serves: 5–7

2 lettuces	salt and pepper to taste	
1 cauliflower	small blade of mace	
4 spring onions, chopped	1 carrot, grated	
1 oz. bacon or rinds, chopped	cornflour with milk to thicken	30 g
2 pints stock, made from cube	grated parmesan cheese	5 cups
bouquet garni		

Wash lettuces and cauliflower then save a few sprigs of cauliflower and a few green lettuce leaves. Chop remaining lettuce and cauliflower, and place in a saucepan. Add onions, bacon, and cook with lid on and shaking constantly for 5 minutes. Add stock, bouquet garni, salt and pepper and mace and simmer for 30 minutes.
   Strain and discard cooked lettuce and cauliflower. Then to liquid, add carrot and remaining lettuce, shredded, and chopped cauliflower. Cook 10 minutes then blend cornflour with milk and add to liquid. Bring to boil then simmer until thickened. Serve with grated cheese sprinkled on croutons.

BAKED CAULIFLOWER

Serves: 4–6

Basic ingredients:

1 cauliflower, broken into fleurettes, cooked and drained
125 g 4 oz. butter
salt and pepper

Variations:

1. grated parmesan cheese
½ cup fresh bread-crumbs

2. 1 cup thick cream
coarsley ground black pepper
grated parmesan cheese
sliced Monterey cheese

3. 1 cup buttered bread-crumbs
crisp fried bits of bacon
chives, chopped
parsley, chopped
paprika

Cook cauliflower fleurettes, drain and arrange in a casserole dish. Then:

190°C
1. Dot with butter, sprinkle liberally with grated parmesan and season with salt and pepper. Sprinkle with bread-crumbs mixed with parmesan and lightly brown in oven at 375°F.

210°C
2. Pour over cream, sprinkle with coarsely ground black pepper, top with grated parmesan and sliced Monterey cheese then place in oven at 400°F until Monterey cheese melts.

220°C
4 mins
3. Using fleurettes or whole cooked cauliflower head, sprinkle liberally with buttered crumbs and bacon bits. Sprinkle with chopped chives and parsley, sprinkle with paprika and heat in oven at 425°F for 5 minutes.

Cayenne

See *Herbs and Spices* p. 73.

Celeriac or Turnip-Rooted Celery

Root celery, resembling a large turnip. Only the root is edible, as the leaves are hollow and extremely bitter. When buying celeriac, pick ones heavy for their size. Light ones are generally hollow or spongy, instead of being firm and fresh.

Preparation: scrub root in a basin of cold water, peel then cut in quarters. May be boiled slowly in vegetable stock for up to 1½ hours or when tender; may be prepared as below.

Use: cooked—
in pieces like *turnip*
in a purée
in hollandaise or béchamel sauce
raw—
shredded and blanched in salad

CELERIAC AND POTATO PURÉE

500 g 1 celeriac, cut into quarters and peeled
30 g salt and pepper

1 lb. potatoes, peeled
top of milk
1 oz. butter

5 cups Cook celeriac in 2 pints water to which 1 teaspoon of salt has been added. After 10 minutes, add peeled potatoes. Cook until potatoes and celeriac are tender. Drain, keeping stock for soup. Press celeriac and potatoes through a fine sieve and put them back into saucepan.

With a wooden spoon, mix sieved vegetables with top of milk added gradually to make a smooth but thick purée. Season to taste then add butter and blend throughout until purée is light. Place over low heat and serve when hot.

CELERIAC, MUSHROOMS AND CHEESE

Serves: 4

125 g 1 celeriac, peeled and cut in slices
60 g 2 oz. butter
1 tablespoon flour
150 ml 5 oz. water
½ teaspoon salt
pepper to taste

4 oz. mushrooms, washed but not peeled, and thinly sliced
2 tablespoons grated parmesan cheese
2 tablespoons fine bread-crumbs

30 g Plunge slices of celeriac into boiling water for 10 minutes. Drain and keep water to add to soup. Melt 1 oz. butter in a saucepan with a tightly fitting lid. Into this mix flour, stir over low heat and allow to become slightly brown.

Add water slowly and season with salt and pepper. Stir and bring to the boil and add celeriac and mushroom slices. Cover and simmer for 25 minutes.

Pour into a casserole dish, sprinkle with a mixture of grated cheese and breadcrumbs. Dot with remaining butter and brown in oven at 425°F.

metric equivalent

220°C

Celery

Originally a wild plant found in marshes of Europe, north Africa and southern Asia, celery seeds were used for medicinal purposes both by ancient Greeks and Romans. Its stalks are thick and juicy and have a distinctive flavour, while the roots are small.

Preparation: cut off roots and wash

Use: in salads, raw
    for flavouring soups, stews, sauces

Cook: braise or stew in veal or chicken stock until tender

CHINESE SAUTÉED CELERY

Serves: 4–6

1 head celery, trimmed of tough outer stems, and leaves, and cut into diagonal strips	2 tablespoons peanut oil 2 tablespoons soya sauce 1 teaspoon sugar chopped parsley

Heat in oil in heavy frying pan, add celery and sauté for 5 minutes, stirring and turning to sauté all sides. Stir in soya sauce and sprinkle with sugar. Cook for 2 minutes more, sprinkle with parsley and serve.

BAKED CELERY AND MUSHROOMS

Time: 1¼ hours
Temperature: 400°F
Serves: 4–6

1 hour
210°C

4 cups celery, diced	2 tablespoons onions, minced
½ lb. mushrooms, sliced	salt and pepper
3 oz. butter, melted	large square aluminium foil

250 g
90 g

Place celery and mushrooms on large square aluminium foil. Sprinkle with onion, salt and pepper and pour over melted margarine. Close foil tightly and bake in oven at 400°F for 1 hour.

metric equivalent

210°C ¾ hr

COOKED CELERY SALAD

Serves: 4–6

1 head celery, with leaves and roots removed and cut in half lengthways. If large, cut each piece in two	vinaigrette (3 parts oil, 1 part vinegar) 1 lettuce, shredded black pepper 1 tin anchovy strips
2 pints chicken stock made from stock cube	2 tomatoes, cut in wedges 12 black olives

5 cups

Place celery in a saucepan, cover with stock and cook until tender. Drain and cool. Place in bowl and moisten well with vinaigrette. Chill in refrigerator. When ready to use, arrange shredded lettuce on a platter or in salad bowl, arrange celery on lettuce, sprinkle with pepper, place anchovy strips over celery, garnish with tomato wedges and black olives.

Celery Cabbage

See p. 35.

Celery Seeds

See *Herbs and Spices* p. 74.

Turnip-rooted Celery

See *Celeriac* opposite page.

Chanar or Chanra

Fruit of a South American tree, used to prepare the alcoholic drink *Aloja de chanar*. May be eaten raw.

Chard: *Swiss Chard; See-Kale Beet; White Beet; Strawberry Spinach*

Originally a southern European plant, related to the beets. Wild chard has dark green or red leaves on yellow stalks. The cultivated variety has long fleshy stalks topped with a dark green spinach-type leaf. In the U.S.A. cardoons are sometimes misnamed chard.

Preparation: trim white fins from chards, setting aside green leaves for other use. Scrape stalks of strings but do not cut. Steam whole and cut only when tender. Large chards must be steamed for an hour, others for a shorter period.

Use: leaves—like *spinach*

stalks—tied in bundles and cooked like *asparagus* or *sea-kale*

Cherries

Small stone fruit from trees related to the plum family. Sweet or table cherries all stem from the wild or bird cherry of Persia and Armenia. They are divided into two groups which now include 600 varieties. The basic stocks are the geans or guignes whose flesh is soft and juice is coloured; and the white-heart cherry (*bigarreaus*) with hard flesh and colourless juice. Sour or cooking cherries which number more than 300 varieties, all stem from the morella, now growing wild in Italy and Greece. These have a dark red skin, semi-translucent flesh, and are tart and acid. The basic sub-groups are the amarelles, pale red fruits with colourless juice; the morellos, dark coloured fruit with acid coloured juice (best for cooking) and damasca, Dalmatian cherries with much smaller fruit from which maraschino liqueur is made. The flesh and juice of damasca are deep red and they are very bitter. Duke cherries are hybrids between sweet and sour varieties and there are 65 varieties.

Preparation: remove stems and wash

Use: eaten whole with skin

in compotes

pies and tarts

to flavour ices and drinks

stoned with slices of nectarines, or peaches, or oranges and plums

metric equivalent

CHERRIES WITH CLARET

Serves: 8

500 g | 1 lb. cherries with stalks removed | cinnamon
| bottle of claret | 3 tablespoons gooseberry jelly
| sugar |

Place cherries in casserole dish and just cover with claret. Add sugar to taste and pinch of cinnamon. Bring to simmering point and simmer gently for 10–12 minutes. Let cherries cool in their syrup. Strain wine syrup then rapidly boil and reduce by one third. Add gooseberry jelly and mix well. Pour over cherries and chill. Serve cold with sponge fingers.

CHERRY FRITTERS

Serves: 4

250 g | ½ lb. stoned cherries | castor sugar
| kirsch | batter

Soak cherries in kirsch and sprinkle with castor sugar for 1 hour. Drain, dip in batter and fry in butter. Serve hot.

CHERRIES JUBILEE

Serves: 4

1 can black cherries | 4 tablespoons cherry brandy
2 teaspoons arrowroot | vanilla ice cream
cold water |

Drain cherries and save the syrup. Pour syrup into saucepan, mix arrowroot into paste with cold water, add to syrup and cook until it boils and thickens. Remove stones from cherries and add to sauce, keeping over a low heat until they are heated. Pour over warmed cherry brandy, ignite it then spoon cherries and sauce over scoops of vanilla ice cream. Serve quickly.

Varieties include

Capulin: Wild Cherry

Sub-tropical fruit of central and South America with

glossy 'cherries'. Fruit has maroon to purple skin and pale green juicy flesh. Flesh is sweet but alleviated by sourer skin.

Use: raw as cherries
     stewed or preserved whole

American Cherries

Member of the *Prunus* group and related to the true cherries, the American cherry is the fruit of a bush-like tree often used for hedges. Its taste is astringent.
Use: for sauces
     in pies

Barbados Cherries

See *Berries* p. 25.

Jamaica Cherry

Globose, cherry-sized fruit of the West Indian fig tree.

Sand Cherry

See *Plums* p. 144.

Surinam Cherry

Name given to two American fruits. They are:
Eugenia uniflora; Pitomba; Perz de Compos

A Brazilian tree now cultivated in other warm American locations, with a red, ribbed, cherry type of fruit. It has a spicy flavour, and is used fresh, or to make jelly.

Malpighia glabra

A tree of tropical America which bears an aromatic edible fruit.

Chervil

See *Herbs and Spices* p. 74.

Bulbous Chervil

Biennial plant grown for its tuberous roots, which are aromatic.

Preparation: use like Chinese artichokes

Chestnut

See *Nuts* p. 115.

Water Chestnut (*Trapa natans*): *Water Caltrop*

Really an aquatic bulb found in pond mud. Reddish brown water chestnuts are known as 'horse's hooves' and may be available fresh in some Chinese shops. Canned varieties, cleaned and peeled, are generally available. Their flavour is delicate and they have a crisp texture, similar to an apple.

Preparation:
    fresh—thoroughly wash and peel
    canned—may be eaten raw, sliced and quartered
Use: with fried pork (*Chow Yuk*) dishes
    like *chestnuts*—roasted, boiled and mashed

PORK AND WATER CHESTNUT DUMPLINGS

Serves: 2

For dough:		
1 egg, well beaten	4 water chestnuts, peeled and minced	
4 oz. water	1 bamboo shoot, minced	½ cup
6 oz. flour	¼ teaspoon salt	185 g
For filling:	¼ teaspoon sugar	
1 teaspoon cornflour	dash white pepper	
4 oz. minced pork	soya sauce to serve	125 g

To make dough: Mix egg, water and flour, knead until smooth and elastic, cover with a damp cloth and stand for 10 minutes.

To make filling: Add cornflour to minced pork and mix well. Add minced chestnuts and bamboo shoot, salt, sugar and pepper. Mix well. Cut wrapping with knife and place heaped teaspoon of filling in centre of each. Bring

edges together and pinch, leaving a wide opening at top to show filling. Place on flat plate and steam for 30 minutes.
Serve hot with soya sauce.

Chicory

See *Endive* p. 55.

Chickling Vetch: *Grass Pea*

European annual plant, grown for its seeds which are white but irregularly shaped. When unripe, they are prepared and eaten like green peas. When ripe, they are dried and used in soups and stews, like chick peas.

Chickweed

Common and tenacious weed, quite edible if cooked like spinach.

Chilis

Hot South American Pepper.
See *Herbs and Spices* p. 74.

Chili (Chile) Powder

See *Herbs and Spices* p. 74.

Red Chilis

See *Herbs and Spices* p. 74.

Chrysanthemum Flowers

Used by the Japanese in salads.

Chufa: *Rush* or *Tiger Nut; Earth Almond; Aya; Zulu Nut*

Edible tubers of the sedge plant, small, brown with white floury flesh. When fresh they are sweet but insipid. The flavour improves as they are kept and dried to be eaten in winter.
Preparation:
    roast whole
    grind and mix with other ingredients

metric equivalent

500 g
1¼ cup 125 g

Use: raw
      roasted as sweetmeats or savouries

Sweet Cicely

Perennial plant whose leaves are aromatic and may be used in salads and stews, finely chopped.

Cinnamon

See *Herbs and Spices* p. 74.

Citrange (*Poncirus trifoliata*)

Citrus fruit, hybrid between the sweet orange (*Citrus sinensis*) and the trifoliate orange.

Citron

Fruit of the citron tree, considered to be the parent stock of both the lemon and lime trees. Fruit is large, like a lemon and strongly aromatic. It has a thick rind especially suitable for candying. This darkens its green outer case and renders the pulp translucent. Slices of citron candied peel are the traditional decoration for Madeira cake. It is also used in mixed peel for fruit cakes. Extensively cultivated in Corsica to make the liqueur *cédratine*.

Citrus Peel

The skins of both oranges and lemons may be used either grated in drinks, cakes and desserts, or as flavourings. They may also be candied.

CANDIED PEEL

4 large lemons and/or oranges	1 teaspoon salt
	1 lb. sugar
½ pint water	4 oz. castor sugar

Choose large ripe fruit. Remove rinds carefully after cutting fruit in half. Keep rinds in halves. If white pith is thick, remove a little but retain enough to keep rinds firm and in shape. Place in bowl and cover with cold water with salt dissolved in it. Soak 48 hours.

Drain in a colander, place in a saucepan and cover with fresh water. Boil gently until tender but unbroken. Boil sugar and ½ pint water for 5 minutes without lid. Place rinds in bowl and cover with syrup. Cover and soak for 24 hours.

metric equivalent

1¼ cups

Strain syrup. Place rinds in pan and boil until clear (about 15 minutes). Sprinkle with castor sugar, remove and place, cut side downwards in warm oven to dry. Turn off oven and leave overnight. When thoroughly dry, store in airtight tins.

CHOCOLATE ORANGE PEEL

90 g

Prepare peel as above, melt 3 oz. dark chocolate in top of a double boiler, dip candied peel in it, coat well with chocolate, then place on waxed paper to cool and set.

HALF ORANGE SKINS

Use: as container to serve fruit salad, topped with whipped cream or top with meringue (1 egg white beaten with 2 tablespoons sugar) and set in oven. Fill with orange or lemon jelly and top with whipped cream.

Clary

See *Herbs and Spices* p. 74.

Clementine

Hybrid of the tangerine and the wild orange of north Africa. Its skin is tight like an orange, it is not quite so sweet as a tangerine and it is practically seedless.

Preparation: remove peel, break into segments and remove pith

Use: eat raw
in fruit salads

Cloudberry

See *Berries* p. 25.

Cloves

See *Herbs and Spices* p. 74.

Coco(a)-plum

See p. 145.

Coconut

See *Palms* p. 128.

Collards

See *Cabbage* p. 36.

Colocasia

See *Herbs and Spices* p. 74.

Comfrey

See *Herbs and Spices* p. 74.

Coriander

See *Herbs and Spices* p. 75.

Cornel: *Cornelian Cherry*

See *Berries* p. 25.

Corn Salad: *Lambs Lettuce; Shepherd's Purse* (*Valerianella olitoria*)

Small annual plant of Europe, north Africa and the Middle East, now grown in the U.S.A., able to withstand frost and useful for winter salads.

Preparation: like *lettuce*—pull whole plant from ground, cut off roots and wash very well to remove all grit.

Use: raw—in salads with chicory, beetroot, celery
cook—like *spinach*

Sweet Corn: *Indian Corn; Maize; Corn-on-the-Cob; Mealies*

Cobs of a tall cereal plant, originally from South America which are used as a vegetable in their partly ripe stage. When fully ripe, the grains (maize) are used to make cornflour, polenta, hominy and grits, and as stock feed. For cooking, select cobs with soft milky grains. Obtainable canned or fresh. Varieties include popcorn, which is a form of New Mexico corn without pods and tassels on its kernels. It is used mainly to make the sweetmeat popcorn and grains are usually obtained dried and in packets ready for frying.

Preparation: remove tasselled top and encasing leaves

Use: boil—in plenty of fresh water for about 15 minutes and serve well brushed with butter and salt. Do not boil in salt water as this will toughen the corn. May also be steamed.

roast—gently under grill brushing with butter and turning until lightly browned all over.

SWEET CORN STEW

Time: 2 hours
Serves: 6

6 corn cobs, with leaves removed	2 onions, chopped fine
1 pig's foot or trotter	2 cloves garlic, chopped fine
½ lb. chick peas, soaked overnight in salt water	2 oz. olive oil
	salt and pepper
2 tomatoes, blanched, skinned and chopped	1 teaspoon fresh mint, finely chopped
2 sweet red peppers, sliced	

250 g   ¼ cup

Place corn in large saucepan of boiling water with pig's foot and soaked chick peas. Water should just cover the top of the corn and should boil vigorously, being kept at same level by adding cold water and keeping on heat until corn grains burst open. Then simmer until chick peas are soft (about 1 hour) and most of the water is absorbed. Simmer tomato, peppers, onions and garlic in oil until they form a thick sauce. Add and mix with stew, season with salt and pepper and cook slowly for 5 minutes.

Serve sprinkled with chopped mint.

Cowslip

See *Herbs and Spices* p. 75.

Cranberry

See *Berries* p. 25.

Cress

Fast growing plant with tiny leaves which are used for garnishing and in sandwiches. This is originally a native of Persia and is different from watercress. Cress is often grown with mustard to make a salad combination. Useful to grow indoors on damp flannel. Varieties include peppergrass and pepperwort.

Preparation: wash cress, dry and chop roughly

Use: serve as hors d'oeuvre with
chopped olives
sardines
boiled beetroot
sliced hard-boiled eggs
in vinaigrette

American Cress: *Land Cress; Belle Isle Cress; Bank Cress; Upland Cress; Hedge Mustard*

Common weed of the U.S.A., easily cultivated and very useful for salads in winter.

Preparation: as for *Watercress* p. 180.

Meadow Cress: *Lady's Smock*

European weed, growing in damp meadows and on stream banks. Leaves have a peppery bite and when picked small, may be used in fresh green salads.

Use: chopped in soups
cooked as for *sorrel*

Crin-crin: *Jew's Mallow*

Leafy vegetable grown extensively in many parts of Asia and West Africa and also in France.

Preparation: leaves are cooked like *spinach*

Crinkleroot

An American toothwort with edible roots.

Preparation: as for *turnips*

Crowberry

See *Berries* p. 25.

Cucumbers

Vegetables of the melon family originally from northern India. There are different types of cucumbers available in different parts of the world. Varieties include pickling types (and or gherkins) 2–3 inches long with small black spines; table cucumbers are smooth-skinned and straight, from 6–20 inches long depending on the variety. In England, foot long cucumbers, often grown under glass, are most common; in Australia, the ground-growing ridge cucumber, rarely more than six inches long, is generally used. Also available are apple cucumbers which have a smooth pale skin and are spherical. Chinese cucumbers are light green with longitudinal white lines. See also *gherkin*.

5–8 cm

15–50 cm

15 cm

To eat: peel the skin and cut into slices or cubes

Use: in salads, either fresh or in vinegar

Methods of cooking: may be cut in pieces and boiled in
  salted water for 20 minutes
  may be braised

CUCUMBER SOUP

Time: 35–40 minutes
Serves: 6

2 ridge cucumbers or 1 English cucumber	1 stalk celery, chopped salt and pepper to taste	
1 medium sized onion, chopped	4 oz. ham, in strips 1 inch long × ½ inch wide	125 g 3 × 1 cm
1 stalk of shallots	2 eggs, beaten	
2 oz. butter	2 oz. onion flakes or dehydrated onion flakes	60 g 60 g
2 pints chicken stock (may be made from cubes)		5 cups

Peel cucumbers, remove seeds and cut into ½ inch wide slices. Brown onion and shallots in butter in bottom of pan and then add stock, celery, salt and pepper and ham. Boil 15 minutes then pour beaten eggs into the boiling soup. Lower heat and simmer 8 minutes. Serve hot with onion flakes on top.

STUFFED AND BAKED CUCUMBER

	metric equivalent
Time: 30 minutes	25 min
Temperature: 375°F	190°C
Serves: 4	

4 cucumbers (6 inches long)	1 small onion, finely chopped	15 cm
2 oz. breadcrumbs	salt and pepper	60 g
1 slice bacon, ½ inch thick, fried and cut into cubes	1 tablespoon tomato sauce	1 cm
	4 oz. chicken stock (made from stock cube)	½ cup
1 oz. bacon fat	1 tablespoon breadcrumbs, baked	30 g
sprig tarragon, finely chopped	1 oz. butter	30 g
sprig parsley, finely chopped		

Peel cucumbers, cut off ends, cut in halves lengthways then scoop away seeds. Mix breadcrumbs, bacon, bacon fat, tarragon, parsley, onion, salt and pepper and tomato sauce. Place cucumber halves in casserole dish, fill them with mixture and pour around chicken stock. Bake in oven until cucumber is tender. Sprinkle with baked breadcrumbs, dot with butter, brown in oven and serve.

KIDNEY SOUP WITH CUCUMBER

Serves: 6–8

12 oz. kidney (ox or lamb) cut into small pieces	1 turnip	375 g
oil for frying	1 large salted cucumber	
4 pints beef stock (made from stock cubes)	2 large potatoes	
	dill seeds	10 cups
2 onions	salt and pepper	
1 carrot	sour cream	

Brown kidney in a little oil. Add stock to kidney, bring to boil then simmer until it begins to soften (about 1 hour). Chop vegetables and add them and dill seeds to kidney. Simmer until vegetables are tender. Add salt and pepper to taste and serve with dessertspoon of sour cream in each bowl.

Snake Cucumber

Variety of melon from Indonesia, long and slender as its name implies and pickled in vinegar as for *gherkins* (see p. 62).

Jersey Cudweed

Common European everlasting plant, now growing in South Africa where natives cook it like *spinach* .

Cumin

See *Herbs and Spices* p. 75.

Cumquat: *Kumquat; Chinois* (France)

Small citrus fruit, similar to tiny elongated or flattened orange, of Chinese or Japanese origin, often grown in large tubs as a decorative shrub. Obtainable preserved whole in thick syrup or fresh in warmer countries.

To eat: fresh like oranges or tangerines

Use: in salads
    marmalade
    in garnish for duck
    in ice cream

Pickle: in vinegar like *gherkins* or *melon*

Preserve: in brandy
        crystallized

Curcuma

See *Herbs and Spices* p. 75.

Currants

See *Berries* p. 25.

Curry Powder

See *Herbs and Spices* p. 75.

D

Dahlia

Tubers of this popular garden plant are edible and have a flavour similar to artichokes.
Preparation: as for *Jerusalem artichokes*

Daikon: *Japanese Radish*

1 metre
11 cm
With serrated leaves and roots growing to 3 feet long and 4 inches diameter, this vegetable is an important food in Asia.

4 cm
Preparation: for salads—cut into matchsticks 1½ inches long. Sprinkle with salt and stand 20 minutes until soft. Squeeze to get rid of excess moisture and mix with 1½ tablespoons vinegar. Squeeze again and use.

Use: raw—like *cucumber*
cooked—parboiled then treated like *turnips*

Dandelion

Common weed with toothed leaves and yellow flowers. Best harvested in winter and spring months. Young leaves of this common weed may be used, but older and larger leaves are too bitter. Best flavour is obtained if young plants are covered by a box to prevent sunshine reaching them. This gives the leaves a pale colour.

Preparation: select only young leaves, wash under cold tap, shake away water.

Use: young leaves may be eaten raw in salads
cooked as for *spinach*
to infuse into a 'tea', in wine, into a gingerbeer

DANDELION PURÉE

1 kg   30 g

2 lb. tender young dandelion leaves	1 oz. butter
1 teaspoon lemon juice	pepper
salt	poached eggs to serve

Hand pick leaves ensuring only young are used. Reject any which seem large or coarse. After washing, place in bowl of cold water with lemon juice added and stand for 1 hour. Drain well and place in a saucepan with salt and

15 g   ½ oz. butter. Place tight lid over saucepan and cook over a low flame, shaking to ensure leaves neither burn nor stick to bottom of pan (15–20 minutes). Chop cooked leaves finely and pass through a sieve. Place remainder of butter in saucepan, sprinkle with pepper and heat purée. Serve with poached egg on top of each mound of dandelion purée.

DANDELION SALAD

1 bunch youngest dandelion leaves, well picked and washed	juice of half a lemon
	1 tablespoon sugar
	½ teaspoon salt
1 bunch watercress, well washed and hand picked	½ teaspoon paprika
	6 small pickled onions,
2 tablespoons salad oil	chopped finely

Arrange small clusters of dandelion leaves and watercress alternatively around a salad bowl. Mix oil, lemon juice, sugar, salt and paprika and sprinkle over the salad. Sprinkle with pickled onions and chill before serving.

Alternative dressing:	½ teaspoon paprika
½ cup cream	1 tablespoon sugar
2 oz. butter	4 tablespoons vinegar
2 eggs, beaten	fried bacon squares to
½ teaspoon pepper	garnish

60 g

Blend cream and butter, add eggs and seasonings, sugar and vinegar and whisk together. Heat until consistency is like soft custard. Pour while still hot over dandelion leaves and toss them until they are thoroughly coated. Garnish with fried squares of bacon. Chill in refrigerator before serving.

Dates

See *Palms* p. 128.

Dessert Date: *Aduwa*

Fruit similar to the date but grown on a small bushy tree in Uganda, Congo, Upper Egypt and Borneo. Its taste is bitter sweet and it is said to have properties as an aperient.

Dewberry

See *Berries* p. 26.

Dill

See *Herbs and Spices* p. 75.

Dock

See *Herbs and Spices* p. 75.

Durian

Spiny oval or spherical fruit of a native Malayan tree, now widely grown in Asia. The fruits weight from 5–10 lb. and are about the size of small coconuts. Their skins are covered with sharp prickles. The flesh is a soft, creamy pulp, with a flavour like that of strawberries or almonds and cream. However, to eat a durian is like eating Port Salut cheese; the nose must be pegged throughout the process. The durian always has a strong smell and if the fruit becomes over-ripe, the smell becomes foul. Its seeds may be roasted and eaten like *chestnuts*.

2·5–5 kg

Eat: raw

Eggplant: *Aubergine; Brinjal*

Originating in India and adopted centuries ago by the Arabs, the fruits of the eggplant are now used by cooks in most countries and are grown wherever it is warm and sunny. The skin is usually a deep purple-black but may be green, yellow, white, ash-coloured or brown. Their shape may be like an egg, a melon or a ball and their weight can vary considerably, some exceeding 1 lb. or more. *(500 g)*

Preparation: cut into slices or cubes and sprinkle with salt for about 20 minutes before using. This removes excess moisture and makes eggplant less tough

Use: mature—fried, sautéed, casseroled, stuffed, baked. As hors d'oeuvre—sautée with chopped garlic, drain on paper towel, cool, place on bed of yoghurt and chill in refrigerator.
Bake whole in oven at 350°F *(175°C)* for 1 hour, remove skin and chop, add chopped parsley, crushed garlic, cinnamon, salt, pepper, crushed dried mint and vinegar and stand for several hours before chilling and serving.
Immature—When 1½ inches *(4 cm)* long, pickle in vinegar with garlic and oregano and eat like pickled *gherkins*.

MOUSAKA I

Serves: 4

The classical eggplant dish adapted from Arabs in most Mediterranean and Middle East countries.

Batter:
2 egg yolks, beaten
½ pint milk *(1¼ cups)*
salt and pepper to taste
Filling:
1 lb. finely minced cooked beef or ham *(500 g)*

3 large onions, sliced
2 cloves garlic, crushed
oil for frying
3 eggplants, sliced but not peeled
½ meat stock cube
4 oz. tomato purée *(½ cup)*

To make batter: Mix beaten egg yolks with milk and season to taste. Cook until it forms a solid custard. Remove and cool.

To prepare filling: Fry sliced onions and garlic in oil until brown. Remove and then sauté eggplant slices (which had been previously salted) until tender. Into a cake tin, 7 inches *(18 cm)* square and 2 inches *(5 cm)* deep (or of equivalent volume) pour some oil and cover the bottom with fried eggplant slices. Cover the eggplant with some minced meat and fried onions. Add other layers of eggplant, meat and onions until all the ingredients have been used. Add meat stock and tomato purée and cover with the prepared batter mixture. Place in an oven at 350°F *(175°C)* for about an hour. The batter should form a crust and be golden brown. Mousaka is usually served hot, but is equally tasty when cold.

MOUSAKA II

Serves: 4–6

This is one of the easiest forms to make and can be prepared in advance.

5–6 tablespoons olive oil
2 medium onions, finely chopped
1 lb. lean beef, raw and minced *(500 g)*
1 teaspoon salt
black pepper, freshly ground
1 × 4 oz. tin tomato purée *(125 g)*
½ stock cube dissolved in 5 oz. water *(150 ml)*

4 medium sized eggplants, peeled and sliced *(185 g)*
6 oz. grated parmesan cheese *(30 g)*
For sauce:
1 oz. butter *(30 g)*
1 oz. flour
½ pint milk *(1¼ cups)*
salt and pepper to taste

Heat 1 tablespoon oil in a saucepan and sauté onion until transparent. Add minced beef, increase heat and brown quickly. Then stir in seasoning, tomato purée and dissolved stock cube. Bring to boil, cover and simmer for 30 minutes. Fry eggplants in remaining oil and if they absorb all the oil, add more so that they cook until tender. Place layer of cooked eggplants in bottom of a casserole dish, sprinkle with some parmesan and add alternate layers of eggplant and grated cheese, saving some cheese for topping. Over the top layer of eggplant, pour the meat mixture.

To make sauce: Melt butter and add flour, blending well and cooking for 1 minute, then gradually add milk and beat well to make a smooth sauce. Season then cook for 5 minutes. Pour over the eggplant and minced beef and top with remaining cheese. Either store in refrigerator or cook immediately in oven at 350°F for 30–35 minutes or until bubbling and cheese is browned. Serve with tossed green salad.

175°C

EGGPLANT PARMESAN

Time: 30 minutes
Temperature: 350°F   175°C
Serves: 6

1 eggplant, cut into ¼ inch thick slices	2 teaspoons dried oregano	6 mm
3 eggs, beaten	2 teaspoons salt	
1½ cups dry breadcrumbs	8 oz. gruyere cheese, sliced	250 g
1 cup olive oil	10 oz. tomato purée	1¼ cups
	grated parmesan cheese	

After salting, dip eggplant slices into egg and then breadcrumbs, coating completely. Sauté them in oil until golden brown. Drain and place into large casserole dish. Using half quantities, place layers of eggplant, salt, cheese slices and tomato purée and parmesan. When this has been repeated, bake in oven at 350°F for 25–30 minutes.

175°C

EGGPLANT CREOLE

Time: 1½ hours
Temperature: 375°F   190°C
Serves: 4

1 large eggplant, skinned cubed, parboiled	1 cup chicken stock (made from stock cube)	
1 green capsicum, chopped	½ teaspoon salt	
1 large onion, chopped	¼ teaspoon black pepper	
2 oz. butter	¼ teaspoon basil	60 g
½ cup rice	1 cup grated parmesan cheese	
4 tomatoes, skinned and seeded		

Parboil eggplant cubes. Sauté capsicum and onion in

butter. Add uncooked rice and sauté until golden. Add tomatoes, stock, eggplant and seasoning and herbs. Bake in a casserole in oven at 375°F for 1 hour. Sprinkle cheese on top after 30 minutes in oven. Serve as accompaniment to main course.

190°C

See recipe for *Okra and Eggplant* p. 120.

Elder

See *Herbs and Spices* p. 75.

Elderberry

See *Berries* p. 26.

Endive and Chicory

Although botanical names have been avoided wherever possible the confusing use of the common names of plants in the *Cichorium* genus and their uses can only be demonstrated in the following table on page 75.

Preparation: heads—remove leaves which are too green or too hard. Cut rest from stump, wash leaves several times. Drain, then blanche for 10 minutes in rapidly boiling salted water. Drain, wash under cold tap, press then chop finely.

BELGIAN ENDIVE WITH CREAM

Serves: 4–6

1 lb. Belgian endive	juice ½ lemon	500 g
½ pint water	½ teaspoon salt	1¼ cups
1 oz. butter	2 tablespoons top of milk	30 g

Cut off brown ends, wash heads without separating leaves. Into saucepan place ½ pint water, 1 oz. butter, lemon juice and salt. Place Belgian endive in pan and bring to boil. Cover and simmer gently for 45 minutes. By then, most of the water should have evaporated. If not, increase heat until water is almost gone. Add top of milk, warm a few minutes, and serve with roast veal or other roast meats.

1¼ cups   30 g

BAKED BELGIAN ENDIVE

220°C	Temperature: 425°F
	Serves: 3

500 g	1 lb. large (not long)	butter
	heads Belgian endive	white pepper
2½ cups	1 pint fast-boiling water	grated parmesan cheese
	1 teaspoon salt	

Cut bottoms off Belgian endives. Wash well without separating leaves. Place heads into saucepan containing

2½ cups — 1 pint boiling water to which 1 teaspoon salt has been added. Cook until tender (about 25 minutes). Drain and dry gently.

Cut in halves, lengthways, and arrange in buttered casserole or fireproof dish with cut surface uppermost. Using only one half of each head, place knob of butter, pinch of white pepper and 1 tablespoon grated parmesan. Cover with other halves of heads and sprinkle them with cheese and add a knob of butter to each.

220°C
15 mins — Place in hot oven (425°F) for 15–20 minutes until cheese is golden.

This dish may be prepared ahead and then placed in oven for 15 minutes to heat thoroughly.

BELGIAN ENDIVE WITH CHEESE AND HAM

500 g	1 lb. Belgian endives boiled	*For Sauce:*
30 g	until tender with 1 cup of	1 oz. butter
	liquid saved	1 tablespoon flour
	8 slices cooked ham	1 cup milk
60 g	2 oz. grated gruyere cheese	endive water
	toasted breadcrumbs	salt and pepper
		grated nutmeg

Boil endives.

To make sauce: melt butter then add flour and blend together. Add milk and mix until smooth over low heat. Add endive water, salt, pepper and nutmeg and after 3 minutes' cooking, remove from heat.

45 g — Add 1½ oz. cheese to sauce. Wrap each endive in slice of ham, place in casserole or ovenproof dish, pour over sauce and sprinkle with remaining cheese and breadcrumbs. Dot with butter and brown in oven or under griller.

Escarole
See *Endive* p. 55.

Eugenia and Minor Myrtaceous Fruits

These are widespread and many varieties may be eaten locally. The best known are:

Abbevillea (Brazil)

Cloves (*E. aromatica*)
See *Herbs and Spices* p. 74.

Feijoa (Brazil)
See p. 58.

Guabiyu (*E. pungens*)
See p. 67.

Jambolan: *Java Plum; Jambu* (*E. jambolana*) (Jamaica)
See p. 91.

Macore: *Macora* (*E. javanica*)
See p. 100.

Malay Apple: *Ohia; Mountain Apple* (*E. malaccensis*)
See p. 6.

Rose Apple: *Brush Apple* (*E. jambos*)
See p. 6.

Surinam Cherry: *Pitomba; Pera de Compos* (*E. uniflora*) See p. 43

Ubajay: *Igbá Jay* (*E. myrcianthes*)
Edible fruit of South America.

Feijoa

Fruit of a Brazilian tree which thrives best in hot climates. Tree is often grown for its ornamental and large red flowers. Fruit is one to three inches long, thin skinned and green with a whitish bloom. The granular flesh surrounds a jellyish pulp containing minute seeds. Its flavour suggests pineapple and strawberry when fully ripe.

2–8 cm

Use: raw
    cooked—stewed
        in jams and jellies

FEIJOA FRUIT SALAD

Serves: 6–8

750 g

500 g

1½ lb. feijoas, sliced	1 cup Chinese gooseberries,
1½ cups water	peeled and sliced
1 cup sugar	1 lb. ripe pears, cooked
juice of 1 lemon	and cubed
2 cups ripe cape goose-	5 bananas, peeled and
berries, halved	sliced
2 cups paw-paw (or	
melon), cubed	

Boil feijoas for 8 minutes in 1½ cups water and with sugar and lemon juice. Pour into a dish and add Cape gooseberry halves, cubed paw-paw, Chinese gooseberries, pears and banana slices. Mix together, and taste. If too sour, add more sugar. If too sweet, add lemon juice. Chill in refrigerator and serve cold.

Fennel: *Florence Fennel; Finocchio (erroneously 'aniseed') (Foeniculum dulce)*

Annual plant originally grown in Italy or other Mediterranean countries for its white bulbous root. For leaves and seeds see *Herbs and Spices*, p. 76.

Preparation:
    fennel—wash, peel and slice the bulb and the tender
        part of the stalk. Cook in boiling salted water
        (25–45 minutes). Sprinkle with salt and pepper
        and pour over melted butter or hot olive oil.
    finocchio—prepare as fennel but never boil. It

should be steamed, or stewed in meat stock. Then treat like *celery*.

Use: raw—sliced and added to salad to which it imparts strong aniseed flavour.

BRAISED FENNEL

Time: 1 hour
Serves: 4–6

500 g

30 g

150 ml

1 lb. fennel roots	salt and pepper to taste
juice of 1 lemon	1 oz. butter
2 tablespoons oil	1 tablespoon flour
¼ pint court bouillon	

Wash and peel roots and cut in halves. Place in casserole dish and pour the lemon juice, oil and stock over roots. Season to taste, cover the casserole dish, bring to simmering point then simmer until roots are tender (30–40 minutes). Remove fennel and keep hot. In a saucepan, melt butter and blend flour with it to form a roux. To this add the juice from the casserole, a little at a time, stirring to blend into a creamy sauce. Cook under low heat for 5 minutes then pour over fennel and serve.

COURT BOUILLON FOR VEGETABLES (I)
or BASIC VEGETABLE STOCK

30 g

1 clove garlic, crushed	2 tablespoons carrots,
1 oz. butter	finely chopped
2 tablespoons onions,	salt and pepper
finely chopped	1 bottle white wine
bouquet garni	

Cook garlic in butter until transparent. Fry onions and carrots in butter until lightly cooked. Season with salt and pepper, add white wine and bouquet garni and bring to boil. Boil for 10 minutes and then add vegetables.

If to be stored, strain, place in refrigerator when cool and use when needed.

COURT BOUILLON FOR VEGETABLES (II)

4 oz. olive oil	Bouquet garni made of	$\frac{1}{2}$ cup
1 pint water	parsley, celery, fennel,	$2\frac{1}{2}$ cups
juice of 2 lemons	thyme, bay leaf	
	12–15 coriander seeds	
	12–15 peppercorns	

Mix oil, water, lemon juice and bring to boil. Add bouquet garni and coriander seeds. Boil for 25 minutes, add peppercorns and boil 5 minutes more. Strain, cool and store.

See also *Greek Sauce* p. 108.

Fenugreek

See *Herbs and Spices* p. 76.

Fern Shoots: *Fiddle Heads; Bracken* (Canada)

The young shoots of certain ferns including bracken (*Pteris aguilina*), the male fern and *Polypodium* are edible. Use only the soft tip of the ferns as you would asparagus tips.

Preparation: boil until tender in salt water to which a few drops of lemon juice have been added.

Use: tossed in butter, then eaten
simmered in cream
tossed in butter, then simmered for a minute in concentrated veal stock

Figs

Fruit of tree, originally from Asia, with thick skins and pulpy flesh. Although there are many varieties, there are four main types—green, white, purple, and red figs. Figs are often available fresh and always dried.

Eat: raw as hors d'oeuvre or dessert with cream and lemon juice
peeled in port wine
with cheese tray
stewed

FIG AND RHUBARB JELLY

Serves: 4–6

1 lb. rhubarb	$\frac{1}{2}$ oz. gelatine	500 g	15 g
2 oz. water	cream, whipped stiffly	$\frac{1}{4}$ cup	
4 oz. sugar	with a little sugar	125 g	
1 lb. fresh figs		500 g	

Cut rhubarb into small pieces and add water and sugar to fruit in a saucepan. Stir over low heat until sugar is dissolved.

Slice the figs and add to saucepan and simmer gently until rhubarb is tender. Soften gelatine in a little water and add to saucepan. Remove saucepan from heat and stir until gelatine is dissolved. Pour into a mould and stand until set. Chill in refrigerator and serve with stiffly whipped cream.

Fines Herbs

See *Herbs and Spices* p. 76.

Flowers

Some varieties of flowers are suitable for crystallizing and those that are proved to be safe are listed below. Others may be poisonous including all those grown from bulbs. If sprays are used, only the flowers should be eaten although leaves may be crystallized for decoration only. Flowers which may be crystallized include: apple blossoms, boronia, cherry blossoms, heather, pear blossoms, plum blossoms, primroses and primulas including polyanthus, roses, violets.

Preparation: select small flowers in perfect bud or bloom, the simpler their shape, the easier they are to crystallize.

Use: to decorate cakes, desserts, jellies, etc.

CRYSTALLIZED FLOWERS

1 oz. powdered gum arabic	obtainable from	30 g
2 oz. rose water, triple strength	a chemist	$\frac{1}{4}$ cup

flowers picked fresh but never wet
castor sugar

Cover gum arabic with rosewater and leave for 24 hours to melt. Place castor sugar in a shaker, or if desired, pass through a blender to reduce the size of the grains. With a small paint brush, hold each flower by the stem and paint the petals and calyx on all sides thinly with the solution of gum arabic and rose water. When every part of the flower is covered, dip in or sprinkle with castor sugar, shake off excess, place on greaseproof paper and dry for 3 or 4 days. Store in airtight tins in a cool place and they will keep for a considerable period.

See also *Acacia* p. 2. *Chrysanthemum Flowers* p. 44, *Tiger Lilies* p. 96, *Waterlilies* p. 96.

Fra-Fra: *Fura-Fura; Potatoes; Fabriama; Daso*

West African plant extensively grown for its edible tubers.

Garlic

See *Herbs and Spices* p. 76.

Garlic Mustard

See *Herbs and Spices* p. 76.

Geranium Leaves

See *Herbs and Spices* p. 77.

Gherkin

4 cm

A small cucumber grown especially for pickling and preserved in vinegar. The best are no longer than 1½ inches long.

Use: for garnishing and savouries
add chopped with paprika to a white sauce

PICKLED GHERKINS

2·5 kg 8 g	5 lb. gherkins	¼ oz. whole allspice
8 g	*Brine:*	¼ oz. cinnamon stick
500 g 8 g	1 lb. cooking salt	¼ oz. whole cloves
20 cups 8 g	1 gallon water	¼ oz. ginger root
8 g	*Spiced vinegar:*	¼ oz. peppercorns
5 cups	2 pints vinegar	

Note: If ground spices are used, allow about 1 level teaspoon of each. However, this makes the vinegar cloudy and the taste may not be so subtle as when using whole products.

Dissolve cooking salt into water. Prick gherkins with a fork and soak for two or three days.

Place vinegar and spice in a china or earthenware (not metal) bowl and cover with a plate. Stand this in a pan of hot water or the top half of a steamer and heat until the vinegar is just simmering. Place to one side and stand for two hours. Pour off vinegar from spices or, if ground spices have been used, strain through closely woven cloth.

Drain gherkins of brine, place into clean jars and fill with spiced vinegar so that there is an inch of vinegar

above the gherkins. Jars must be covered with material which will prevent vinegar evaporating but will not be attacked by vinegar. Nowadays, plastic sheeting would seem to be better than greaseproof paper. Pickled gherkins improve when stored and should be kept at least two months before using. If well sealed, they will keep for several years if needed.

Ginger

See *Herbs and Spices* p. 77.

Gooseberry

See *Berries* p. 26.

Cape Gooseberry: *Ground Cherry; Strawberry Tomato; Jamberberry; Brazil Cherry* (India); *Tomatillo* (Mexico); *Husk Tomato*

A variety of plants of the *Physalis* family, related to the tomato. The fruit looks like small tomatoes with thin outer husks. The tomatillo or ground cherry is a native of southern U.S.A., Mexico, Peru and Chile where it grows wild. The Cape Gooseberry is of the same family but gained its name because it was extensively cultivated in the Cape of Good Hope area of South Africa. It is now cultivated in the hills of northern India and in Australia. The fruits are round, golden or red or purple berries, enclosed in a calyx which looks like a dead leaf. The fruit is piquant, sub-acid and can be made into jams which have a distinctive flavour. Obtainable raw, tinned in syrup, sometimes as jam.

Use: stewed
in jam
with berries dipped in fondant as a sweetmeat
in fruit salad

GLACÉ CAPE GOOSEBERRIES IN CARAMEL

150°C Cape gooseberries   sugar syrup cooked to 310°F
powdered gum arabic

Remove berries from calyxes, roll in powdered gum arabic, then dip in sugar syrup. Remove with perforated spoon and cool on lightly buttered metal tray.

CAPE GOOSEBERRY COMPOTE

Serves: 6–8

2 lb. Cape gooseberries	peel of a lemon	1 kg
1 lb. sugar	kirsch or apricot brandy to	500 g
1 cup water	taste	

Place sugar and water in a pan and bring to boil. Remove calyxes from fruit and add berries. Cook for 5 minutes. Remove and drain fruit and place in an ovenproof bowl.

Place lemon peel in middle of fruit. Replace syrup on heat and reduce to thicken. Pour over the fruit then chill. Before serving, sprinkle with kirsch or apricot brandy.

Chinese Gooseberry: *Kiwi Fruit* (*Actinidia chinensis*)

Brown-skinned oval fruit, grown from a vine and now particularly cultivated in New Zealand, although originally a native of southern China. Each sausage-shaped fruit, is 3 inches long and 1½ inches in diameter and covered with stiff hairs. Flesh is pale to emerald green, juicy and has soft brown edible seeds. Its flavour is unusual, slightly reminiscent of a gooseberry, but distinct.   8 cm   4 cm

Preparation: rub away hairs or peel before scooping out flesh.

Use: eat raw
   fresh in fruit salads or trifle
   cooked in jam and in chutney
   as flavouring for cakes

CHINESE GOOSEBERRY DESSERT

Serve peeled or sliced, sprinkled with lemon juice and castor sugar, or with cream or cold custard.

CHINESE GOOSEBERRY FRUIT SALAD

Serves: 6–8

1 pineapple, peeled and cut in cubes or 1 large tin pineapple cubes	fresh or bottled strawberries 3 Chinese gooseberries, sliced
3 bananas, sliced	syrup made from
1 orange, or 2 mandarines, broken into segments	1 tablespoon sugar boiled in 1 cup water
juice of 1 lemon	

Place pineapple, bananas and orange segments in a bowl and pour lemon juice over them. Add strawberries (or other berries if preferred). Saving some slices of Chinese gooseberries for decoration, blend rest of slices among other fruits. Pour over syrup and top with Chinese gooseberry slices. Stand to allow flavours to blend. Chill in refrigerator. Serve with fresh cream in a separate container.

CHINESE GOOSEBERRY TRIFLE

Serves: 4–6

stale sponge cake	½ cup hot water	
8 Chinese gooseberries, stewed with sugar	½ pint syrup from stewing Chinese gooseberries	1¼ cups
3 teaspoons gelatine	1 tablespoon lemon juice	

Place cake in bottom of bowl and top with stewed Chinese gooseberries. Dissolve gelatine in hot water, add to Chinese gooseberry syrup and add extra sugar if necessary. Squeeze in lemon juice, allow to thicken slightly, then pour over cake and fruit. Chill and serve with custard or ice cream.

OTHER WAYS TO USE CHINESE GOOSEBERRIES

Raw slices to decorate ice cream.
Place spoon of cooked pulp in dessert dish, top with ice cream sprinkled with grated preserved ginger
Decorate cake icing with raw slices of Chinese gooseberry.
Rub steak with peeled Chinese gooseberry a few minutes before grilling. It will enhance flavour and tenderize the meat.

Otaheiti Gooseberry

See *Grosela* p. 67.

Goumi

See *Berries* p. 26.

Gourilos

See *Endive* p. 55.

Gourd

Family of creepers with large fruit. Includes marrows, squash, pumpkin, barbarine and the cushaw of Canada. Today, the term usually refers to ornamental but inedible varieties of this family.

Calabash or **Bottle Gourds**

Fruit of the calabash tree with hard green shell and acid white pulp. In West Indies, the pulp is used to make syrup. Gourds are also dried to make pipes and other articles.

Use: may be roasted whole (Peruvian dish)
      stuffed with rice and chopped meat and boiled (Asian dish)
      stuffed and roasted when green (Middle Eastern dish)

Cucumbers
See p. 47.

Loofah Gourd: *Snake Squash; Dishcloth Gourd* (*Luffa cylindrica*)

Slender fruit of the cucumber family used in Chinese cookery. Cucumber may be used in its place.

Use: as with *cucumber*

Marrows or **Vegetable Marrows**
See p. 101

metric equivalent

35–40 cm
10–13 cm

7 cm

26 cm

Melons

See p. 104.

Pumpkin

See p. 149.

Round Gourds

Yellow flowering gourds, usually eaten when green or unripe.

Squash

See p. 171.

Wax Gourd: *White Gourd; Tallow Gourd*

Oblong, cylindrical fruit of Asian creeper, usually 14–16 inches long and 4–5 inches in diameter. Flesh is slightly floury and white and can store well.

Zapallito

Gourd from South America with round, glossy mahogany coloured fruits, now grown in England and other countries. Flesh is golden and firm but they should not be used when more than 3 inches in diameter.
Preparation and use: as for marrows.

Granadilla: *Grenadilla; Passion Fruit*

Fruits of vines found in various parts of the world, often very popular for use in salads, drinks, ices and desserts. The best known varieties are:

Giant Granadilla: Barbardine (France) (*Passiflora quadrangularis*)

An American vine whose fruit is used as a dessert fruit. The moist pulp is scooped from the elongated, thick shell (which is up to 10 inches long) and mixed with sherry or fresh cream and sugar. It may also be eaten raw.

Passion Fruit

See p. 132.

Parchita or *Sweet Granadilla* (*P. ligularis*)

From central America and Venezuela. Has a strong shell and a translucent whitish pulp.

Sweet Cup or *Sweet Calabash: Kuruba* (*P. maliformis*)

A West Indian variety.

Water Lemon: Yellow Granadilla; Pomme d'Or; Golden Apple; Jamaica Honeysuckle; Belle Apple (*P. laurifolia*)

Native of Hawaii and the West Indies.

Grapefruit: *Pomelo* or *Shaddock; Pamplemouse* (France)

Large juicy citrus fruit, globose and usually pale yellow. Originally from China and then brought to the West Indies by a Captain Shaddock, after whom they were called shaddocks. Today, cultivated varieties are grown in most warm climates of the world. It is said to be the first citrus fruit brought from the East to Barbados in the West Indies. The flesh of most is a translucent lemon colour but others have a pink or red flesh. Coloured varieties are known as pomelos or pomels and are sweeter.

Preparation: cut in half and separate fruit from skin and slice in sections.

Use: in half shell or skin, sprinkled with sugar and then chilled, for breakfast
as hors d'oeuvre
in marmalade
sprinkle with butter, brown sugar, mixed spice and sherry and heat under grill or in oven.
raw in fruit salads with grapes and bananas; with apples and pears.

GRAPEFRUIT JELLY

Serves: 4

½ cup water	¼ cup orange juice
½ cup sugar	¼ cup lemon juice
1 tablespoon gelatine soaked in ¼ cup cold water	¼ teaspoon salt
	2 cups grapefruit sections, fresh
¾ cup grapefruit juice	whipped cream to serve

Boil water and sugar for 3 minutes and dissolve gelatine and water in it. Cool and add juices and salt. Pour into mould, add grapefruit sections last. Cool then refrigerate. Serve topped with whipped cream.

GRAPEFRUIT CHEESECAKE

Serves: 4–6

For crust:	2 eggs	
10 oz. sweet biscuits	¾ cup sugar	315 g
¼ teaspoon grated nutmeg	pinch salt	
¼ teaspoon powdered cinnamon	1 tablespoon gelatine	
	¼ cup cold water	
5 oz. butter, melted	1 lb. cream cheese	155 g 500 g
For filling:	2 teaspoons lemon juice	
3 grapefruit	½ teaspoon grated lemon rind	
½ teaspoon grated grape-fruit rind	½ cup cream	

To make crust: Crush biscuits finely and blend with nutmeg and cinnamon. Mix in melted butter to form shortbread and press against bottom and sides of an 8-inch diameter cake tin. Cool while filling is prepared.   21 cm
To make filling: Peel grapefruit, removing all pith and membrane and saving juice. Grate rind. Save 8 segments of grapefruit for garnishing, and cut rest into small pieces. Separate 1 egg, saving the white to be stiffly beaten. Add yolk to the other egg, sugar, salt and 1 tablespoon of grapefruit juice. Mix and cook in a double boiler until thick and smooth. Soften gelatine in cold water and stir into cooked mixture until dissolved. Cool mixture. Press cream cheese through sieve and blend with remaining grapefruit juice, grapefruit and lemon rind and lemon

juice. Mix with cooled mixture and fold in grapefruit pieces, stiffly whipped cream and stiffly beaten egg white. Spoon into prepared casing, garnish top with grapefruit sections and chill in refrigerator overnight.

GRAPEFRUIT AND PRAWN COCKTAIL

Serves: 2

1 grapefruit, cut in halves with flesh cut away from skin	lettuce leaves, shredded 1 tablespoon tomato purée or paprika
125 g — 1 × 4 oz. packet frozen prawns or shrimp	mayonnaise parsley, finely chopped

Chop grapefruit flesh and mix with most of prawns and lettuce. Tint mayonnaise with tomato purée or paprika until it becomes a pale salmon colour. Mix mayonnaise with grapefruit mixture and refill half-skins with this. Garnish with chopped parsley, and remaining shrimp, sprinkle with a little paprika, chill in refrigerator and serve on bed of crushed ice.

See recipe for *Persimmon and Grapefruit Entrée* p. 141.

Yuzu

Japanese variety of grapefruit. Where stipulated in recipes lemon may be used instead.

Grapes

Small globular fruit, growing in bunches from a stem on the grape vine. While the bulk of grapes grown throughout the world are used to make wine, brandy and vinegar, the only varieties relevant here are those used for cookery. These include exclusively dessert grapes (such as muscats) and others which, when dried become raisins, currants and sultanas.

Preparation: wash on the bunch and serve to be picked at the table.

Use: as fresh for desserts
      peeled and seeded to garnish Sole Veronique and
         other dishes
      to make grape jelly

in fruit salads with orange slices; or nectarines or plums; with pineapple; with grapefruit

SPATCHCOCKS AND GRAPES

Serves: 2–4 (depending on size of birds)

2 spatchcocks (small chickens) cleaned and trussed as for roasting	4 rashers bacon bouquet garni
1–1·5 kg	2–3 lb. under-ripe seedless grapes, peeled
salt and pepper	

Clean and dress the spatchcocks and season inside and out with salt and pepper. In a fireproof dish with lid, or a baking tin with lid, gently cook the rashers of bacon until their fat just begins to become transparent. Remove from heat and place the two spatchcocks and a bouquet garni in the pan. Then pour in grapes to the height of the spatchcocks, or the top of the pan if lower than the top of the birds. Replace lid and simmer very gently for 1 hour or until the spatchcocks are tender. Remove spatchcocks and place on a hot platter. Discard bouquet garni. Arrange grapes around them with bacon rashers on top. This recipe may also be used for duckling, partridges, and other game. Serve with crumbly boiled long-grained rice.

Riverside Grapes

See *Berries* p. 26.

Grape or Vine Leaves

Throughout the Middle East, Caucasia and Armenia, leaves from grape vines are considered an essential vegetable, especially as a wrapping for a savoury filling. With large numbers of grape vines grown in many places, there seems no reason why their leaves should not be utilized more often to provide a few stuffed dishes with a difference. Preserved grape leaves (in brine) are often available from Greek delicatessens.

Preparation:
      fresh grape leaves—pick small and tender leaves,
         wash in boiling water for 10 minutes until leaves
         become tender.

Apple and cream cheese tart (Page 5)

Lamb chops and apricots (Page 7)

Brussels sprouts and chestnuts (Page 30)

Cucumber soup (Page 47)

Dried leaves—need only be washed in a colander with cold water and then drained.

Use: stuffed grape leaves
in tomato pulp, after cooking
as hors d'oeuvre

STUFFED GRAPE LEAVES (I)

Makes: 30 rolls
Time: 1½ hours

1 cup olive oil	½ cup chopped parsley,
3 large onions, chopped	retain parsley stems
1 teaspoon salt	5–6 shallots chopped
¼ teaspoon pepper	2 lemons
1 cup rice	2½ cups water
1 tablespoon chopped fresh dill or 1 teaspoon dry dill	½ lb. grape leaves in brine, or fresh grape leaves 250 g

Heat half the olive oil and sauté onions with salt until they are transparent. Add pepper and rice and cook 10 minutes, stirring occasionally. Add dill, parsley, shallots, juice of 1 lemon and ½ cup water. Cook 10 minutes or until liquid is all absorbed.

Rinse grape leaves and if in brine, separate carefully, placing shiny side down. Place 1 teaspoon filling on each leaf near the base. Starting from the base, fold over once, then fold in the sides and continue rolling towards the tip. Arrange rolls in a large saucepan with stems of parsley between the layers. Add remaining olive oil, juice of 1 lemon and 1 cup of water. Weigh down with a heavy plate and simmer 25 minutes. Add remaining water, simmer a further 25 minutes. Cool and serve with more lemon juice.

STUFFED GRAPE LEAVES (II)

½ lb. prepared grape leaves	2 cups cooked rice	250 g
1¼ lb. minced lean pork	1 tablespoon salt	625 g
¾ lb. minced lean beef	1 teaspoon freshly and	375 g
½ lb. onions, chopped	coarsely ground black	250 g
½ lb. lard	pepper	250 g

Combine pork, beef, onions, lard, rice, salt and pepper. Put balls of this into leaves as described in previous recipe.

For saucepan:	2 tablespoons butter
6–8 rashers bacon	2 tablespoons flour
beef stock (made from beef cube)	½ cup beef stock
	½ cup fresh cream
2 onions, chopped or minced	½ cup warm sour cream

Cover bottom of heavy saucepan with bacon rashers and on them arrange layers of stuffed leaves. Add enough stock to reach rim of weighted plate. Cover and cook over low heat for 1 hour.

In another pan sauté onions in butter until golden, add flour and blend, add ½ cup beef stock and fresh cream, stirring constantly till thick. About 15 minutes before serving add to juices in saucepan with grape leaves, and continue simmering. When ready to serve, drain sauce from stuffed grape leaf rolls, and arrange them on a platter. Mix sour cream with liquid, pour over the stuffed leaves and serve hot with more sour cream as side dressing.

Grosela or Otaheiti Gooseberry

Greenish acid fruit growing on stems of tree found in Pacific Ocean region.

Use: stewed with sugar

Grumichana

Native fruit of Brazil, now cultivated in south Florida.

Guabiyu

Fruit of South America, eaten mainly by native Indians.

Guarana

Seed of a Brazilian climbing shrub, with high tannin and caffein content.

Use: ground to make a dry paste
to flavour drinks

Guava (*Psidium* spp.)

Fruit of a South American or Indian tree or ornamental
bush, now widely grown in tropical countries. Particular
varieties include black guava in Jamaica, the guayobo or
pineapple guava of Argentina and Chilean guava. The
fruit is usually pear shaped but sometimes like an orange
or strawberry. Its rind varies from yellow to purple and
flesh is pulpy varying from white to salmon red. Flavour
is pleasantly acid and musky though some claim it is too
insipid for their tastes. It is available fresh in tropical areas
and canned elsewhere.

Preparation: cut in half and remove flesh from skin

Use: may be eaten raw
  for guava jelly (see medlar jelly)
  jam or stewed
  after making jelly, remaining pulp is served as
  guava 'cheese', *goibada* of Brazil
  shells may be stuffed with cream cheese and served
  as dessert

GUAVA CUSTARD PIE

190°C

Temperature: 375°F
Serves: 6

1 tin guava 'nectar' or syrup	*For custard:*
½ cup stewed guavas, cut small	4 tablespoons cornflour
1 prepared and cooked pie crust	¾ cup cup sugar beaten into 2 egg yolks
	2 egg whites beaten stiff with ½ cup castor sugar
	½ cup grated desiccated coconut

Mix cornflour with a little cold water and make into a
smooth paste. Boil the guava nectar and pour on to the
cornflour paste. Cook in a double boiler for 10 minutes.
Add sugar and beaten egg yolks. Cook for 5 minutes then
add chopped guavas and mix well. Pour into a baked pie
crust. Beat egg whites adding ½ cup castor sugar to stiffen
them. When stiff, top custard with egg whites and sugar
and sprinkle with desiccated coconut. Bake in oven at

190°C

375°F until coconut and meringue begin to brown.
  Serve hot or cold.

Hackberry

See *Berries* p. 26.

Hamburg Parsley

See *Herbs and Spices* p. 79.

Hartshorn: *Bucksthorn Plantain; Star of the Earth*

European weed cultivated for its edible green leaves which are added raw to salads when young and tender. Wild variety is found in sandy and stony locations, often near the sea.

Herbs and Spices

Aromatic and sometimes pungent vegetable substances used for seasoning food. While they may all be invaluable in cookery, some herbs and spices should be used sparingly or they can spoil a dish. Often, certain herbs and spices can be used effectively only with particular foods. Many herbs can be grown in pots or in a garden. For most effective use, they should be picked early in the morning while still wet with dew, and when their oil content is greatest. For preserving or drying, herbs should also be picked early in the morning, just before the first blossoms appear. Dry in oven at 200°F until brittle. Herbs should be stored in wide-mouthed jars with lids. Storing in bundles in the open makes them too dry and they become covered with fine dust and lose their flavour.

95°C

Culinary herbs belong to two botanical families. The *Labiatae* have leaves impregnated with glands containing volatile oil, present also to a lesser extent in their flowers. They produce a characteristic fragrance when crushed. This class includes balm, basil, lavender, marjoram, mint, rosemary, sage, and thyme. Plants belonging to the *Umbelliferae* have oil present mainly in the seeds excepting parsley, fennel, chervil and lovage where leaves or fronds are most fragrant. Others in this class are anise, caraway, coriander, cumin and dill.

The exceptions from these orders are the tarragons and related plants in the Compositae and the Boraginaceae (borage) and the Lauraceae (the laurels), all containing oils in leaves and flowers. To release the essential oils, chopping, bruising and pounding are employed, as is the application of heat.

The Italians usually add finely chopped basil to the crushed garlic when heating oil for sautéing meat, or the rice for risotto. Hot oil releases the oils of herbs more effectively than simmering or boiling in water.

Certain herbs are often used together such as *bouquet garni* and *ravigote*. Others are associated with certain vegetables, e.g. onions, carrots, celery for giving distinctive flavours to stews and casseroles. The French *mirepoix* (p. 85) is typical.

In Imperial China, seasonings were included under five classifications—salty, sweet, sour, peppery, and spicy. A sixth, natural, indicating the flavour of raw foods was included by some Chinese chefs.

In the hot climates where they originated, spices not only enhanced many foods but were originally used as preservatives or to disguise poorly preserved foods in the days before refrigeration. They also stimulate the appetite and aid the sweat glands in warm climates. Wherever they are used, provided discretion is applied, they can enhance and add variety to the finest basic foods.

Most Common Herbs and Spices and Vegetables they match

	Basil	Bay Leaf	Caraway Seeds	Celery Seeds	Chili	Chives	Curry Powder	Dill	Garlic	Ginger	Mace	Marjoram	Mint	Mustard	Nutmeg	Oregano	Parsley	Rosemary	Tarragon	Thyme
Beans	X				X				X						X				X	X
Beetroot			X	X				X						X					X	
Broccoli	X								X					X	X	X				
Brussels sprouts	X			X			X							X		X				
Cabbage			X			X		X							X		X		X	
Capsicum	X								X								X			
Carrots	X	X					X		X	X	X	X	X		X		X	X		X
Cauliflower	X		X			X					X					X	X			
Celery	X																X		X	
Cucumber								X		X										
Eggplant	X							X	X			X				X		X		
Mushrooms	X					X			X								X			
Potato								X			X							X		
Peas						X			X				X							
Spinach	X								X		X	X		X						
Tomato	X			X	X				X							X	X		X	
Turnip	X								X	X		X								

		Use with:
Agi or **Aji**	Dwarf red pimento, grown in Peru.	
Alecost: *Costmary*	South European chrysanthemum-balsam whose leaves are used.	Veal stuffing; soups; stews.
Alisander	Celery flavoured herb. Must be blanched before using.	In place of celery.
Alliaria: *Jack-by-the-Hedge*	Garlic flavoured European wild herb.	In salads.
Allspice: *Jamaican Pepper*	Seeds of West Indian pepper-myrtle or pimento plant said to possess flavours of cinnamon, cloves and nutmeg.	Game and poultry stuffing; 2 or 3 seeds in pea soup; in pickles, marinades, stews, chutneys. Also to flavour sauces for egg and fish.
Angelica	Handsome plants growing to 6 feet high whose green stalks are used.	With cooked orange; crystallized to decorate cakes and desserts; with stewed rhubarb and pears.
Anise	Seeds of Mediterranean plant, source of aniseed (its oil). Has liquorice flavour, said to aid digestion.	In Asian dishes with fish and game; crushed seeds in cakes and custards; with carrots and cabbage.
Balm	Perennial plant with lemon-scented foliage.	In stuffings; add fresh sprig to long summer drinks; leaves may be made into tisane (herb tea) or added to ordinary tea; in salads; with roast duck, turkey or ham.
Bannet		Substitute for cloves.
Basil	Annual plant, originally from India with flavour similar to bayleaf, very pungent when freshly bruised leaves are used. Flavour is slightly peppery.	Excellent with tomatoes; mix with oregano and chives in spaghetti butter sauce; add to lamb chops and liver; use with chives or parsley with eggs, in potato salad, cold rice.
Bay Leaf	Aromatic leaves from bay tree, often dried	Cook with salt pork, mutton and beef; with tongue; milk puddings. See recipe for *Mirepoix* p. 85.
Bergamot: *Bee Balm*	Perennial, highly scented herb, originally from North America. Aroma combines pungency of sage with scent of rosemary.	Young leaves added to tossed green salad; with roast pork.
Borage	Perennial garden herb whose flowers and leaves may be used fresh, with fragrance reminiscent of cucumber.	Add fresh sprig to wine cups; in long summer drinks in place of mint; chopped young leaves in a salad.

Bouquet Garni — Traditional faggot or bunch of tied sprigs of parsley, thyme and bay leaf. If dried, use in muslin bag. May also contain marjoram and mace. — Insert in stews, soups and casseroles and remove after cooking.

Yellow Broome — Preserve buds in vinegar. Use instead of capers. — Use: as *capers*.

Burnet — Meadow plant used fresh and young, with slight cucumber flavour. — To flavour vinegar (see *Tarragon* vinegar p. 86) and in salads and sauces.

Capers — Buds of bush originally grown in Sicily. The smaller the capers, the more delicate their flavour. — Obtainable bottled in vinegar. Used mainly to flavour sauces: caper sauce for mutton; tartare sauce; as garnish for hors d'oeuvres. See also *Broom, Nasturtium Seeds*.

Capsicum: *Sweet* or *Bell Peppers; Poivrons* (France); *Paprika* (central Europe) — Large, bell-shaped, fleshy fruit of an annual plant, originally from central America, now widely cultivated. They are said to contain a cure for stomach and kidney ailments and counteract flatulence. Red ones are claimed to be slightly hotter than the green (or younger) variety but little difference seems noticeable in the fresh capsicum. Paprika is made from the red ones. Names of varieties vary according to shape and colour of the skin when ripe, e.g., long pepper, bonnet pepper. See also *Pepper Chilis* p. 80. — Preparation: cut round stalk and pull out removing core and most of seeds. Remove skin: hold pepper on a fork over a flame until skin blisters. It can then be removed easily. Use: raw—cut in slices or other shapes in salads, as garnish, etc. See recipes for *Capsicum Purée* and *Stuffed Capsicums* p. 84.

Cardamom — Small black seeds in white pods of several tropical plants belonging to ginger family. Pungent, aromatic spice, reminiscent of eucalyptus. — Used in curry powder. Crushed can be sprinkled sparingly on melon, in black coffee; with iced beetroot; baked pears.

Caraway — European plant, related to parsley, grown for its pungent aromatic seeds. — Use with allspice in red cabbage; crushed in cakes, bread and biscuits; cheese dips; with fish.

Cassia Bark — Cheaper substitute for cinnamon, but lacking its subtlety of flavour. — Use: as *cinnamon*.

Catmint: *Catnip* — One of many different varieties of mint, of which at least 14 varieties are grown in England. — Use: as *mint*.

Cayenne — See *Red Pepper*.

73

Celery Seeds	Dried seeds of celery plant ground and mixed with salt to make celery salt.	In pickles, soups, tomato juice, seafood cocktails; white sauce; mayonnaise.
Chervil	Biennial plant of eastern Europe with feathery leaves, related to parsley. Use fresh and chopped, slight aroma is lost when dried. Dittany is a substitute in U.S.A.	With eggs and fish; in hollandaise sauce, in French dressing; in mashed and other potatoes; in tomato juice; with haricot beans. See recipe for *Sorrel and Chervil Soup* p. 86.
Chili (Chile) Powder	Mixture of hot spices.	See recipe p. 84.
Chilis: *Hot South American Peppers*	Slender red elongated fruits of tropical plants, originally from South America. They are hot, pungent, tongue burning and eye smarting and known as chilis or cayenne. They are related to the milder *capsicums* and *pimento*. Cayenne pepper and chili (or chile) powder are made from ground and dried red chilis of various kinds.	Use: mixed in small quantities with beans and tomatoes; in hot pickles
Chinese Five Spices	Ready prepared mixture of Chinese star anise, fennel, Chinese anise pepper, clove, and cinnamon.	Chinese dishes.
Chives	See *Green Onions*.	
Cinnamon	Rolled bark of tree from Ceylon, sold in sticks or powdered.	In small quantities with fish and fish sauces; also with pork and game before roasting; all forms of cooked apples; cakes, biscuits, and pastry.
Clary	Related to sage and similar in flavour.	For soups, stuffings and savouries where sage could be used; with onion.
Cloves	Dried flower bud of tree grown in Moluccas, highly aromatic, used whole or ground. Remove stalk except for sticking in ham for baking, or in onion.	Use sparingly when boiling ham; with onion; with apples; ground cloves in cakes, biscuits, etc.
Colocasia	Tuberous herb of the Moluccas now grown in the West Indies.	Tuberous roots are cooked like yams. Leaves like cabbage.
Comfrey	English 'pot herb'.	Use: in soups and stews.

Coriander: *Dhanya;* *Chinese Parsley* — Valuable herb which can be grown from more common seeds, sweet yet acid tasting, in seed; fresh resembles taste of chervil. — Seeds—in curries; with pork; with dried bean recipes; also with cream cheese; in pickles and chutney. Fresh—in salads and soups. Crushed—with juniper and cloves in beef casserole; to garnish baked fish. See recipe for *Cold Stewed Okra and Coriander* p. 120.

Cowslip — European wild flower. — Wine making; flavouring vinegar (see *Tarragon vinegar* p. 86).

Cumin (Cummin): *Jeera* — Strongly aromatic seeds of annual Mediterranean plant, resembling flavour of caraway but stronger. — Seeds—in curries; in meat loaf; with dried beans; with chicken sparingly. Flowers—as garnish.

Curcuma — Indian plant with yellow rhizome with acrid flavour, a cross between saffron and ginger. — Powdered in curry powder and in English mustard.

Curry powder — Mixture of spices, yellow and usually very hot. — See recipe p. 84.

Dill — Herb resembling fennel, leaves used for garnishing, stalks for flavouring pickles. Said to help the digestion. — Add chopped to potato salad; to mayonnaise; serve with fish; when preserving cucumbers; with rice; with cabbage.

Dock — Some varieties of dock leaves may be used as herbs. — Cook young leaves as with *sorrel*.

Elder — Flowers of European elder plant. — Flowers—give delicious flavour to muscat grapes, fruit salad, strawberries; or stewed in bag with gooseberries; also in fritters—see *Acacia*.

Endive and Chicory

COMMON NAME	BOTANICAL NAME	HOW CULTIVATED	USE
Belgian Endive or **Endive** (France and U.S.A.): *Chicory* (England; *Chicoree de Bruxelles, Witloof, Barb-de-boec* (Belgium)	*C. endiva*	Stems blanched while growing.	Only stems or hearts used, either raw or cooked. Quarter and cut in ½ inch slices. Cook: braise like *celery*.
Chicory or **Curly Endive** (U.S.A.)		Curly leaves growing in flat heads, tied to blanch those in centre.	Leaves used raw in green salads.

2 cm

75

Succory (England)
or **Escarol** (U.S.A.)
C. intybus

Grows to a height of 6 feet,
has china blue flowers.

Finely shredded leaves may be
added raw to lettuce in a green
salad giving it a bitter yet
pleasant taste.
Root may be cooked like *parsnip*;
or dried, roasted brown and
ground to adulterate coffee.

Gourilos or
Moelle de Chicoree

Stumps of curly endive.

Blanch in salt water containing
lemon juice: then cook in butter
or cream in covered pan until
tender; fry after soaking in oil
and vinegar and dipping in
batter; grilled with cheese.

Fennel

Fresh leaves or seeds of *Foeniculum vulgare*,
a feathery herb with aniseed or liquorice
flavour (see also p. 58).

Use sparingly in fish sauces; liver, kidney and
pork recipes; seeds in pastry.

Fenugreek

Seeds of unusual Asian *Trigonella* plant with
slightly bitter flavour.

Used in curry powder.

Fines Herbes

Term used to refer to very finely chopped
sweet herbs. Can include parsley, shallots,
chives, mint, basil, tarragon, chervil and
savoury.

To flavour an omelette; in Remoulade
sauce; for stuffing fish.

Garlic

Pungent root of a perennial plant of the
onion family, essential in many forms of
cooking. Roots are usually dried and a
section or 'clove' or two are removed for use.
Use of garlic seems to be determined by a
cook's sensibility. For most dishes, sparing
use imparts a subtle but distinct flavour.
However, in parts of Europe, and elsewhere,
many people like crushed garlic on toasted
bread and are indifferent to the distinctive
smell which is retained on the breath. Like
onions, garlic is also reported to have
valuable medicinal properties though no
modern scientists seem to have confirmed
or denied these reports by earlier herbalists
and others.

Preparation: remove required number of
cloves, skin them, then crush or slice before
using.
Use: rub wooden salad bowl with crushed
garlic before adding other ingredients; rub
steak with crushed clove before frying or
grilling; when frying, gently sauté crushed
or sliced garlic in oil to extract its flavour in
the oil, then remove before adding other
ingredients; when roasting lamb and mutton,
nick the flesh and insert tiny slivers of garlic.
See recipes for *Garlic Butter*, *Garlic Toast*,
Garlic Soup and *Mirepoix*, p. 85.

Garlic Mustard or **Sauce
Alone**

Pot herb, grown in England.

Geranium Leaves, Scented	Leaves of certain varieties of geranium with distinctive scent. They include nutmeg, apple, rose, lemon, peppermint, and coconut.	In cakes, jellies, custards, baked apples.
Ginger	Hot, pungent root of ginger plant, originally from India and now grown in many places. Obtained green, or dried and crushed or ground.	With other spices—in chutney, curries, and sauces. Ground—with apple; for sprinkling over steak before grilling; in cakes and biscuits; in Chinese fish cookery; pickled with carrots, parsnips, onions, and cucumbers.
Horseradish	Hot tasting root of European horseradish plant, used grated and mixed with lightly whipped cream (horseradish sauce).	Horseradish sauce with roast beef and fish used fresh—grated over cold beef and beetroot salad. See recipe for *Apple and Horseradish Salad* p. 5.
Hyssop	Aromatic herb of ancient origin.	In green salads; to flavour liqueurs.
Sweet Javril	Perennial herb of America with aromatic roots.	
Juniper	Blue berries from small fir-type of shrub with pungent spicy taste. Used fresh or dried, but crushed first.	Add dry berries to marinades for game; to flavour gin; in stuffing for poultry; in *sauerkraut* and *cole slaw* (p. 35).
Kuchay: *Kiu-Ts'ai*	Chinese variety of garlic, now widely established by expatriate Chinese wherever they have settled and available from Chinese stores. 　As well as using the cloves, the leaves can be used like chives and even the flowers have a subtle flavour of garlic coupled with a sweetness which makes them a valuable component of any green salad.	Use: cloves—as garlic; leaves—as with chives; flowers—in green salads
Lovage	Perennial south European herb related to angelica with grey-green serrated leaf and taste of celery.	Young leaves may be chopped and added to salads; in soups and sauces.
Mace	Dried crimson coating of outside of nutmeg kernel. Whole (blade) or ground. Flavour similar to nutmeg but of greater intensity and with hint of cinnamon.	Blade mace—to flavour curries, pickles, spiced vinegar (see *Tarragon* vinegar and milk for béchamel sauce, and sauce supreme for fish. Ground mace—added to cakes and puddings; sprinkled lightly on fish or puréed potatoes, creamed spinach, and young carrots; with chocolate dishes.

Sweet Marjoram	Annual herb with strong, slightly bitter taste. Use fresh or dried.	In stuffings for veal and lamb; in omelettes with fish; with spinach, carrots, turnips; with chives and parsley.
Masha: *Sour-Sour; Indian Sorrel*	Oriental herb used widely, with rather bitter flavour.	In soups and stews, salads and curries.
Melilot	Perennial leguminous plant of England and France with aromatic leaves and flowers, usually used dried and crushed.	In marinades and stews; in stuffing for baked rabbit; to flavour cheese.
Mercury: *Dog's Mercury; Allgood; Good-King-Henry; Goosefoot; Wild Spinach*	Annual herb, found in England and South Africa.	Cook in two waters, throwing away first which extracts very green and bitter fluids. Young shoots may be eaten like *asparagus*.
Milfoil	European woodland plant.	Tender leaves added to salads.
Sweet Mint	Originally native of Europe, now found everywhere but used mostly in Britain and U.S.A. Many varieties are grown, with different flavours including apple, eau-de-cologne, pineapple, wild spearmint.	With vinegar and sugar in mint sauce for lamb; with peas; in salads; long summer drinks; in stuffings and aspics.
Mugwort	Hardy European perennial with strongly aromatic leaves but a bitter taste.	Use: in stews and stuffings.
Mustard	Ground seeds of Brassica type plant which are mixed with water or vinegar to form a hot paste. English mustard is sold as flour with turmeric added. French mustard is a prepared paste, milder than English variety, with herbs and vinegar added.	Ideal with roast beef, steak; in mayonnaise and salad dressings; whole seeds used in pickles. For use of leaves see p. 110.
Myrtle	Evergreen shrub, wild in parts of Europe, whose aromatic leaves, seeds and berries have been used since ancient Rome. Leaves are substitute for bay leaves, berries in place of pepper.	In marinades and stews to impart alternate flavour.
Nettle or **Stinging Nettle**	Common weed must be gathered with gloved hands when shoots are young and tender.	Cook as for *spinach*; young leaves may be used in salads; may also be used in home-made beer.
Nigella: *Fennel Flower; Devil-in-the-Bush*	Plants of *Ranunculus* family with aromatic pungent seeds, sometimes used instead of pepper, and cultivated and used in Egypt.	As a *pepper* substitute.

Nutmeg — Fruit or kernels of Indonesian tree, available as whole kernels or ground. Nuts should be grated finely. See also *Mace*. — Strong spice, used sparingly with apples, sauces, and desserts. To give lamb a different taste.

Oregano — Leaves of wild marjoram obtained in Italy but stronger than marjoram. — Mixes well with tomatoes in any form; sprinkled on baking onions; roasting lamb or pork; in stuffing for poultry and meat; in marinades.

Paprika — Ground powder blended from ground sweet red peppers, used extensively in Hungary, Morocco and Spain. See also *Capsicum*. Its flavour is spicy but not hot. — Use in goulash; with chicken and veal; for garnishing crab, eggs, cheese, hors d'oeuvres.

Parsley — Biennial herb with tight curly leaves, and distinct flavour. — Used extensively as garnish; finely chopped to enhance soups, sauces, stews and in stuffings; also fried.

Hamburg Parsley: *Turnip Rooted Parsley* — Variety of the common herb with roots resembling a turnip and grown mainly in Europe. — Use: as vegetable, leaves prepared like *spinach*. Roots prepared as for *celeriac*.

Cow Pea: *White-Eyed Pea; Black-Eyed Pea; China Pea (Vigna sinensis)* — Sprawling herb, growing wild in most tropical countries and extensively cultivated in the southern States of the U.S.A. as cattle food. The dried seeds are also used for food. There are two types, white and black.

Pennyroyal — Type of mint used for similar purposes, fresh or dried. — Add to stews; use with parsley.

Pepper — True pepper is made from grinding the small round seeds of berries grown on a vine distantly related to the elm-tree, grown in South-East Asia.

Black Pepper — Dried unripe fruit of Indonesian plant. Quickly loses aroma and taste when ground and best flavour is obtained if peppercorns are milled when needed.
   Hot and sweet peppers are fruits of tropical annual plants originally from tropical America. — More pungent and aromatic than white pepper; whole peppercorns added to soups, stews and casseroles; to boiling salt pork, mutton or beef.

Red or **Cayenne Pepper** — Ground product from various types of dried hot red peppers or chilis, very hot, pungent and biting. — Sparingly used with cheese, eggs, fish, shell-fish, salad dressing. Also added to curry and in making hot sauces, e.g., Newburg.

Pimentos (Pimientos):
Spanish Peppers; Canned or Bottled *Sweet Peppers*

A sweet pepper but is smaller and more triangular in cross section than the capsicum. Occasionally canned or bottled sweet peppers are seen on sale in gourmet stores and no one seems to know what to do with them. One brand from Mexico are known as *chiles poblanos*. See recipes p. 84.

Poppy Seed

Fine grey seeds of type of poppy flowers. Available whole or ground.

To garnish rolls and bread before baking; with cakes and strudels.

Purslane: *Pussley*

Annual herb with mildly aromatic foliage. In South America, the tuberous roots of garden purslane or rose moss are an important article of food. Sea purslane or notch weed may be used like spinach or pickled like vinegar as a condiment. Two varieties cultivated in Asia are Philippines spinach and which are cooked as spinach. Another variety is winter purslane, grown in central America and the West Indies and used in the same manner.

Use fresh shoots in salads or vegetable soups in place of sorrel. Cooked as for spinach. Leaves may be pickled as with nasturtium seeds.

Rape

European herb of the cabbage family whose leaves may be gathered in spring.

Use: as for *spinach*.

Ravigote

Combination of tarragon, chervil, parsley, burnet, and chives.

Use fresh ingredients, finely chopped in salads; or in butter for sauce with steaks or fish.

Rocket

Garden herb whose leaves, like cress, have a peppery taste when gathered young and added to green salads. Rocket salad sold in the U.S.A. is the winter cress, a variety of watercress. Turkish rocket, a native of western Asia is grown in France and is used to produce green salads earlier than other salad plants.

When its leaves become too coarse, they may be cooked as for spinach.

Rose Hips

Seed cases or fruit of the wild English rose, rich in Vitamin C.

To make rose-hip syrup, obtainable commercially; used in jellies by adding water, sugar, claret, port or sherry and gelatine 1 oz. to 1 pint liquid.

30 g   2½ cups

Rosemary — Leaves of an evergreen shrub with an aromatic pine flavour. Flowers also used to garnish salads. — To flavour fish and stuffings; sprig inside roasting fowl can replace stuffing; good with rabbit and lamb; freshly chopped in salads or when sautéing potatoes.

Rose Water — Obtainable from south-east European shops, and chemists, provides a delicate and unusual flavour. — In desserts, pastries and cool drinks.

Rue — Strongly aromatic Mediterranean plant. — Add to stews; sometimes to salads; in brown bread sandwiches.

Saffron — Dried stigmas from a species of crocus, originally from Asia, used as yellow dye with a warm, bitter aroma. One pinch is enough for a dish. Soak in 2–3 tablespoons of warm water for 30 minutes before use. Obtainable from chemists—rather expensive as 200,000 needed to make 1 lb. weight. — Traditional Cornish addition to make saffron buns; in Italy for saffron rice; in Spain for *paella*; in France for *bouillabaisse* and other fish soups.

500 g

Sage — Leaves of a perennial shrub with pungent but pleasing aroma. Use fresh or dried. — Ideal with rich meats such as pork, goose, and duck; for sage and onion stuffing; to wrap round cream cheese to flavour it; in marinades. See recipe for *Sage Claret* p. 85.

Salt — The chemical sodium chloride, usually obtained from solar evaporation of sea water, sometimes from rock salt, and for table use often with other chemicals added to ensure free flow in damp conditions. — Add to most savoury dishes and sometimes in small quantities to sweet ones.

Sauce Alone — See *Garlic Mustard* p. 76.

Savory — Peppery sage or rosemary flavoured herb. A summer variety is an annual plant; the winter variety, perennial. — Use: with broad beans; for stuffing; when stewing liver, tripe and sausage; for seasoning poultry; with trout.

Sesame Seeds — Seeds of annual plant known from Middle East and Orient, used to make sesame oil (available from Chinese shops). Both black and white sesame seeds available. — Seeds used in biscuits and cakes; in halva in Middle East; fried in butter and mashed with potato or avocado; sprinkled on roast chicken.

Simsim (Africa): *Sesame Seed*

The small oblate flattish seeds of the sesame plant, best known as a source of oil which is extracted from them and is known as sesame, benne or gingli oil. It is used as a flavouring agent in margarine and soap manufacture and to dilute olive and other expensive oils. The sesame plant is believed to have originated in the Malaysia-Indonesia archipelago but is now grown widely. Seeds are sold in the U.S.A. under the name bene seeds. In parts of Africa they are used extensively in cookery.

Preparation: Use 4 tablespoons water to 1 cup simsim then rub to remove skins. Put seed in pan over heat and stir so that it does not burn. Cook for 20 minutes. When seeds begin to pop they are cooked. Grind cooked simsim into a paste and mix with other ingredients. 1 cup simsim is enough for 6 serves.

Sorrel: *Sour Grass*

Plant or herb of the dock family cultivated in Europe with acid-fresh taste. The degree of bitterness varies with the variety. Wood or mountain sorrel is the strongest and French sorrel is the mildest.

Preparation: pick and wash in running water to remove all dirt. Shake then chop up fairly small, and place in saucepan with no extra water. Cook for about 15 minutes, then add salt and pepper and butter.
Use: as purée to serve with eggs, carp and hake, rich meats including veal; mix with spinach; add to various soups.
See recipe for *Sorrel and Chervil Soup* p. 86.

Wood Sorrel: *Alleluia*

Common weed of Europe whose young leaves are added to green salads for their slightly bitter taste. A Mexican variety has fleshy white roots which may be cooked like parsnips but which have little flavour. The leaves of the Mexican variety may be prepared as for sorrel.

Spearmint

A variety of mint.

As *mint*.

Spignel

Herb with celery flavour.

Use: fresh in salads or stews.

Spikenard

Indian flavouring obtained from root of an Asian species of valerian. There is also an American variety with a powerful and pleasing fragrance but a bitter flavour.

Spice still used in Malayan cookery.

Sumac

Sour tasting powder from plant of rhus family

Used with kebabs or other grilled meats.

Tansy

English roadside plant with bitter aromatic flavour, akin to ginger.

To flavour cakes and puddings, especially in Yorkshire at Easter.

Mousaka (Page 54)

Walnut meringues (Page 118)

Stuffed olives dip (Page 121)

Pineapple duck (Page 142)

Tarragon	Perennial herb with delicate though pungent taste, should be used only fresh but may be used dry.	For flavouring wine vinegar; for chicken; in salads, stews and omelettes; in aspics; in Bearnaise sauce; green mayonnaise; in marinades for meat and fish. See recipe for *Tarragon Vinegar* p. 86.
Thyme	Ordinary and lemon flavoured herb, used fresh or dried.	Lemon thyme especially good with eggs, scrambled or creamed; in butter with shellfish; in soups and stuffings; with salt and black pepper sprinkled over beef, lamb, and veal before roasting; in a *bouquet garni*. See recipe for *Mirepoix* p. 85.
Lemon Thyme	Lemon flavoured variety of *thyme*.	Substitute for lemon in stuffing or forcemeat.
Turmeric: *Haldi*	Dried and powdered root of a ginger family plant from Ceylon, bright yellow, aromatic, slightly bitter and peppery	Essential ingredient in curry powder; in some pickles and sauces; in fish kedgeree and devilled eggs.
Udo: *Oudo*	Japanese herb with edible shoots, possessing a delicate aromatic taste.	Preparation: blanch in hot water as for asparagus with hot butter sauce; cold in vinaigrette.
Vanilla	Dried beans from the pods of an orchid, originally from Mexico but now grown in many tropical countries. When split, tiny black seeds have strong aromatic flavour. Usually obtained as a pure essence though synthetic vanilla is now also on sale.	In flavouring many types of dessert dishes including milk puddings, cakes, etc.
Yarrow	Strongly scented species of milfoil, used fresh.	Use: instead of *chervil*.

STUFFED CAPSICUM I

Time: 1 hour

175°C Temperature: 350°F

Serves: 3–6

6 large capsicums	salt and pepper
2 tablespoons onion, chopped	1 cup rice, boiled
	2 oz. tomato purée
1 lb. finely minced steak	
little oil for sautéing	

500 g ¼ cup

Cut stem and core from capsicums, remove all seeds. Dip in boiling water for 5 minutes then drain. Sauté onions and minced steak in a little oil until lightly browned. Season with salt and pepper, mix with rice and moisten with a little water. Fill capsicums with mixture and arrange in casserole dish.

175°C   Mix tomato purée with double the quantity of water and pour over capsicums. Bake in oven at 350°F until peppers are tender, basting with sauce once or twice. This should take about 35 minutes. Can be prepared the day before and baked when needed.

STUFFED CAPSICUM II

Time: 1½ hours

175°C   Temperature: 350°F

Serves: 6

6 green capsicums, medium sized	¼ teaspoon ground cinnamon
1 cup cooked chopped lamb or ½ lb minced steak	1 tomato, peeled and chopped
1 cup cooked rice	1 dessertspoon olives, chopped
1 onion, chopped	salt and pepper
1 tablespoon almonds, skinned and in slivers	1 cup chicken stock, made with stock cube
1 teaspoon coriander seed, crushed	

250 g

Slice top off each capsicum, scoop out seeds, but save tops. Mix together lamb, rice, onion, almonds, coriander, cinnamon, tomato and olives and season with salt and pepper. Stuff the capsicums with this mixture, place capsicums in a casserole dish, replace capsicum tops,

pour over the stock. If any stuffing mixture remains, form into balls and add to casserole dish. Bake in oven for 1 hour, basting frequently.

CAPSICUM PURÉE

Remove cores, seeds and skins from capsicums, then place fresh in boiling salted water for 15 minutes. Drain and pulp with a fork, or press through a sieve. May be used with salt as a filling for sandwiches.

CHILI (CHILE, CHILLI) POWDER

Blend of hot spices pounded and mixed together like curry powder, widely used in Mexico and the southern States of the U.S.A.

Ingredient quantities vary according to taste but include:

black *peppercorns*	*paprika*
white *peppercorns*	*cumin seeds*
red *peppercorns* (dried chillis, bird's eye peppers)	dried *garlic* *oregano*

CURRY POWDER

A blend of many different herbs and spices differing widely in formulae and quantities depending on the type of food to be curried and the area where the powder is made. Its hot quality depends on the proportions of ginger, and/or hot pepper and its colour on turmeric.

HOME MADE CURRY POWDER

75 g	2½ oz. powdered turmeric	13 cloves, knobs only (or
15 g	½ oz. powdered ginger	equal weight in allspice)
60 g	8 g	2 oz. coriander seed	¼ oz. powdered cayenne
8 g	¼ oz. whole black peppers	pepper
8 g	¼ oz. whole cardamom seeds	

Pound all ingredients in a mortar until very fine then mix thoroughly with powdered ingredients. Store in tightly closed jar or use immediately.

metric equivalent

GARLIC TOAST

slices of wholemeal bread   garlic butter
or long French stick

Toast slices and spread with garlic butter; cut half slices of stick, spread cuts with garlic butter, wrap in aluminium foil and heat in oven until crisp.

GARLIC BUTTER

		metric equivalent
4 cloves garlic, crushed or pounded	4 oz. butter	125 g

Whisk garlic and butter together until well blended then pass butter through a fine sieve. Add to sauces, stuffings, to butter bread for savouries and aperitifs.

GARLIC SOUP

Time: 35–40 minutes
Temperature: 450°F   230°C
Serves: 4

1 tablespoon olive oil	salt	
3 cloves garlic	¼ teaspoon paprika	
2 tomatoes	3 thin slices of bread, cut	
½ bayleaf	into fingers	
1½ pints boiling water	3 eggs	3¾ cups

Heat oil in pan and gently brown cloves of garlic. Fry tomatoes and bayleaf in the oil, then add boiling water and season with salt and paprika.

   Place bread fingers into a large casserole and break eggs over them. Strain soup from pan and pour over bread and eggs. Place casserole in oven until a brown crust forms.

Note: Onions may be used to replace garlic.
      Boiling water may be replaced with beef or chicken stock made from meat or from stock cubes.

MIREPOIX

2 carrots	1 clove garlic	
2 onions	¼ lb fat bacon	125 g
2 shallots	¼ lb raw ham	125 g
2 bay leaves	oil for cooking	
sprig thyme	1 glass red wine	

Mince all ingredients together except wine and mix thoroughly. Place in pan with little hot oil and sauté for a few minutes. Add red wine and increase heat to allow its flavour to be added to the other ingredients. This is used as a basis for braising, sauce or casserole.

PIMENTO CREAM

4 pimentos   1 egg white
1 cup cream

Rub pimentos through a sieve and place at one side. Whip cream until thick and beat the egg white until stiff. Fold egg whites into cream and combine and then fold in sieved pimentos. Use as salad dressing or dip.

Alternate uses

1. Mix small can of sweet corn with equal quantity of diced cheddar cheese and a smaller amount of chopped pimento and fill inside peppers. Beat yolks of three eggs, add a little cream and pour over peppers. Dot with pieces of cheese and bake at 325°F until hot and cheese has melted.   160°C
2. Stuff peppers with savoury minced meat (mince meat with herbs, spices, salt and pepper to taste), dip in batter and deep fry in hot oil. Can be served hot or cold.
3. Marinade peppers in olive oil, lemon juice and salt overnight. Drain and stuff with shredded sardines, mixed with peeled and chopped tomato, minced green onions, a little oregano and some of marinade. Serve sprinkled with grated parmesan cheese. Tuna or shrimp may replace sardines or sild.
4. Marinade peppers as for (3) above. Stuff with chopped cooked meat or chicken mixed with chopped almonds and raisins. Place in dish and spread with mashed avocado, cooked and mashed baby marrow moistened with some of the marinade. Salt to taste and serve cold.

SAGE CLARET

2 oz. fresh sage leaves	1 pinch cayenne pepper	60 g	
1 oz. fresh lemon rind	few drops of lemon juice	30 g	
1 oz. salt	1 pint claret	30 g	2½ cups

Add ingredients to claret and stand for 14 days, shaking the bottle well every day. Allow to stand and then strain claret into a new bottle and cork tightly.

Use: added to juices of roast pork, duck and goose to
make gravy;
added to goulash;
add to onion sauce

SORREL PURÉE AND EGGS

Time: 25 minutes
Serves: 4

500 g	1 lb sorrel, prepared as above

butter
4 eggs, poached

Chop finely the prepared sorrel, add a little more butter, and cook for another 10 minutes. Place on individual plates, and on each nest of sorrel place one poached egg. Serve hot.

SORREL AND CHERVIL SOUP

Time: 1¼ hours
Serves: 4

125 g	4 oz. sorrel
	1 tablespoon chopped chervil
60 g	2 oz. butter
5 cups	2 pints chicken stock (made from stock cubes)

yolks of 2 eggs
salt and pepper
croutons

Pick and wash sorrel and chop small. Pick chervil from stalks and chop. Put these in saucepan with butter. Simmer gently for 30 minutes. Add stock and use tightly fitting lid. Simmer another 30 minutes. When ready to serve, beat egg yolks, add a little of the hot liquid to the eggs and gradually mix together, stirring constantly. When slightly thickened, remove from heat, season to taste. Add butter and serve with croutons.

Alternately, replace chervil with 2 large potatoes, add 1 tablespoon of flour before adding stock and use only 1 egg.

TARRAGON VINEGAR

1 large, wide-mouthed jar
filled with fresh tarragon
leaves, picked on a dry
day when plant is due to
flower

white wine vinegar,
sufficient to cover
leaves

Cover leaves with white wine vinegar and stand for 5 or 6 hours. Strain vinegar through a cloth and cork it tightly in the bottle.

Use: for mixing mustard
in Tartare sauce
an ingredient in fish sauces

Hondapara

Fruit of an Asian tree. A thick fibrous shell covers the fruit which has a tomato-like centre. Flavour is very acid and flesh must be cooked before use.

Honey Tree: *Japanese Raisin Tree; Cock's Claw*

Fruit of deciduous shrub or small tree of eastern Asia, also grown in parts of South America. Its reddish, false fruit (really fruit-bearing peduncles) are edible.

Hop Shoots

The flowers or panicles of the male hop plant are eaten in traditional hop growing areas. The tip of the panicle is broken off similar to an asparagus tip.
Preparation: boil until tender in salt water with a few drops of lemon juice added.

Use: always tossed in butter
simmered in fresh cream
simmered a short while in concentrated veal stock

Serve: as vegetable
as garnish with omelette and poached eggs

Horseradish

See *Herbs and Spices* p. 77.

Huckleberry

See *Berries* p. 26.

Huevo de Gallo

Fruit of native *Salpichroa* tree, occasionally sold in markets in Argentina.

Hyssop

See *Herbs and Spices* p. 77.

IJK

Ibas

Variety of fruit from the Obas tree, originally from Gabon, Africa. It is similar but inferior to the mango grown in West Africa and eaten by natives there. The kernel is used to make *dika* or *odika* bread. Seeds are processed to extract *dika* butter, fat or oil with a flavour reminiscent of cocoa. It is now grown in some parts of Europe.

Igba Purú

Native *Myrciaria* tree of Brazil with deliciously flavoured fruit.

Eat: raw
    use in jellies
    ferment into alcoholic beverage

Imbu

4 cm

Tree of *Spondias* genus, native to N.E. Brazil, similar to a greengage plum, about 1½ inches long and yellow. Flavour of the soft, melting, almost liquid flesh suggests a sweet orange. It is the basic ingredient of *imbuzado* made by adding the purée to boiled, sweetened milk and producing a greenish white dessert.

Use: fresh
    in jellies

Inga

Edible fruit of a tree native to Brazil and Argentina but now grown in West Indies where it is called 'guava'. Fruit is purple and grows on both trunk and branches. Their white pulp is said to be delicious though jams, jellies and pastes made from Inga are claimed to be inferior to those made from the true Guava.

Use: as with *guava*.

Isiqwashumbe: *Hedge Mustard*

Variety of wild mustard eaten to prevent scurvy by natives in South Africa, particularly eastern Cape Province.

Izibo

Tuber of African plant, eaten by natives in S.W. Provinces of South Africa. In Senegal, the seeds too are fried in oil.

Jaboticaba

4 cm

Grape-like fruits growing from the trunk of a south Brazilian tree. Related to the guava, its maroon-purple fruit grow to 1½ inches in diameter. The skin is thicker than a grape and the flesh is a translucent white or rose-tinged pulp.

Use: in jelly
    to make wine

Jackfruit

25 kg

Variety of breadfruit originally native to southern Asia but now widespread in the tropics. The fruit weighs up to 50 lb. In Ceylon, the smaller African Jackfruit is cultivated solely for its seeds which are ground into a meal or flour to make cakes, bread and a form of almond milk.

Preparation: remove skin and eat pulp raw

Use: pulp cooked in oil and with curry
    dried and preserved
    seeds may be roasted like *chestnuts*

JACKFRUIT SOUP

1 lb green jackfruit pulp	1 packet chicken noodle
¼ lb salt beef	soup
1 pig's trotter	½ lb flour
1 lb yam	salt and pepper
1 slice pumpkin	

500 g
125 g
250 g
500 g

Pick and wash jackfruit in salt water or lime (lemon) juice. Boil jackfruit in water. When tender, drain, add salt beef and pig's trotter, and cover with fresh water, simmer 1 hour, or until meat is tender. Add yam and pumpkin, bring to boil and simmer. Add packet of chicken noodle soup mixed with flour and cook until yams and pumpkin are tender. Season with salt and pepper, serve hot.

Variation: in place of pumpkin and chicken noodle soup
—add 2 vegetable pears, milk from 1 coconut
and 2 carrots.

Jambolan: *Java Plum*

Fruit of a *Eugenia* tree, native to Indonesia, New Guinea
and northern Australia and most islands of the south
Pacific. It resembles a plum and has astringent seeds.

Eat: cooked in tarts and puddings

Jujube: *Chinese Dates; T'sao*

Fruit of the jujube tree, originally from Syria but now
grown in many warm climates including California and
China. There are many varieties but the date-like fruit is
generally oval, about the size of an olive with a smooth
leathery red skin. The flesh is yellow, sweet but
comparatively dry and crisp, surrounding a long pointed
stone. The Chinese use three types of jujubes in their
cooking. Red are the most common but there are also
white 'honey' jujubes or 'dates' and black 'dates'. All are
sweet and are cooked in soups, fish dishes and desserts.
Available dried from some Chinese suppliers.
Preparation: soak dried jujubes for 1 hour before using.

Use: in pickles
    stewed
    candied as a sweetmeat
    in puddings
    jellies
    cakes and bread
For recipe see *Lotus Root* or Stem Soup, p. 97.

Kale: *Borecole; Collards; Coleworts; Spring Greens*

Members of cabbage family with curly leaves which do
not form a heart. Kale has blue green leaves while collards
or coleworts have leaves which are generally yellow green
and smooth instead of crinkly. Always make sure that the
kale is crisp and fresh.

Quantities: use 2 lb raw kale to serve 4 people.   1 kg

Preparation: thoroughly wash, shred and serve raw as a
    green salad, with lettuce, endive, vinegar and oil.

Cook: as for *cabbage*.

Kamachile: *Kamanchile*

Prized edible fruit of a tropical American *Pithecolobium*
tree. The tree also yields good timber, a yellow dye and a
mucilaginous gum.

Kohlrabi: *Cabbage Turnip*

Root vegetable with blue-green leaves, similar to kale.
Flesh is really an above-ground swelling containing a
pithy flesh with a slight flavour of celery.

Preparation: root—as for *turnip*, mash and serve mixed
    with a little milk and butter and chopped parsley;
    tops—as for spinach
    like *celeriac* for use in salads or hors d'oeuvres.

SAUTÉED KOHLRABI WITH PORK

lard	1 breast of pork, cubed
2 onions, chopped	salt and pepper
1 lb kohlrabi, peeled and	½ bottle white wine
sliced	meat stock (from cube)

500 g

Heat sufficient lard in pan to soften the onions then add
the kohlrabi. When kohlrabi is nearly cooked, add pork
and season with salt and pepper. Add white wine and
stock and simmer until reduced by half.
    Serve hot as entrée.

Kudzu (Japan); *Fan-kot* (China)

Starchy edible roots of an Asian ornamental vine, used
widely in Japan and China and also by nationals of these
countries in the U.S.A. and other countries where
communities have been established.

Lamb's Quarters: *Pigweed; Goosefoot*

A common weed originated in Europe and Asia and is found in many places. Young stalks and leaves may be eaten raw or cooked as for *spinach*.

Lawton Berry

See *Berries* p. 26.

Leeks

A hardy biennial plant known in ancient Egypt and Rome, and the national emblem of Wales for 1400 years. Nero and other Romans claimed that leeks helped to improve the voice and ate them specially for that purpose. The Welsh too, eat a large number of leeks and also have particularly sonorous voices. Leeks are grown in trenches to blanch the stalk. The flavour is delicate and resembles but differs from an onion.

Preparation: cut off roots and outer leaves and split down the middle. Wash thoroughly, boil for 30 minutes. Can also be braised or deep fried.

Use: hot with white or cheese sauce
cold with vinaigrette or mayonnaise

LEEK SOUP

Time: 70 minutes
Serves: 4–5

3¾ cups	6 leeks	1½ pints water or beef
	bacon rinds	stock made from cubes
1¼ cups	salt and pepper	½ pint white sauce
	¼ turnip, chopped	1 carrot, grated

Trim and chop leeks, wash well in colander and place in saucepan with bacon rinds, seasoning, and chopped turnip. Cook slowly for 5 minutes but do not allow ingredients to be browned. Add stock, cover and simmer for 1 hour. Strain vegetables, save stock, and rub vegetables through a sieve. Return purée to stock, add white sauce and grated carrot. Cook slowly for 10 minutes and serve hot with croutons.

LEEK FRITTERS

Serves: 4

3 cm	8 leeks, less than 1 inch diameter	pinch salt
		1 egg
2½ cups	1 pint water	½ teaspoon oil
	1 teaspoon salt	milk or water
	oil	lemon quarters or wedges
	For batter:	for garnishing
	2 tablespoons flour	

2½ cups / 13 mm

Cut roots and green part from leeks and cook in 1 pint boiling water to which teaspoon of salt has been added. When almost tender, remove from heat and drain.

Place half inch of oil in heavy frying pan and heat. When ready, dip leeks individually into the batter and then place in frying pan, keeping flame gentle to allow batter to turn golden slowly. When cooked on one side, turn to brown the other. Drain and keep hot and serve with quarters of lemon.

To make batter: Make well in centre of flour, add salt and break egg in it. Beat egg and work flour into it. Add oil and enough milk or water to make the batter a thick creamy consistency. Stand 1 hour before use.

Lemon

Originally from India, and now grown in most warm climates, the lemon is the most useful of all citrus fruits in the kitchen. Rind and juice are used to flavour all forms of preparations, and the acid juice is superior to vinegar. Many varieties are available.

Use: with fish
for cold drinks
after sweetening
as a flavour in sweet and savoury dishes.

To extract juice easily: heat or roll between hands until skin is soft before squeezing.

LEMON MERINGUE PIE

Serves: 4–6
Time: 35 minutes
Temperature: 325°F for 15 minutes

		metric equivalent
1 packet frozen short pastry	2 lemons, rind grated finely and juice extracted	160°C
1 tablespoon cornflour	2 eggs, yolks and whites separated	
5 oz. water		150 ml
4 oz. castor sugar	3 teaspoons castor sugar	125 g

Line a round, vertical sided pie dish or shallow cake tin with rolled pastry. Prick bottom and bake about 15 minutes at 425°F. Mix cornflour and water in small saucepan and cook until simmering, add sugar, rind of both lemons, and lemon juice, and cook slowly for 5 minutes. Allow to cool then stir in egg yolks, mix well and pour into cooked pastry case. Whisk egg whites until stiff, add 3 teaspoons of castor sugar slowly and whisk thoroughly. Pile on top of the lemon and egg mixture then bake in oven at 325°F until meringue is set and a golden brown (about 15 minutes). Serve hot or cold.

(12 mins 220°C, 160°C)

Lemon Thyme

See *Herbs and Spices* p. 83.

Lentils: *Dhal* (India) (*Lens esculenta* (*culinaris*))

Dried leguminous seed (similar to peas and beans) originally from central or south-west Asia with exceptionally high protein content. Many varieties available including golden and brown. The smaller ones cook more quickly. They are considered an excellent substitute for meat.

Preparation: soak but not for more than 1½ to 2 hours. Longer causes fermentation which spoils the flavour and can induce toxicity.
Put in deep saucepan with plenty of cold salted water. Bring slowly to the boil and cook until tender (35–40 minutes). Do not let them burst and become mushy. Flavour can be improved by adding an onion stuck with cloves and a bay leaf to the salted water.

LENTIL CURRY

Time: about 70 minutes
Serves: 4

		metric equivalent
8 oz. lentils	1 teaspoon curry powder	250 g
salt	4 dried red chilis (hot) seeded, and finely chopped	
freshly ground black pepper		
2 oz. butter	2 green capsicums, seeded and chopped	60 g
3 onions, chopped		
2 cloves garlic, chopped finely	1 lb thin sausages, fried or meatballs	500 g

Prepare and cook lentils in water seasoned with salt and pepper. Drain saving a little of the cooking water, then rub lentils through fine wire sieve to make into a thick purée.

Heat butter in heavy frying pan and fry the onions and garlic until golden. Then add curry powder, chilis and capsicum. Add the lentil purée and moisten with a little of the water from cooking the lentils. Heat, mixing thoroughly. Garnish with meatballs or fried sausages.

LENTILS AND FISH CAKES

Time: 1 hour
Serves: 4–6

		metric equivalent
3 oz. lentils, cooked and mashed	pinch of grated nutmeg	90 g
	salt and pepper	
6 oz. cooked fish (flake, cod or what you prefer) flaked	1 egg, beaten	185 g
	breadcrumbs	
	oil for frying	
1 teaspoon anchovy sauce	slices of lemon and parsley	
grated lemon rind		

In a large bowl, mix mashed lentils and flaked fish with anchovy sauce, lemon rind, nutmeg and salt and pepper to taste. Form into cakes and dip into beaten egg then breadcrumbs. Fry in hot oil, drain and serve with slices of lemon and garnished with parsley.

May be served with white sauce if preferred.

Lettuce

Plant with tender green leaves, which originally grew wild in China and Egypt but is now cultivated universally. There are many varieties but the best known are the round cabbage lettuce and the somewhat sweet-corn shaped vertical Romaine (France) or cos (England) or leaf variety. In America there is also the Boston loose headed and the coarser leafed varieties. One peculiar form is the Asparagus or Pamir Lettuce which never forms a head and has long and narrow leaves. Its thick, swollen stem may be cooked when about one foot high.

Use: fresh and sometimes in cooking
    mostly in salads

Preparation: Pamir lettuce—boil for 25 minutes, drain,
    remove fibrous outside cover and eat the inside pith
    with melted butter.

LETTUCE SOUP

Time: 15 minutes
Serves: 6

30 g

5 cups

1 oz. butter	2 chicken stock cubes,
8 green outside lettuce	crushed
leaves, shredded	2 pints water
½ cup chopped shallots	2 teaspoons salt
½ cup chopped parsley	pepper

Melt butter in bottom of saucepan and add lettuce, shallots and parsley. Fry 1–2 minutes, shaking constantly then add crushed stock cubes, water, salt and pepper. Bring to boil, reduce heat and simmer 3 minutes.
    Serve hot topped with some fresh chopped parsley.

SAUTÉED LETTUCE

Serves: 4 as side dish

5–8 cm

1 tablespoon oil	2 large onions, chopped
1 clove garlic, crushed	rind of 2–3 inch length of
8–10 green outside lettuce	cucumber, chopped
leaves, shredded	finely

Heat oil in frying pan and add garlic and onions and

cucumber rind. Cook until onion is transparent, add shredded lettuce, reduce heat and sauté 3–5 minutes.
    Serve as vegetable with chicken or veal.
    See recipe for *Cauliflower and Lettuce Soup* p. 39.

Indian Lettuce

Round leaved winter green, grown in U.S.A.

Preparation: as for *spinach*.

Indian Tree Lettuce

Coarse lettuce growing in the West Indies.

Preparation: as for *spinach*.

Tiger Lilies: *Gum Jum*

The dried flower bud of the tiger lily is a Chinese specialty, often used in conjunction with mushrooms and other dried ingredients. These golden buds are called 'golden needles' in Chinese.

BRAISED CHICKEN WITH MUSHROOMS AND TIGER LILIES

Serves: 4

750 g

¾ cup

12 dried tiger lilies	2 tablespoons dry sherry
4 dried Chinese	or saki
mushrooms	1 teaspoon green ginger,
1 spatchcock, cut into	minced
joints or 1½ lb chicken	6 oz. chicken stock (made
pieces	from stock cube)
2 tablespoons peanut oil	salt to taste
1 tablespoon soya sauce	

Soak dried lilies and mushrooms separately in warm water for 15 minutes. Clean, rinse and dry. Slice mushrooms into strips. Brown chicken in hot peanut oil then add soya sauce, sherry and ginger. Add lilies and mushroom strips and stock. Cover and braise until chicken is tender. Season with salt to taste.

Water Lily (*Nymphaea stellata*)

Tropical water plant, cultivated in India for its roots,

flowering stem and its seeds. Other edible water lilies are grown in Africa where natives boil and eat the roots. In northern Australia, Aboriginals also prepare water lily roots as food.

Use: roots—eaten both raw and cooked
    young stems—added to curries
    ripe seeds—roasted and ground and added to cakes
      (see recipe for winter melon soup p. 103.)

Lime

Small oblong greenish yellow fruit of the lime tree, one of the citrus family, now cultivated in all sub-tropical and tropical countries. Both juice and rind are used in cooking in the same way as lemon. A variety is known as sweet lime. Juice of both is used in cordials but green limes have the best flavour.

Use: juice—for cordials along with grape, grapefruit or
      orange juice
    as basis for yeast culture
    like lemons
    flowers—to flavour pastry, confectionery and
      desserts

LIME JULEP

Serves: 4

4 sprigs mint, freshly picked	castor sugar to taste
	crushed ice
juice of 8 limes, squeezed or 1–2 tablespoons bottled lime cordial	4 jiggers brandy
	soda water

Crush sprigs of mint at bottom of each glass. Pour in the juice of two limes (or cordial). Stir in sufficient sugar to sweeten. Add a tablespoon of crushed ice, jiggers of brandy and fill with soda water.
    This is a particularly refreshing drink in hot weather.

Loganberry

See *Berries* p. 26.

Longan: *Lungan; Dragon's Eye (Nephilium longana)*

Pulpy fruit of Indian tree, related to the *lychee*, about 1 inch diameter or smaller with a light brown or cinnamon outer shell. Obtainable fresh, dried and canned, often from Chinese shops. Canned longan may be called *Seen Loan-Ngon* and dried longan *Loan Ngon-Gon*.

Use: for desserts

Loquat: *Japanese Medlar (Eribotrya japonica)*

Oriental tree related to the rose with rich, orange-coloured fruit, now grown in Mediterranean countries, southern U.S.A. and Australia. The fuzzy-surfaced fruit grow in clusters and each resembles a small plum or olive. The flesh is rich though acid-sweet and refreshing, the flavour akin to a cherry.

Eat: raw.

Use: preserved as a sweetmeat
    in jams and preserves

Lotus *(Nelumbo nucifera)*

Egyptian or Indian water lily used extensively in Chinese cookery. Fresh lotus leaves are used to wrap certain foods to which they impart their flavour. Its starchy red-brown roots or stems, of about 2 inches diameter are sliced to reveal an interior of holes running along the length. Lotus seeds are boiled with sugar to form a thick mixture known as lotus jam, used as a filling in lotus cakes and other Chinese pastries. Lotus seeds are sold candied as a sweetmeat. May be obtained canned or sometimes fresh from Chinese shops.

LOTUS ROOT OR STEM SOUP

Serves: 6–8

1 lb fresh lotus root or 1 small can lotus stems	6 jujubes or dried Chinese dates (if not available, 3 slices fresh green ginger)	500 g
2 pints cold water		5 cups
½ lb stewing steak, cut into ½ inch cubes	salt to taste	250 g
	1 tablespoon soya sauce	2 cm

5 cm

Cut lotus root or stems into round slices, ¼ inch thick. Boil water and add lotus root, beef and jujubes (or ginger). Reduce heat and simmer. Fresh root needs 3 hours, canned stems about 45 minutes. Add salt and soya sauce when ready to serve.

STUFFED LOTUS ROOTS

Serves: 4–6

peanut oil
4 oz. minced pork
2 onions, finely chopped
1 slice fresh green ginger, chopped
2 tablespoons soya sauce
1 tablespoon cornflour

10 slices or rounds of lotus root, each ⅛ inch thick
For batter:
1 egg
3 oz. flour
¼ teaspoon salt
oil for deep frying

125 g · 5 cm
90 g

Mix ingredients for batter together and stand until ready to use.

Heat 1 tablespoon peanut oil in pan and when very hot, add pork, onion, ginger, soya sauce and cornflour and sauté well together. Remove to a plate. Spread pork mixture between sandwiches of two slices of lotus root. Dip in batter until well coated. Lower into the boiling oil for deep frying and fry until golden brown. Remove and drain on absorbent paper.

Serve very hot.

Lovage

See *Herbs and Spices* p. 77.

Lychees (also *litchi*, *leechee*, *lichee*)

A Chinese fruit, now found in many parts of Asia, Australia and the U.S.A., growing in bunches like cherries and about the same size but covered with a thin shell. The flesh is white tinged with pink, reddening as it ripens. It has the delicate flavour and texture of muscat grapes. Lychees are sometimes available fresh from Chinese shops in places where the climate is warm but are more often sold tinned in syrup. Sometimes they may be obtained, dried in the shell, when they resemble raisins and are known as lychee 'nuts'.

To eat: remove the outer shell and the small hard seed, leaving the edible translucent, jellyish pulp. They may be eaten raw or poached gently in a syrup of sugar and water until tender.

Use: served with cream or ice cream
  in a mixed fruit salad
  in sweet chicken and duck dishes in Chinese cooking

BREAST OF CHICKEN WITH LYCHEE AND PINEAPPLE

Serves: 3

2 chicken breasts, sliced thinly across grain
peanut oil
1 tablespoon soya sauce
2 tablespoons dry sherry or saki
1 teaspoon fresh green ginger, minced

3 oz. canned pineapple pieces
3 oz. canned lychees
3 oz. pineapple juice
3 oz. lychee juice
cornflour
water

90 g
90 g
100 ml
100 ml

Sauté chicken in oil until slices curl. Add soya sauce, wine, ginger, pineapple and lychees and braise 2 minutes. Add fruit juices, boil, thicken with cornflour and water and serve immediately it is thickened (after 4 more minutes of cooking).

M

Mace

See *Herbs and Spices* p. 77.

Macore: *Macora*

Red cherry-like fruit with aromatic qualities, grown on tree in Indonesia, related to Surinam cherry.

Mallow

Common European weed with pale mauve flowers. Young leaves are used.

Preparation: as with *spinach*.

Mamoncillo: *Spanish Lime; Quenette; Knepe*

South American relative of the lychee, dragon's eye and rambutan. Plum-sized fruit has leathery green exterior enclosing a large seed and surrounded by edible yellow, semi-sweet and juicy pulp.

Eat: raw when ripe

Manduvira

Fruit from South American tree.
Preparation: toast before eating

Mangaba: *Mangabeira*

Fruit from Brazilian tree, resembling a persimmon.

Mangel: *Mangold; Mangold-Wurzel; Mangel-Wurzel*

Variety of common beet used mainly as stock feed. Small or young mangels may be eaten.

Preparation: as with *turnips*

Mangoes

Fruit of trees cultivated for more than 4,000 years in many warm countries, probably originating in Indonesia and Malaysia. Fruit is oblong, somewhat pear-sized, at first green and ripening to orange-yellow with red on the sunny side. Flesh is orange-yellow, very juicy and

250 g

1¼ cups
500 g

125 g

originally fibrous. Flavour is sweet but slightly acid and mangoes are now being cultivated to eliminate fibres and develop different flavours. Fresh mangoes lose aroma and colour very quickly and must be used immediately. Obtainable also as canned fruit or pulp.

Eat: raw or cooked

Preparation: cut in halves and remove stone

Use: green—in chutneys, curries
pickled with capsicum, salt and oil
ripe—in jam, mango fool
stewed
in pies
for jam
salted—in fish curries.

MANGO SHERBET

Serves: 4–6

1 cup sugar	1 tablespoon lemon juice
3 tablespoons water	1½ cups milk
8 oz. mango pulp	1 egg white, beaten

Dissolve sugar and water and stir over gentle heat until a drop of syrup can be formed into a soft ball after dropping in cold water. Cool slightly then pour on to mango pulp, to which lemon juice has been added and mix well. Add milk slowly until it is mixed in. Fold in egg white then pour mixture into freezing trays and place in refrigerator deep-freeze compartment. When mixture begins to freeze at edges, whip with a fork to make fluffy and break up ice crystals.

MANGO MOUSSE

Time: 20 minutes and chilling
Serves: 8

1 tablespoon gelatine	1 teaspoon ground ginger
2 tablespoons cold water	½ pint cream
1 × 16 oz. can mango pulp or 2 large ripe mangoes	sliced fresh or canned mangoes or canned peaches
1 tablespoon lemon juice	
4 oz. sugar	

Soften gelatine in cold water and add to mango pulp with lemon juice, sugar and ginger and mix thoroughly. Whip cream and fold into mango mixture. Spoon into individual serving glasses and chill until set. Decorate with more whipped cream and sliced mangoes or peaches.

MANGOES ROYALE

2 large ripe mangoes
castor sugar
kirsch, curacao or brandy

champagne
maraschino cherries and candied angelica

Cut mangoes in half and remove stones and skins. Slice and dip each slice in sugar. Cover with kirsch or curacao or brandy and soak for about an hour. When ready to serve, place slices in long-stemmed glasses and pour over champagne at the table and top with a maraschino cherry and a piece of candied angelica.

MANGO DIP

1 lb sirloin steak cut in 1 inch cubes marinaded 3 days in mango juice
butter
2 ripe mangoes, sliced

2 chilis, sliced
1 teaspoon caraway seed
salt and pepper to taste
boiled rice to serve

500 g
3 cm

After marinading, place beef on skewers and grill or barbecue. In frying pan, melt butter and sauté mangoes, chilis and caraway seeds. Season with salt and pepper and pour over steak kebabs.

Serve with crumbly boiled rice, and roast breadfruit or sweet potato.

MANGO CHUTNEY

2 pints wine vinegar	1 lb preserved ginger, diced	5 cups	500 g
3 lb cooking apples, peeled, cored and sliced	2 cloves garlic, crushed	1·5 kg	
	2 tablespoons salt		
1 lb brown or raw sugar	4 oz. mustard seed	500 g	125 g
1 oz. chilis, chopped finely	2 tablespoons powdered ginger	30 g	
1 cup seeded raisins			
1 lb preserved lemon peel, cut finely	1 lb mangoes, peeled and seeded	500 g	500 g

Sterilize sufficient bottling jars with rubber rings and screw lids. Boil vinegar and in it cook apples and add other ingredients. Cook together for 8 minutes. Put hot chutney into warmed preserving jars and seal while hot.

Mangosteen: *Mangistan*

Malayan fruit now grown extensively in Ceylon, India, Indonesia, North Queensland and the West Indies. The variety grown at Cape York, Australia, is known as Coochin-York. The fruit resembles an apple, having a short stem and four thick leaf-like bracts which form a rosette encasing the brownish-purple fruit. The flesh has the consistency of a greengage and a flavour suggesting a mixture of pineapple, apricot and orange. Mangosteen is a delicate fruit which must be picked ripe and eaten soon after picking. Its flavour is sweet with a refreshing acid after-taste.

Eat: raw
Use: in tropical fruit salad
     in Indonesia to make vinegar

Langsat: *Lanzone; Boboa*

Inferior type of mangosteen growing in Malaya and the Philippines.
Use: as with mangosteen

Santol: *Santul*

Fruit of a Malayan tree, described as an inferior mangosteen.

Sweet Marjoram

See *Herbs and Spices* p. 78.

Marrow: *Vegetable Marrow; Squash*

Large, sausage shaped member of the gourd family, usually green skinned and white fleshed. It is best used when small and the flesh is delicate and tender. The flesh is rather tasteless and is enhanced by strongly flavoured stuffings, spices or sauces. A form of squash.

Preparation: peel smaller ones then cut in slices: large marrows should be cooked whole and peel removed when cooked.

Cook: vegetable marrow is best if steamed, baked or fried. Boiling is not advisable.

steam in a double boiler until tender then serve in white sauce; or mash into a purée mixed with a little tomato purée; or sprinkled with paprika.

stew gently in butter and serve with chopped herbs or parsley.

dip round slices, not peeled, in egg and breadcrumbs then fry in butter. Season and serve hot; or skinned cut in strips and dipped in egg and breadcrumbs and fried.

STUFFED MARROW

Serves: 4–6 as entrée

2½ cups — 11 cm — 1 marrow, not more than 4 inches diameter	1 pint boiling salted water
1 length thin sausage (cabana)	2 bacon rashers, chopped
	1 large onion, finely chopped
sprigs of parsley, slices of tomato for garnishing	salt and pepper
For rice filling:	1 tablespoon parmesan cheese
1 cup long-grained rice	2 tomatoes, cut in cubes

To make rice filling: Wash rice and cook gently in boiling water for 10 minutes. Drain then wash under cold tap and dry. Fry bacon and onion until onions are golden, add rice to pan and sauté until rice is tender. Season with salt and pepper, sprinkle with parmesan and add tomato cubes.

Peel marrow, cut off one end and scoop away the core. Insert length of cabana sausage into cavity and around it spoon in the rice filling. Replace end of marrow and tie in place with string. Salt outside of marrow, paint with oil, wrap in aluminium foil, then place in oven at 400°F for 1½ hours. *(205°C)*

Serve hot garnished with sprigs of parsley and slices of tomato.

MARROW PIE

Serves: 4–5

1 marrow, peeled, seeded and cut into small cubes	1 cup raisins
juice of 1 lemon	prepared pastry, deep frozen
1½ cups castor sugar	

Sprinkle marrow with lemon juice and mix with sugar and raisins. Line pie dish with pastry, add marrow mixture and cover with more pastry. Cook in oven at 425°F but when pastry is beginning to turn golden, cover with brown paper, reduce oven heat to 300°F and cook until marrow is cooked (about 20 minutes more). *(220°C / 150°C)*

Varieties of marrow include:

Baby Marrows: Italian Marrows or *Squash; Zucchini* (U.S.A.)*; Courgette* (France)*;* also *Courgeron; Coucouzelle; Zuchetti*

As their name suggests, immature vegetable marrows. Preparation: may be skinned or not, depending on use. When peeled, cut into slices or into sticks.

Use: steam
deep fry
sauté

SAUTÉED BABY MARROWS

Serves: 4

500 g — 1 lb baby marrows, with skin left on, cut in quarters	2 tablespoons olive oil
	1 clove garlic, crushed
	salt and pepper to taste

Take marrow quarters and soak in cold water for 20 minutes. Heat olive oil in saucepan and add garlic for a minute or two. Add marrow and turn during cooking so that it browns lightly all over. Remove garlic, season to taste and serve at once. They should be crisp when eaten.

If preferred, add 2 peeled and seeded tomatoes to pan and cook with baby marrows and pour sauce over them when served.

SAUTÉED BABY MARROWS WITH CHEESE

Serves: 4

4 or 5 small baby marrows, cut in ¼ inch thick slices	1 teaspoon black pepper, coarsely ground	1 cm
3 tablespoons olive oil	4 eggs, beaten	
½ teaspoon salt	2 oz. parmesan cheese, grated	60 g

Sauté baby marrow slices in hot olive oil for 5 to 6 minutes, turning once. Add salt and pepper to beaten eggs and then add parmesan to the eggs. Pour into the pan over the baby marrows and cook slowly until eggs are set. Remove frying pan and brown top of eggs under the grill.

May be served hot or cold.

BABY MARROW PANCAKES

Mexico's *Tortas de calabacitas*

Serves: 4

1 lb baby marrows	salt	500 g
3 oz. plain flour	1 egg, well beaten	90 g
1 teaspoon baking powder	butter for frying	

Peel raw baby marrows and grate into a bowl. Sift together flour and baking powder and add to bowl. Add salt to taste and beaten egg and mix well. Make pancakes from the mixture, each 2 to 3 inches in diameter and fry in butter. (5–8 cm)

Serve hot or cold. A classic Mexican dish, often eaten cold on outings.

Barbarine

Variety of marrow, usually cucumber shaped, yellow or yellow striped with green.

Preparation: as marrows and cucumbers

Hairy Melon or Hairy Brinjal

Long green vegetable marrow with fine white fuzz on the skin, sometimes available fresh from Chinese stores. Cucumber is a satisfactory substitute.

HAIRY MELON AND CHICKEN SOUP

1 large hairy melon (or cucumber)	1 teaspoon soya sauce	
1½ pints chicken soup	1 teaspoon monosodium glutamate (optional)	3¾ cups
8 oz. diced chicken meat, raw	salt to taste	250 g

Skin the melon and cut flesh into ½ inch cubes. Boil chicken soup and add melon and chicken. Simmer 15 minutes, then add soya sauce, MSG and salt. (2 cm)

Chinese Winter Melon: *Doan-Gwa* (*Benincasa cerifera*)

Large vegetable marrow, similar in size and shape to a water melon with a white frosted green rind. Meat is white with yellow seeds. Has delicate flavour. May be available from Chinese shops.

Use: for Winter Melon and other soups
preserved in sugared cubes as a sweetmeat

WINTER MELON AND HAM BROTH

1 lb winter melon	4 pints water	500 g	10 cups
½ lb boiled ham		250 g	

Remove rind and seeds from melon and cut into 2 inch long strips, ¼ inch square in section. Cut ham into ½ inch cubes. Add melon and ham to cold water and bring to boil. Simmer 30 minutes and season with salt and pepper. (5 cm / 1 cm / 2 cm)

WINTER MELON SOUP

6 lb winter melon, top sliced off 2½ inches deep, lengthways, and hollowed in centre. Retain top	2 fresh mushrooms, cubed	3 kg
	1 tablespoon boiled ham, cubed	6 cm
3½ lb chicken, boned and cut into ½ inch cubes	1 can lotus seeds	
	2 pints chicken stock (made from stock cubes)	1·6 kg / 5 cups
1 small tin Chinese mushrooms, cubed	½ teaspoon salt	2 cm
	pinch pepper	

Place chicken, mushrooms, ham, lotus seeds, stock, salt and pepper in a saucepan and bring to boil.

Place melon in deep casserole dish. Pour soup mixture into the melon and replace top of melon. Place casserole dish in steamer and cover and steam for 3 hours. Serve the soup and the melon walls from the melon at the table.

Masha

See *Herbs and Spices* p. 78.

Mastuerzo

South American tree whose aromatic leaves are particularly rich in vitamin C.

Use: washed but raw, in salads

Medlars

Fruit of a small European tree, about the size of a plum with brown skin and firm flesh. After gathering, the fruit must be kept until the flesh is over-ripe and begins to disintegrate.

To eat: squeeze flesh from skin on to a spoon and eat raw
    or they may be stewed.

Use: in jelly
    medlar cheese
    in jam, or bottled

MEDLAR JELLY

Time: 45–55 minutes

2 kg   2 cm

4 lb ripe medlars	½ inch stick cinnamon
sufficient water to just	rind and juice of 1 lemon
cover fruit	sugar

Wipe fruit and place in large saucepan with water to just cover fruit. Add cinnamon, lemon rind and juice and bring to boil. Simmer until fruit breaks apart, mashing against sides of pan occasionally. Strain and add ¾ lb sugar to each pint of liquid. Bring strained liquor to boiling point and boil rapidly for 15–20 minutes. Test to see if it sets. When cooled, pour into jars and cover when cold.

375 g

Note: This recipe may be used for *guava* jelly and other similar fruit jellies.

Rock or Savoy Medlar: *Sweet* or *Grape Pear*

Small fruit of native European bush closely related to American juneberry. See *Berries* p. 27.

Melilot

See *Herbs and Spices* p. 78.

Melloco

Root vegetable of the high Andes of South America, where it is almost as important as potatoes as a staple food. However, it is little known elsewhere.

Melon

Fruit of gourd family with crisp, sweet flesh, originally from Asia but now widely grown. Varieties include:

Cantaloup

Medium to large globular variety with rough skin, naturally divided into sections, originally grown at Cantalupo near Rome. Flesh is pinkish and has peach-like flavour.

Casaba: Honey Dew or Winter Melon in U.S.A.

Variety of musk melon with green or whitish flesh.

Charentais

Small, sweet smelling melon with pale green skin.

Citron Melon

Grown for rind and used in preserves.

Egyptian or Jerusalem Melon

Native melon of Egypt with sweet and juicy flesh, valued as a thirst quencher. Used to make ices and bombes, or eaten as dessert or hors d'oeuvre as other varieties.

Honeydew Melon

Large, globular rough-skinned variety of the casava with white rind and much desired golden flesh.

Jerusalem Melon

See opposite.

Musk, Nutmeg or Rock Melon: Cantaloup in U.S.A.

Variety with netted or lacy patterned rind, related to the cantaloup with white, green, yellow or red flesh.

Nutmeg Melon

See opposite.

Persian Melon

Variety from the Middle East, globular with finely netted greenish skin and orange flesh with sweet mild flavour.

Preserving Melon

See Citron Melon opposite.

Rock Melon

See above

Spanish Watermelon or Honeydew

Bright yellow skinned and globular variety with sweet flesh.

Watermelon

Elongated with smooth, dark green skin and brilliant crimson flesh studded with dark brown seeds. Has little flavour.

Use: unripe like marrow
    boiled, fried or stuffed

Selection: tap and listen if it sounds hollow; smell stalk
    end and buy only if it smells sweet. Ripe melons also
    have a crown around the stem.

Use: sliced and chilled, eaten raw
    seasoned with salt and ginger as an hors d'oeuvre
    or with sugar and grated nutmeg
    preserved as for *gherkins*

Serve: with wedges of lemon

MELON SURPRISE

Serves: 4–6 as dessert

1 large sweet melon (but not a watermelon)	grapes, seedless
bananas, sliced	castor sugar
cherries, stoned	kirsch or Cointreau
pineapple, in wedges or cubes	ice chips
	mint to garnish

Cut 7 inch wide piece off top of melon and remove all seeds and strings. Remove flesh by scraping into balls. Combine melon balls with any other fruits available such as bananas, cherries, pineapple, and grapes. Sprinkle with castor sugar and flavour with kirsch or Cointreau. Fill melon with well-mixed fruits, replace piece from top, chill thoroughly and serve in a bed of ice and garnished with mint.   *18 cm*

ICED MELON SOUP

Serves: 4–6

4 oz. stale breadcrumbs	1 dessertspoon vinegar	*125 g*
3 cloves garlic	1 medium sized melon, cantaloup or rock	
salt and pepper		
2 tablespoons almonds, ground	½ lb crushed ice	*250 g*

Grate bread into crumbs. Crush garlic and salt and pepper to taste. Pound almonds and breadcrumbs together in mortar with garlic and add vinegar. Skin melon and chop in finger-sized slices. Place ice in soup tureen, cover with melon and pour over mixture in mortar. Cool together and serve when sufficient ice has melted.

MINT SYRUP FOR FLAVOURING WATERMELON

handful of young tender mint leaves	half a lemon watermelon balls and
2 cups of water	ice cream to serve
1 cup sugar	

Crush mint leaves and boil them in 2 cups of water, for 10 minutes. Add sugar and juice of half lemon and cook 5 minutes more. Cool then pour over balls of watermelon and serve them with balls of ice cream.

WATERMELON GLACÉ

Known in Yugoslavia as *slatko*, this preserve will keep for a year when stored in a glass container in a refrigerator.

Serves: 8

4 lb watermelon rind	3 pieces vanilla bean, each
4 lb castor sugar	4 inches long or ½ tea-
13 oz. water	spoon vanilla essence
2 lemons, thinly sliced and seeded	

Remove outer green skin from rind and the inner pink flesh leaving only the lightest part of the rind. Cut into ½ inch cubes. It should make about 8 cups. Cover cubes with cold water in a large saucepan. Bring water to boil, then pour off. Add more cold water, boil and drain again. Repeat, but this time simmer for 20 minutes before draining rind in a colander.

Replace rind in the saucepan and cover with sugar and 13 oz. water. Add lemon slices and vanilla and cook over a medium heat, shaking frequently until all sugar has melted. Simmer uncovered for about 2 hours or until

syrup temperature is 234°F or forms a soft ball when dropped into cold water.

Cool and store in a glass container.

Serve in a small dish as a dessert or as you would serve preserves.

Bitter Melon: *Balsam Apple* or *Pear; African Cucumber* (*Mormodica charantia*)

Cucumber-sized vegetable with green wrinkled skin, used in Chinese cooking. Flavour is cool and slightly bitter due to quinine content, an acquired taste. Available fresh, diced or canned (Foo-Gwa) from Chinese shops.

Preparation: remove layer of white spongy pulp inside.

Shoots may be used as a green vegetable.

Use: in soup
braised with meat
stuffed
in curries

BRAISED BEEF AND BITTER MELON

Serves: 4–6

1 lb bitter melon, fresh	½ teaspoon sugar
2 teaspoons black soya beans, fermented	2 tablespoons sherry (or saki)
1 clove garlic, crushed	salt to taste
peanut or soya oil	6 oz. beef stock
¼ lb fillet steak (tenderloin) sliced thinly	(made with cube) cornflour to thicken
2 teaspoons soya sauce	

Cut the melon in two, scoop out seeds and slice the flesh. Boil for 3 minutes then drain. Wash beans, drain and mash with garlic.

Heat oil in pan, add garlic, bean pulp and stir for ½ minute. Add bitter melon and sauté 2 minutes. Add beef and sauté 1 minute. Add soya sauce, sugar and sherry. Season with salt, add stock and braise for 1 minute. Thicken with cornflour and serve.

Melon de Malabar

French name for the Siamese pumpkin.

Preparation: as for *pumpkin*

Mercury

See *Herbs and Spices* p. 78.

Milfoil

See *Herbs and Spices* p. 78.

Mint

See *Herbs and Spices* p. 78.

Miraculous Fruit

See *Berries* p. 26.

Mistol

Fruit of South America, said to be edible in its raw state, but mainly used to prepare alcoholic beverages from its fermented juice.

Moelle de Chicoree

See *Endive* p. 55.

Red Mombin (Mexico): *Ciruela* (Philippines); *Jocote, Spanish Plum*

Race of *spondias* with 1 to 2 inch long fruit, red to yellow externally and similar to an olive. Its flesh is also yellow and very soft and juicy, its flavour acid sweet and reminiscent of an orange. Another variety ambarella (yellow mombin or hog apple) has a thin bright yellow skin.

Preparation and use: as with *ambarella*

Monkey Bread: *Baobab*

Fruit of baobab tree of Africa and N.W. Australia. Pulp is sweet and slightly acid flavour. Leaves may be dried and crushed to form a herb, mixed with food in Africa.

Use: pulp can be made into refreshing drink

Monstera Deliciosa: *Ceriman; Tropical Fruit Salad Plant*

Elongated conical fruit of a large-leaved climbing plant, originally from Mexico and Guatemala but now widely grown for its decorative qualities as an indoor plant. The fruit ripens gradually and is eaten in sections, the thick octagonal segments of rind being removed and the adhering pulpy flesh used. Its flavour is reminiscent of a combination of almost every type of tropical fruit and its aroma similar to pineapple. Unfortunately, Monstera leaves an unpleasant aftertaste due to small needle-shaped crystals (raphids) which enter the tongue.

Use: monstera pulp and water, strained through thick cloth, to make ices and drinks

Moringa

Fruit of horseradish or ben-nut tree, a shrub native in Egypt. Fruit are about the size of hazel nuts and the fresh ripe pods are edible and added to food to enhance its taste.

Mugwort

See *Herbs and Spices* p. 78.

Mulberry

See *Berries* p. 26.

Mushrooms

Common form of fungi, easily recognized by thick stalks, skin which readily peels and undersurfaces (gills) ranging in colour from pink, when fresh, to black. Found wild in pastures and meadows in autumn, usually about a week after heavy rains. Now they are extensively cultivated, or may be obtained dried from Chinese stores. Tiny button mushrooms are known as *champignons* and may be obtained canned. Larger mushrooms, fully opened, may be known as *cepes*. There are also many other forms of edible fungi but expert advice should be sought for identification. A good preliminary guide may be found in *Plats du Jour* by Patience Gray and Primrose Boyd (Penguin Books, London 1957). This also lists other books on the subject.

Preparation: mushrooms lose much of their flavour if peeled. Rinse under a tap to remove loose grass and dirt, then wipe with a damp cloth, and dry. Cut off stalks, peel and save for other dishes (see below). However, tough skins of old mushrooms must be peeled or scraped.

3–5 cm

Use: raw—when very young, thinly sliced and dusted
with fine salt
or thinly sliced, tossed in oil and vinegar for 15
minutes
served alone or with finely sliced tomatoes, or red
and green capsicum, chicory, or lettuce
Cooked—sautéed
grilled
stuffed
in soups and sauces

SAUTÉED MUSHROOMS

Serves: 4–6 as entrée

500 g

1 lb mushrooms, whole if small	5 tablespoons oil
	salt and pepper to taste

Wash, rub and dry mushrooms whole if small, or cut into
small pieces. Sauté in oil over a low flame, turning once,
until tender (6–10 minutes). Season with salt and pepper
and serve on hot toast.

Variations

After sautéing mushrooms, add 2 tablespoons chopped
parsley and ¼ cup fresh cream. Heat through but do not
simmer or boil.
First sauté 1 clove garlic, sliced; add mushrooms and
seasoning and when ready to serve, add 1 teaspoon
Worcestershire sauce.
Sauté 3 shallots, finely chopped, add sliced mushrooms.
When tender add 3 tablespoons finely chopped parsley
and 1 cup sour cream. Stir and heat but do not simmer or
boil.

MUSHROOM STALK PURÉE

Serves: 4–6

30 g

mushroom stalks with bottoms removed and peeled and/or large or old mushrooms, mashed and peeled	1 oz. butter
	½ teaspoon salt
	pepper to taste
	2 tablespoons fresh cream
	croutons to serve

Wash and dry peeled stalks and/or mushrooms. Mince
together then place in saucepan into which butter has

been melted. Cook five minutes under moderate heat
then increase flame to evaporate water. Season, add
cream and keep warm, but do not cook any more.
Serve with fried croutons.

MUSHROOMS IN GREEK SAUCE

a la grecque

Serves: 4–6

For Greek sauce:

500 g

2 cups

2 tablespoons olive oil	1 clove garlic
juice of 1 lemon or 1½ tablespoons wine vinegar	1 lb small mushrooms, washed, rubbed and dried
½ teaspoon salt	less than 1 pint of boiling water
bouquet garni	

To make sauce: Place ingredients except mushrooms and
water in a saucepan and heat until simmering. Add
mushrooms and enough boiling water to just cover them.
Bring to simmering point and poach 8 minutes. Remove
mushrooms and set aside.
Strain sauce then reduce under heat until half the
original amount. Pour over the mushrooms, allow to cool
then chill in the refrigerator.

This sauce and cooking method may be used for the
following vegetables:
tiny artichokes, trimmed and soaked 1 hour in water and
lemon juice
celery hearts, halved and washed
cauliflower, cut in small florettes
baby onions
egg plant, skinned then cut in small sticks
baby marrows, sliced or in quarters

GRILLED MUSHROOMS

Serves: 4–6

500 g

1 lb mushrooms, large, equal sized, washed, rubbed and dried	oil

Place mushrooms in heatproof dish with top facing upwards. Paint with oil and grill for 5 minutes. Turn upside down, paint with very little oil and grill a further 5 minutes. Before serving, place a ball of *maitre d'hotel* butter on each mushroom. (See below).

MAITRE D'HOTEL BUTTER

2 oz. butter	salt and pepper	60 g
1 teaspoon parsley, finely chopped	few drops lemon juice	

Cream butter with parsley, salt and pepper. Add lemon juice, whip again with fork and roll into tiny balls.

Variation

In place of *maitre d'hotel* butter use:

BEURRE D'ESCARGOT

2 oz. butter	1 teaspoon salt	60 g
1 tablespoon parsley, finely chopped	¼ teaspoon freshly ground black pepper	
1 teaspoon garlic, sliced and pounded to paste	pinch mixed spices	

Whip butter with fork, fold in parsley, garlic, salt, pepper and spices. Whip until well mixed then form into small balls. As the name suggests, this is used mainly with snails (*escargot*) but it is equally delicious with grilled mushrooms.

MUSHROOMS AND CHICKEN LIVERS

Time: 30 minutes
Serves: 4–6

½ lb chicken livers	2 tablespoons chicken stock, made from stock cube	250 g
1½ oz. butter		45 g
1 teaspoon chives, chopped		
½ rasher bacon, chopped	salt and pepper	
1 teaspoon flour	12 oz. or 6 medium, cup-shaped mushrooms	375 g
1 teaspoon chutney		

Spread livers on a board and remove green bag (gall bladder) when present. Wash in cold water, dry and chop.

Melt half butter in a frying pan and add livers, chives and bacon. Fry slowly, shaking constantly, for 5 minutes. Blend flour with stock in a mixing bowl, add to frying pan. Add chutney, salt and pepper and stir until bubbling. Keep over very low heat. Wash mushrooms, clean skins and remove stalks. Turn mushrooms upside down and place a little butter on each. Place in grill (or broiler) and cook for 10 minutes.

Serve mushrooms on plates and place spoonful of livers on each and serve on hot buttered toast.

An alternative is to cook livers for 5 minutes, and to them add chopped mushrooms and seasoning. Simmer for a further 10 minutes then add flour and stock, bring to boil, cook over low heat for 5 minutes and serve over freshly boiled rice.

MUSHROOMS, KIDNEYS AND BACON

Time: 30 minutes
Serves: 4–6

1 lb or more mushrooms, freshly picked; or bought, though they haven't the same flavour	1 lb sheep kidneys, skinned, halved and finely chopped and tossed in seasoned flour	500 g	500 g
2 rashers of bacon, cut in small slices	salt and pepper		

Sort mushrooms, washing all dirt away. Clean skins, cut off stalks and cut tops into slices. Prepare kidneys. Place bacon in a heavy frying pan and gently heat to extract fat. Apply stronger flame, toss in kidneys and brown quickly. Reduce flames and add mushrooms. Simmer gently with lid on pan for 10 minutes. Sprinkle with salt and pepper. Serve piping hot on thick slices of toast made from fresh bread. This is a personal favourite and there seems nothing more enjoyable after rising at dawn, collecting mushrooms in foggy pastures for an hour or two, and then preparing this with mushrooms which still have dew adhering to them.

MUSHROOMS PARMESAN

Serves: 4–6

155 g 5 oz. butter	½ teaspoon salt
500 g 1 lb mushrooms, sliced	¼ teaspoon grated nutmeg
60 g 3 tablespoons plain flour	2 oz. breadcrumbs
¾ cup 6 oz. milk	½ cup grated parmesan
¾ cup 6 oz. cream	cheese

60 g   Melt 2 oz. butter in heavy pan and add mushrooms. Cook over low heat until wilted. Blend remaining butter and flour in a small saucepan, then add milk, cream, salt and pepper, and nutmeg. Stir over very low heat until thickened. Place mushrooms in a casserole dish, pour sauce over them, sprinkle with breadcrumbs and parmesan then brown in hot oven (400°F).

205°C

STUFFED MUSHROOMS

Time: 30 minutes
Serves: 6

12 large champignons, washed and rubbed and dried	2 eggs
	1 tablespoon onion, finely chopped
For stuffing:	½ teaspoon salt
60 g 2 oz. dried breadcrumbs	¼ teaspoon pepper
60 g 2 oz. quick dried oats, soaked a few minutes in a little water	½ cup canned crab meat or minced chicken
	butter
1 tablespoon parsley, finely chopped	grated parmesan cheese

Mix ingredients, turn mushrooms upside down and fill caps. Sprinkle with more breadcrumbs, dot with butter and sprinkle with grated parmesan cheese. Place mushrooms in lightly oiled baking dish, place in moderate oven (375°F) for 15–20 minutes until mushrooms are just tender.
    Serve on fried toast.

190°C

See recipes for: *Celeriac, mushrooms and cheese* p. 40.
    Baked celery and mushrooms p. 41.
    Braised chicken, mushrooms and tiger lilies p. 96.
    Spinach and mushroom entree p. 170.

Mustard: *White Mustard*

European plant with small, tender green leaves usually cut six or seven days after sowing and often grown indoors on damp flannel.

Use: with *cress* in sandwiches and for garnishing. For use of seeds see p. 78.

Chinese Mustard Greens: *Goy Choy*
(*Brassica cernua*)

Oriental vegetable, usually available from Chinese stores in canned form (and salted) but occasionally available fresh. It is widely used in Asia and in Indonesia is known as sujur asin.
    Fresh plant is green often with yellow flowers on the tops of the central stalk. Its taste is slightly bitter.

Preparation: wash then sauté or use in soup

MUSTARD GREENS SOUP

Serves: 8

1 head mustard greens	4 slices fresh green ginger
5 cups 2 pints meat stock (from packet)	root
	1 teaspoon monosodium
125 g 4 oz. pork, finely chopped	glutamate (optional)
1 teaspoon soya sauce	salt and pepper to taste

Wash the greens and slice obliquely. Heat soup stock and add pork and ginger. Boil for 5 minutes, add mustard greens and boil another 3 minutes. Add soya sauce, MSG and season with salt and pepper.

Salted Mustard Greens; Chinese Mustard Cabbage
(*Brassica cernua*)

Varieties of this green, preserved in salt, are obtainable with individual flavours. They are usually obtainable in cans, sometimes in bulk. Best known are:

    Salted Mustard Greens; Harm-Choy
    Fermented Mustard Greens; Muy-Choy
    Winter Vegetable; Doan Choy
    Onion Pickled; Choan-Choy
    Red- Inside-Snow; Sewt-Lay-Hoan

If obtainable in bulk, cabbage must be washed clean, squeezed dry and sliced.

Use: steamed or sautéed with meat and fish
in soups

STEAMED MINCED PORK AND SALTED CABBAGE

Serves: 4

		metric equivalent
1 small can 'Winter Vegetable' salted cabbage or other variety to taste 1 teaspoon cornflour	½ lb pork fillet, coarsely chopped 1 teaspoon peanut oil 1 teaspoon soya sauce	250 g

Chop the cabbage finely and mix with other ingredients. Form into a thin pancake in a dish and place dish in a steamer. Steam for 30 minutes and serve.

SALTED MUSTARD GREENS AND PORK

Serves: 4

2 lb pork fillets (belly slices)	2 pints water	1 kg	5 cups
2 slices ginger root			
1 × 8 oz. can salted mustard greens	salt to taste	250 g	

Slice meat into 1 inch cubes and place in saucepan. Add 3 cm
salted mustard greens, water, ginger and salt. Bring to
boil then simmer 40 minutes or until meat is tender.
Serve with boiled rice.

Leaf Mustard: *Chinese Mustard (Brassica juncea)*

Plant of the brassica or cabbage family, either with cabbage-like or curly leaves, cultivated in France in winter. See also *Chinese Cabbage* p. 36.

Preparation: as for *spinach*

Myrtaceous Fruits

See *Eugenia* p. 56.

Myrtle

See *Herbs and Spices* p. 78.

Nangka

Edible fruit of a tree from the Philippines.

Preparation: boil or roast and eat like *chestnuts*

Use: young fruits

Nangkaboom

Fruit of tree related to the jack fruit.

Use: when fruit is very young it is used in soup in
Malaysia and Vietnam

Narcissus Bulbs

Edible bulbs of well known flower, sometimes used as
food.

Preparation: as for *Jerusalem artichokes*

Nasturtium: *Indian* or *Mexican Cress*

Decorative garden plant, mostly grown for its flowers.
Petals and leaves taste similar to watercress.

Use: leaves—when young. Flower petals may be added
to salads for a different flavour
tender buds, when young, can be pickled in vinegar
and used as *capers*
dried seeds—ground to make a form of mustard

Tuberous-rooted Nasturtiums

Perennial plant of South America with tuberous roots
about the size of a hen's egg and striped in yellow and red.
Cultivated in Bolivia where they are considered a delicacy,
although an acquired taste.

Use: as for *parsnips*

Nectarine

Stone fruit of peach family, grown in warm climates but
with smooth skin, smaller size and firmer flesh. Colour
usually greenish-red and the flesh soft and delicious, pink
to red near the stone.

Use: as for *peaches* but best eaten whole as a dessert

metric equivalent

175°C

175°C

BAKED NECTARINES

Temperature: 350°F
Serves: 3–4

6 or 8 ripe nectarines, peeled, covered with cold water with lemon juice added	1½ cups sugar 1 cup water 6 or 8 cloves

Boil sugar and water together for 5 minutes. Remove
each nectarine from water, dry and stick with a clove.
Arrange nectarines in a baking dish and pour the syrup
over them. Bake in oven at 350°F for 25 minutes, basting
every 5 minutes with syrup. Cool then chill nectarines in
refrigerator and serve with cream.

Nettle

See *Herbs and Spices* p. 78.

Newberry

See *Berries* p. 26.

Nigella

See *Herbs and Spices* p. 78.

Nutmeg

See *Herbs and Spices* p. 79.

Nuts

The fruit of certain trees which have a hard shell
covering an edible kernel. Though nuts are mostly used
for dessert, they are often rich in oils.

Almonds

Kernel of the seed from the fruit of a tree related to the
peach. There are two varieties, the edible sweet almond
and the bitter almond which is poisonous in all except the
smallest quantities. Valued for the table and in cooking.

To blanch: stand in boiling water for 5 minutes or until skins wrinkle. Drain and rub off skins.

Use: toasted at 350°F in oven for 20 minutes   *175°C*
    sautéed in butter for 5 minutes until lightly browned.

SPANISH ALMOND SOUP

Time: 20–30 minutes
Serves: 6

24 almonds, peeled and blanched	3 peppercorns
2 tablespoons olive oil	1 sweet red pepper, chopped
3 cloves garlic, chopped	1 teaspoon saffron
2 slices bread	2 pints water, boiling *5 cups*
1 teaspoon parsley, chopped	salt

Fry blanched and peeled almonds in hot oil then remove and drain. Fry chopped garlic, bread, parsley, peppercorns, chopped sweet red pepper and saffron together in oil. Remove and drain, place with almonds in a mortar and pound to a pulp. Place mixture in a saucepan and gradually stir in boiling water. Season with salt, simmer to keep hot and serve.

Javanese Almond

See *Pili* p. 117.

Beech Nuts

Fruit of the beech tree, its flavour between that of the hazel nut and the chestnut. Raw taste is rather astringent but this is ameliorated by roasting.

Brazil: *Cream; Niggertoe; Jigger Nuts*

Triangular seeds of the fruit of a large tree, originally grown in Brazil. Up to 32 seeds or nuts found in each fruit and each has an exceptionally hard shell with three sharp edges and a pure white kernel, rich in oil. Taste is similar to the coconut and hazelnut. Seldom used in cooking but popular as a dessert.

Cashew Nuts

Kidney shaped seeds of a tree originally from tropical America. Kernels are usually fried in butter, or roasted, and then salted and eaten as cocktail nuts. They may also be crushed and added to a véloute sauce to serve with chicken or turkey.

VELOUTÉ SAUCE

Serves: 4

		metric equivalent
1 oz. butter	salt to taste	30 g
1 oz. flour	mushroom stems	30 g
½ pint chicken stock (made from stock cube)	4 oz. cashew nuts lemon juice	1¼ cups 125 g

Melt butter and add flour. Cook for 5 minutes, stirring constantly until it is a straw colour. Add hot chicken stock and salt and maintain heat, whisking until thoroughly blended. Add mushroom stems and cook until sauce is two-thirds the original quantity. Add crushed and pounded cashew nuts and blend in until desired thickness is achieved. Add lemon juice just before removing from heat.

Chestnut: *Spanish Chestnut*

Fruit of the Spanish or 'sweet' chestnut tree and also the Japanese chestnut, found inside a prickly husk. Nuts of the Australian Moreton Bay Chestnut (*Castanosperum australe*).

Eat: freshly roasted
    grated in stuffings
    pounded into flour
    for cakes and purées
    in *marons glaces*

Use: roasted, boiled, steamed or grilled—after which the kernel becomes sweet and floury.

BOILED CHESTNUTS AS A VEGETABLE

Slit skin on flat side and place in saucepan of boiling salted water. Boil until tender (about 30 minutes), drain, cool and remove shells. Toss in hot butter and serve as a vegetable with roast poultry or beef.

Roast chestnuts with skins removed may be used as a garnish for veal cutlets.

VEAL AND CHESTNUT PUDDING

Serves: 4–6

metric equivalent			
250 g	250 g	8 oz. veal, cooked and minced	8 oz. tomatoes, skinned
	500 g	1 or 2 slices boiled ham or 2–3 rashers bacon, minced	1 lb chestnuts, skinned and boiled
	1 cup		salt and pepper
185 g	30 g	6 oz. baked or fried breadcrumbs	8 oz. stock from veal 1 oz. butter

Butter a pie dish and put in a layer of meat, a layer of sliced tomatoes, a thin layer of breadcrumbs, a good layer of chestnuts. Repeat until all ingredients are used, seasoning each with salt and pepper. Pour in stock, cover with a thin layer of breadcrumbs dotted with butter. Bake in oven at 375°F for 30 minutes.

190°C   35 mins

See recipe for *Brussels Sprouts and Chestnuts* p. 30.

Chilean Nut or Chile Hazel

Coral red fruit of a Chilean shrub, similar in taste to the hazel nut.

Coconuts

See *Palms* p. 128.

Filberts: *Cob Nuts*

Large oval nuts with an outer husk, sold for dessert purposes. From the same family as the Hazelnut but a different species.

Gingko Nuts

Starchy seeds of the maidenhair tree, used in Chinese and Japanese cookery. Available canned or dried from Chinese shops. Seeds are originally prepared by fermenting away outer flesh and then roasting or boiling them. Touching the raw seeds may cause dermatitis.

Preparation: dried—crack shells with nut cracker, soak nuts in hot water for 10 minutes, peel away inner skin.

Use: in soups, especially winter melon soup and vegetarian dishes where numerous mixed ingredients are added.

GINGKO NUT SWEETMEATS

40 gingko nuts
$\frac{1}{3}$ teaspoon salt
$\frac{2}{3}$ teaspoon sugar

monosodium glutamate
20 cocktail sticks

Remove hard shells from nuts and place nuts in $\frac{1}{2}$ cup water and boil. While boiling, rub nuts with spoon to remove thin skin from nut. Drain, add cold water and drain again. Mix $\frac{1}{3}$ teaspoon salt with $\frac{2}{3}$ teaspoon sugar and monosodium glutamate. Stir nuts in mixture until all are well covered. Pierce two nuts at a time with cocktail stick and store in a jar.

Chili Hazel

See *Chilean Nut* this page.

Hazelnut

Small round nuts, the fruit of the hazel tree. Kernels should be lightly baked before use and the skins rubbed away. These are used more for cakes and confectionery than for dessert purposes.

Barcelona Nut

Small round hazelnut kernels.

Hickory Nut

Fruit of some American hickory trees, used in the U.S.A. for confectionery manufacture.

Jamaican Cob Nut

Sweet edible seed of a West Indian tree.

Macadamia or Queensland Nut

Originally from Australia, the tree bears fruit with a particularly hard shell. Recent crosses from Hawaii have produced trees whose nuts have softer shells. The oil content of macadamia nuts is 78 per cent, the highest for any type of nut. It is used for confectionery and desserts. It can also be made into a rich oily paste similar to peanut 'butter'. Flavour is rich and crisp, similar to the hazelnut but sweet and mellow.

Monkey Puzzle Nut: *Pino*

Nuts of two varieties of the South American *Araucarias* or monkey-puzzle tree, found originally in Chile and Peru. They are large, hard and oily.

Oysternut (*Telfuria pedata*)

Large flat seeds from the fruit of an African vine now used as a dessert nut.

Peanut: *Ground Nut; Monkey Nut; Earth Nut; Carachis*

Valuable fruit of a ground-growing Brazilian herb which develops underground. Two kernels grow in each nut which has a soft shell. Before using, the pinkish skin should be removed. They may be eaten raw, roasted, fried and salted. They are also used to make peanut oil and peanut 'butter'. Ground peanuts are used in Africa and Asia to make the staple peanut cake.

PEANUT SAUCE

Serves: 4

½ lb peanuts, roasted, with skins removed	1 onion, minced or finely chopped and fried until	250 g
1½ pints boiling water	golden	3¾ cups
2 medium sized tomatoes, skinned and sieved	curry powder to taste (optional)	

Pound peanuts into a paste and then sieve. Mix with boiling water. Add tomatoes to onion and simmer together. Pour peanut sauce into pan and heat through over low heat.

When ready to serve, season with curry powder if desired.

PEANUT CRISPS

Quantity: 2 dozen

4 oz. butter or margarine	2 eggs, beaten	125 g
4 oz. sugar	8 oz. peanuts, chopped	125 g 250 g
¼ teaspoon ground or grated nutmeg	self-raising flour to thicken	

Cream butter and sugar and nutmeg, add the eggs then the peanuts and enough self-raising flour to make a stiff batter. Beat well and drop spoonfuls on a well-greased flat baking tray, leaving room for each biscuit to spread. Bake at 350°F until a golden brown (about 10–15 minutes).   175°C

See recipe for *Plum and Peanut Pie* p. 144.

Pecan Nuts

Smooth, oblong, thin-shelled nut of a type of hickory tree found in the western and southern States of the U.S.A. Shelled nuts resemble walnut kernels and are becoming increasingly popular for dessert use.

Pili or Javanese Almond

Thick shelled, fatty nut from the seed of a Javanese wild plum. Only the kernel within the seed is edible. It may be eaten raw or roasted.

Pine Nuts: *Pinon; Pignoli* (*Pinus edulis*)

Edible seeds or kernels of cones of some species of pine trees, natives of semi-arid areas of south-western U.S.A. and Mexico. They are the equivalent of pine nuts in Asia and Europe. If not available, almonds may be used as a substitute as they have a similar flavour.

Pistachio Nuts

Seeds of a deciduous tree, originally from the Middle East which have an edible kernel, olive-sized within a thin husk. The kernel splits in two halves, each covered by a reddish skin. The nut is brilliant green in colour. To retain colour, blanch by covering with cold water, bring to boiling point, strain then cover again with cold water. Remove skins and dry slowly, either in halves or chopped finely. To retain colour after drying, store in green bottle or light-proof tin. The flavour is sweet and slightly aromatic. They are used extensively as a flavouring in cookery, pork butchery, pastry making and confectionery (such as nougat). They may also be fried and salted for cocktail savouries.

Queensland Nut

See *Macadamia* above.

Sapucaia Nut

Fruit of the Palmito tree of tropical America (not a true palm). The nut is used extensively as food in the highlands of South America.

Souari: *Swarri, Butter, Paradise* or *Guiana Nuts*

Tropical South American nuts contained in woody capsules resembling cannon balls when ripe. The thick shell containing the kernel is very difficult to break but when the nuts are extracted, they resemble brazil nuts but have a richer flavour.

Tiger Nut: *Earth Almond*

Small corms of a West African plant, gathered wild and eaten raw or roasted, especially in Nigeria.

Walnuts

Walnut trees have been transplanted to many parts of the world from their European homelands. Lucky is the person who can boast of a fruiting walnut in his garden, for the nuts' uses are endless. Like most nuts, the walnut has a smooth outer green husk which is removed when ripe nuts are picked and sold. The outer shell is removed and only the kernel is eaten. However, one of the best forms of walnut is the unripe nut which is harvested while the kernel, shell and husk are still soft and then pickled.

Use: pickled—as a garnish with cold meats, boiled pork and anything which tends to be bland and rich;
ripe kernels—whole for eating or decoration on cakes, chopped or ground for use in stuffings and cakes.

Pickled Walnuts

Prepare brine and spiced vinegar as for *pickled gherkins* p. 62. Use only walnuts whose shells have not begun to form. Fruit may be tested by piercing right through with a fine needle. If not over-ripe, the needle will easily pass through. Prick walnuts with a fork and stand immersed in brine for about a week. Drain and place on an old tray lined with clean white paper. Stand in light, preferably in sun, turning once or twice so that they become blackened all over. Do not handle walnuts more than necessary as the stain is persistent. When black all over, pack walnuts into jars, cover with cold spiced vinegar with at least 1 inch of vinegar above walnuts, cover with polythene sheet and tie down and use after two months.

WALNUT MERINGUES

Quantity: 3 dozen approx.
Temperature: 325°F

2 egg whites	½ cup castor sugar
1 cup walnuts, finely chopped	½ cup raw sugar
	1 teaspoon baking powder

Beat egg whites, gradually adding castor sugar until they are stiff. Mix walnuts with raw sugar and baking powder and fold into egg whites. On a greased baking tray, place teaspoonfuls and bake in oven at 325°F for 20–30 minutes.

3 cm

165°C

165°C

118

Oca: *Occa; Okaplant*

South American plant, grown in Peru and Bolivia and related to wood sorrel. Its edible tubers are also cultivated in England, Wales and France.

Preparation: after harvesting, dry in sun several days to remove calcium oxalate. Then wash and simmer in salted boiling water for 15 minutes.

Use: lightly fried in butter
in white sauce
casseroled
mashed like potatoes
boiled and candied
dried and powdered in soups

Okra: *Gumbo; Lady's Fingers; Bamia* (Middle East)*; Quimbombo* (West Indies and South America)

Green pods of an Ethiopian hibiscus plant, also grown in India, West Africa, Turkey, America and other warm countries. Young green pods resemble gherkins and are used to make a stew called *gumbo*. Available fresh where grown or in tins. Leaves of the native New Guinea Okra can be used like *sorrel*. Dried seeds may be used as *dried haricot beans* steeped in water before use. In India, dried seeds are pickled.

Preparation: pods should be blanched first in salt water
then boiled like *asparagus*
roasted seeds as substitute for pearl barley.

Use: in curry or a sauce based on tomato purée
sliced and dipped in corn meal and fried
in soups and stews
pickled in salads
uncooked in oil

Gumbo

Soup based on pork and okra. It may contain vegetables, chicken, beef, oysters, shrimp, crab but always has the okra.

FRIED OKRA RINGS

Serves: 6

metric equivalent		
¾ cup	6 oz. milk	cornmeal or flour
	2 eggs, beaten	salt and pepper
750 g 60 g	1½ lb fresh okra, sliced	2 oz. butter

Mix milk and eggs and into them dip okra, and then dip it in the cornmeal to thoroughly cover. Season with salt and pepper and sauté in butter until golden, turning when needed.

OKRA AND EGG PLANT

Time: 30 minutes
Serves: 4

12 okra pods, washed and sliced	2 large tomatoes, skinned and sieved
1 egg plant, medium size, diced	½ oz. butter
	salt and pepper
1 onion, peeled and sliced	parsley, finely chopped

(15 g)

Place okra, egg plant, onion and tomatoes into a large saucepan in which butter has been melted. Season and add parsley, stir well and simmer until cooked.

Serve hot or use as filling for open tart or as separate vegetable course.

COLD STEWED OKRA WITH CORIANDER

Serves: 6

8 cloves garlic, crushed	10 baby white onions
1 teaspoon salt	3 tomatoes, sliced
1 teaspoon coriander seeds, crushed	½ cup lemon juice
	½ cup cold water
3 cups young okra pods	½ teaspoon sugar
oil for frying	½ teaspoon pepper

(2 cm)

Crush garlic, salt and coriander seeds together. Remove stems from okra, wash and dry, then gently fry okra in ½ inch oil until tender but still green. Drain okra and fry onions in oil until golden. Drain oil from pan and when dry, add another teaspoon of oil. In this cook garlic/coriander mixture for 1 minute, and remove from heat.

In a casserole dish, place a layer of tomato slices and a layer of okra. In the centre make a depression and fill with onions. Sprinkle with garlic/coriander mixture and then add mixture of lemon juice, water, sugar and pepper. Bring to boil and simmer 10 minutes with lid in place. Remove lid and continue simmering until most of the liquid has been absorbed. Cool then refrigerate and serve cold.

Olives

Fruit of the olive tree, originally a native of the Mediterranean region but now grown in many similar climates including Australia. Olives are also grown widely in France, Spain, Greece and Italy. Spanish olives are the largest. Obtainable as green olives preserved in brine, or black olives (the ripe fruit), also pickled in brine and packed in oil. Green olives, stoned and stuffed with a pimento or anchovies are often available in bottles.

Preparation: marinade pricked black or green olives in the following marinade for two days before using.

1 cup olive oil
3 teaspoons oregano
1 teaspoon thyme
1 teaspoon peppercorns, crushed

Mix together well in a jug. Place olives in a screw top jar, pour over marinade and, if necessary, add oil to cover topmost olives.

STUFFED OLIVES DIP

Serves: 4 as entrée

		metric equivalent
1 cup white sauce	*For white sauce:*	
2 teaspoons anchovy sauce	2 oz. butter	60 g
1 teaspoon tomato purée	2 tablespoons flour	
1 teaspoon Worcestershire sauce	1 cup chicken broth (made from cube)	
2 eggs, hard boiled, shelled and chopped	½ teaspoon salt cayenne pepper	
10 stuffed olives, sliced, saving some for garnish	4 oz. cream	125 g

To make white sauce: Melt butter in a saucepan then mix in flour, heating a little, but not browning. Add chicken broth gradually, stirring until mixture thickens and bubbles. Season with salt and cayenne and cook for 5 minutes over a low flame. Stir in cream and keep hot for 5 minutes more. Do not allow to boil.

To white sauce, add anchovy sauce, tomato purée, Worcestershire sauce. Fold in eggs and olives and spoon into an ovenproof ramekin. Heat in oven and serve hot, garnished with olive wedges, on slices of toast.

BRAISED DUCK WITH OLIVES

Serves: 4–6

		metric equivalent
4 oz. butter	½ pint chicken stock, made from stock cube	125 g 1¼ cups
1 duck	bouquet garni	
2 onions, sliced	2 rashers bacon	
2 carrots, sliced	salt and pepper	
1 stick celery, sliced	½ lb black olives	250 g
½ bottle white wine		

Heat butter in heavy saucepan and brown duck on all sides. Remove duck and then brown onions, carrots and celery. Place duck on cooked vegetables, pour the wine over it and reduce wine to half its original quantity. Then add the chicken stock, the bouquet garni and place the bacon rashers over the duck. Season to taste. Cover, reduce heat and simmer until duck is tender. Blanch olives in boiling water for 3 minutes then drain. Remove duck from its cooking stock, strain the stock and remove excess fat. Then return stock to saucepan and thicken by reducing. Add olives and allow to heat. Place duck on a platter and pour over the olives and reduced stock.

Chinese Olives: Java Almonds

Stone fruit of tree cultivated in the Philippines, Malaya and Indonesia. It is harvested for the fragrant resin which is extracted from it, but the fruit is also dried and salted and used in vegetarian dishes. It may also be eaten as a savoury.

121

Olluco

South American perennial with branching, creeping stem which roots where it touches the ground. From the base of the stem it produces oblong to round yellow tubers, with smooth yellow flesh. They are gathered in autumn and eaten like potatoes.

Preparation: as for *potatoes*

Onions and their relatives

Onions are one of the most valued flavourings which were known and used in Egypt at least 4,600 years ago. Extremely strong essence is contained in the concentric skins and as well as its flavour, it is reputed to have therapeutic qualities. Main types of onions available are:

Brown Onions: *Spanish Onions*

Large and often with purple-tinted flesh, having good keeping qualities.

Green Onions

Various forms of green or spring onion types of vegetable are available. They are:

Chives

Although usually considered to be a herb, chives are of the onion (*Allium*) genus and are conveniently grown in pots or in herb borders. They grow as clusters of tiny roots but only the green shoots are used. They are particularly useful as they will grow perennially and have a delicate onion flavour. The French term *ciboule* also refers to a type of chive which is also known as 'Welsh onion', (though it originally came from Siberia) or the Japanese *nebuka*.

Rocambole or *Sand Leek*

European variety of the Welsh onion, found wild in Denmark (from which its name derived—*Rockenbolle* or onion-on-the-rocks) and the British Isles with a mild garlic-type flavour.

Shallots

Small onions with mild and delicate flavour which multiply by increasing the number of bulbs. Their outside skin is red-brown and the flesh is slightly purple tinged. In some places, shallots are called *scallions*.

Similar plants include Welsh onions or *stone leeks*, and the Scottish *syboes*.

Spring Onions

Usually thinnings of ordinary onion plants.

Use: spring onions and shallots by cutting off rootlets and stripping outermost skin
Chives: by cutting the green shoots

Zibet

Variety of chives from tropical Asia.

Use: as chives

Small Onions: *Button* or *Silver Skin Onions*

Used for pickling.

Tree Onions

These produce large bulbs underground and have small onions on top of aerial shoots. They are best used for pickling.

White Onions

Not so strongly flavoured, can only be stored for short periods and include odourless varieties.

Preparation: cut away rootlets and remove outer layers of peel.

Use: raw—either sliced, grated or chopped in salads or with other ingredients in sandwiches
cooked—sautéed, fried, grilled, baked, boiled either on their own or with other ingredients.

FRIED ONION RINGS

Time: 25 minutes
Serves: 8–10

4 onions, peeled	*For batter:*	
deep oil for frying	4 oz. flour	125 g
batter	½ teaspoon salt	
	1 egg	
	10 oz. milk	1¼ cups

To make batter: Sieve flour and salt through a sieve or dredge. Make hole in centre and drop in egg. Mix a little flour with it then add milk slowly, mixing in the dry flour from the sides. Beat or whisk until mixture is smooth and continue until batter is full of bubbles. Add more milk stirring constantly, until consistency is that of cream.
To cook onions: Place whole onions in boiling water and cook for 15 minutes. Drain, cool and cut onions into rings. Dip rings into batter and fry in deep oil until batter is golden brown. Drain and serve hot.

PICKLED ONIONS

2 lb small silver onions or tree onions or shallots	1 dessertspoon allspice berries	1 kg
1 dessertspoon peppercorns	2 pints brown vinegar	5 cups
	1 dessertspoon salt	

Skin the onions and place into jars. Bruise peppercorns and allspice and add to vinegar, together with salt. Pour spiced vinegar over onions until half an inch of liquid stands above top of onions. Seal jar with waxed paper or screw top and store. Onions remain crisp in this pickle. See recipes for *Sauteed Carrots and Onions* p. 38.
Vegetable Pears, Tomatoes and Onions p. 137.

2 cm

Orach: *Orache; Mountain, Mexican or French Spinach; Sea Purslane; Bonne Damme; Fat Hen*

Common names for several species of plants in the goosefoot family grown both wild and cultivated, especially in France, for their edible leaves.
Preparation and cooking: as for *spinach*
Use: alone or mixed with spinach

Oranges

Globular citrus fruits, generally with orange coloured skins. However, some varieties have skins ranging from dark green to red. Navel oranges are noted for their sweetness and absence of seeds but there are many other varieties. Seville oranges (*bigarade* in France) are a very sour variety, used mainly to make marmalade. They may also be made into bigarade sauce to serve with duck and game.
Use: fresh with skin removed and in segments
squeezed for their juice
sliced and baked in the oven to garnish roast duck
in salads with: grapes, nectarines and pears;
pineapple; strawberries; bananas; custard apple;
grated coconut; avocado; for flavouring cakes
and biscuits, sauces and desserts.

BIGARADE SAUCE

Serves: 4

1 meat cube and water to dissolve it or juices from game	1 teaspoon redcurrant jelly juice of 1 Seville orange shredded rind of 1 Seville
¾ cup claret	orange

Dissolve meat cube in water (or game juices), boil rapidly to reduce it to a thick syrup. Add other ingredients and mix well under a low heat. Boil to thicken then pour over game or duck.

ORANGE AND ASPARAGUS CASSEROLE

Time: 1½ hours
Temperature: 350°F — 175°C
Serves: 4

1 × 16 oz. can asparagus tips	3 spring onions, chopped finely	500 g
juice of 1 lemon	salt and pepper	
2 large potatoes, boiled and sliced	¼ pint basic white sauce	150 ml
grated rind of 2 oranges	½ cup breadcrumbs	

Drain asparagus, sprinkle with lemon juice and stand for

30 minutes. Place alternate layers of sliced potato and asparagus in a casserole dish. Sprinkle each layer of potatoes with grated orange rind, chopped spring onions, salt and pepper. When filled, pour over white sauce and sprinkle top with breadcrumbs. Bake in oven at 350°F for 30 minutes.

175°C

VEAL À L'ORANGE

Time: 1½ hours

175°C Temperature: 350°F

Serves: 6

6 oranges	3 teaspoons capsicum,
¾ pint white sauce	skinned, seeded and
4 cups cooked veal,	chopped
chopped	1½ cups uncooked long-
3 teaspoons orange juice	grained rice
3 teaspoons chopped	2 teaspoons grated orange
parsley	rind
salt and pepper	

475 ml

Wash oranges and cut a slice from each end. Scoop out flesh with a grapefruit knife. Save the pulp. Heat white sauce and add veal, orange juice, parsley, half the orange pulp, salt and pepper. Place chopped capsicum in cold water and bring to boil. Drain and stir into the white sauce mixture. Replace slice at one end of orange case, place cases in casserole or baking dish, and fill with spoonfuls of veal and white sauce mixture. Heat in oven at 350°F for 20 minutes. Boil rice and grated orange rind in salted water until rice is crumbly. Strain, mix with remaining orange pulp and serve with veal in orange cases.

175°C

ORANGE SEGMENTS IN SPICED CLARET

Serves: 6

½ cup sugar	5 oranges, peeled with all
½ cup water	pith removed and outer
1 cup claret	membrane of segment.
2 cloves	Then, with sharp knife,
2 inch stick cinnamon	remove flesh in
3 thin slices of lemon	segments without
	membrane, removing
	any pips.

5 cm

Place sugar in saucepan with water and claret. Stir over low heat until sugar has dissolved. Bring to boil and add cloves, cinnamon and lemon slices tied in muslin. Simmer for 5 minutes. Pour hot syrup over orange flesh and allow to cool. Refrigerate and serve very cold.

BRAISED PORK IN ORANGE SAUCE

2 oz. butter	1 cup dry white wine
2 lb loin pork, boned and	salt and pepper
rolled	3 oranges
2 carrots, cut in chunks	flour
2 tablespoons brandy	buttered rice to serve

60 g
1 kg

Melt butter and sear outside of pork roll. Add carrots, pour in brandy and flame. Add white wine, season to taste, cover with aluminium foil and bake in oven at 350°F for 2 hours. Remove pork and carrots from baking dish and keep warm. Add grated rind and juice of 1 orange to baking dish. Thicken juices with a little flour and cook until gravy is thick. Peel remaining oranges and cut into ¼ inch thick slices. Serve slices of pork, glazed with orange sauce and topped with a slice of fresh orange. Serve with buttered rice.

175°C

1 cm

Kaffir Orange

Fruit of Portuguese East African tree with hard shell-like rind and brown glistening pulp, similar to over-ripe banana flesh, which has an aromatic flavour. Not botanically related to the orange which it resembles in shape and size.

Eat: raw

Oregano

See *Herbs and Spices* p. 79.

Ortanique

Citrus fruit, hybrid between an orange and a tangerine, grown in the West Indies.

Use: as for *oranges, tangerines*

Oyster Plant

See *salsify* p. 166.

Pacuri

Edible fruit of a South American tree.

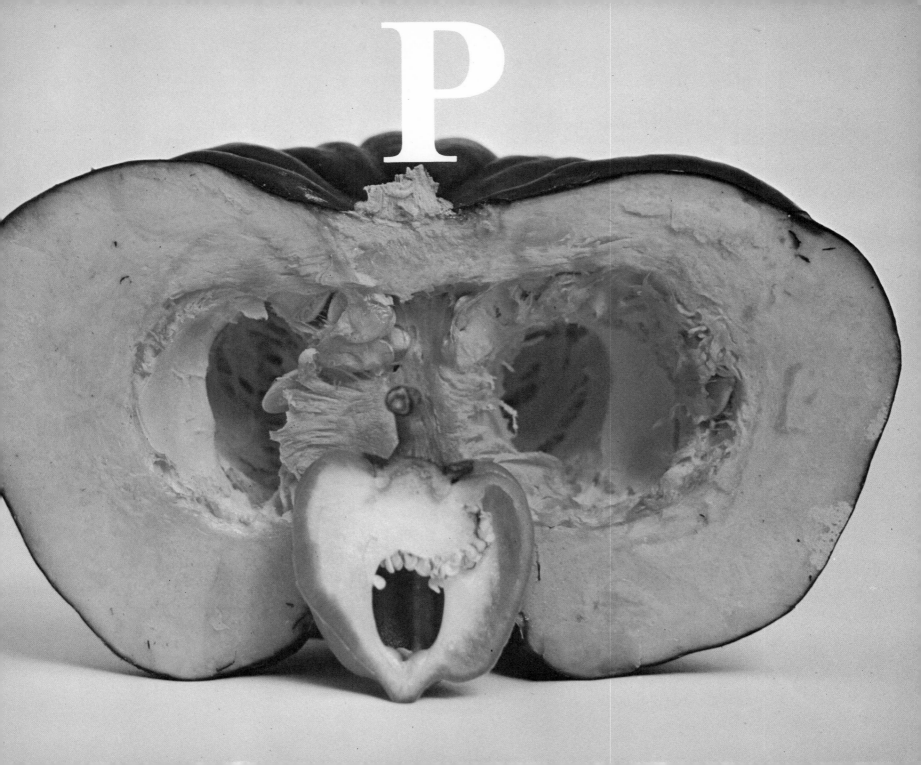

Palms

Large family of trees and shrubs (*Palmae*), widely grown in the warmer climates, some of important culinary value and others of major commercial value. Locations mentioned are where they are believed to have originated and many are now grown widely throughout the tropics.

Arenga Palm

See *Sugar Palm* p. 131.

Awarra Palm

From tropical South America. Oil is extracted from kernel of nut, excellent for frying fish. 'Butter' is also made from kernel.

Betel Palm

Small bunches of Areca or Betel nuts are harvested by natives who chew them with lime, producing a bright red juice and possibly obtaining some type of narcotic effect. Betel leaves are used to make a refreshing drink.

Carnauba Palm

From Brazil and Bolivia yielding 'toddy' or sap. This is obtained by tapping the trunk. Both sugar and vinegar are made from the toddy.

Coconut Palm

Most extensively cultivated palm. The coconut consists of an outer fibrous husk and a nut containing the flesh and a refreshing fluid (coconut milk). The 'milk' is often used as a substitute for water or cow's milk when preparing puddings. The flesh can be eaten fresh as coconut or cooked to extract its oil. The kernel can be drained of its milk by spiking the soft eyes in the top. In the wild, coconuts must have the outer husk removed and discarded. The kernel may be split with a heavy blade or hammer and the nutty lining removed for use. The dried kernel is known as copra which is grated (desiccated coconut) to use with rice, in curries and made into sweetmeats.

Use: to make coconut butter; coconut cream
     for flavouring and garnishing
     in salads and desserts
     in sauces

CHICKEN IN COCONUT HALVES

Time: 1 hour
Temperature: 425°F
Serves: 4

1 fresh coconut	1 capsicum, chopped finely
1 chicken, cut into sections and boned	2 shallots, chopped finely
	dried rosemary
salt	2 oz. coconut milk
pepper	2 oz. tomato purée
2 oz. flour	packet of pie pastry
4 tablespoons oil	milk

Drain coconut milk and save. Cut coconut in half, leaving the flesh in the shell. Dust chicken with salt and pepper, roll in flour, and sauté in oil until well browned. Warm coconut shells in the oven. Add capsicum, shallots and rosemary to browned chicken and cook a further 3 minutes. Place chicken mixture into warmed coconut halves. Mix coconut milk and tomato purée over a low heat and pour over the chicken.

Roll pastry and cover the filled shells, brushing pastry with milk. Bake in oven at 425°F for 20 minutes and serve.

COCONUT BUTTER

Grate the flesh of a fresh coconut and toast in an ungreased skillet until golden brown and crisp. Grind or mince twice until it becomes a fine butter. Can be stored in a tightly sealed jar in a refrigerator for several weeks.

metric equivalent

215°C

¼ cup
60 g

60 g

215°C

BEEF WITH COCONUT BUTTER

Serves: 6–7

		metric equivalent
2 lb shank beef cut in 1½ inch cubes	salt to taste	1 kg
16 oz. coconut milk	1 onion, finely chopped	3 cm
3 tablespoons coconut butter	2 cloves of garlic, pounded	2 cups
1 tablespoon ground chili	2 oz. tamarind juice or lemon juice	¼ cup
½ tablespoon turmeric	8 oz. vegetable oil (peanut, safflower or maize)	1 cup
10 mint leaves		

Wash and drain the meat and place in a frying pan. Add all ingredients except the oil. Bring to boil and cook over medium heat for about 25 minutes. Keep stirring until meat has absorbed all the juice. Add oil and fry, stirring constantly until mixture is light brown.

If desired, the mixture may be stored in a refrigerator and then heated just before serving with freshly boiled rice.

COCONUT CREAM

This is not the juice found inside the coconut kernel but an infusion made as follows:

Grate the fresh meat of 1 coconut or obtain ½ lb desiccated grated coconut and place in a bowl. Cover with boiling water and stand for 20 minutes. Drain the liquid and then place grated coconut in cheesecloth. Squeeze and add to other liquid and allow to hang until all moisture is extracted. [250 g]

COCONUT AND PINEAPPLE SAUCE

Serves: 4

		metric equivalent
1 × 12 oz. tin pineapple, crushed	2 teaspoons arrowroot cold water	375 g
1 tablespoon desiccated coconut	1 tablespoon rum	

Place pineapple, juice and coconut in a small saucepan. Mix arrowroot to a paste with a little cold water then add to saucepan and heat over a moderate flame until it reaches boiling point. Simmer for 3 minutes, remove from heat and add rum. Serve with vanilla ice cream, or with pies and other desserts, or over sponge cake.

CHOCOLATE MACAROONS

		metric equivalent
Temperature: 350°F		175°C
Quantity: about 1 dozen		
4 oz. cooking chocolate	pinch salt	125 g
½ cup peanut butter	1 dessertspoon vanilla	
1 cup sweetened condensed milk	3 cups flaked coconut	

Chop chocolate and melt in double boiler. Add peanut butter and stir with wooden spoon until smooth. Add condensed milk, salt, vanilla and coconut, one at a time and stirring each thoroughly into the mixture.

When thoroughly blended, drop teaspoons of mixture onto well greased oven plate and bake in oven at 350°F for 10–15 minutes. Remove from oven and while still warm, lift macaroons from oven tray. Store in tin with tight lid. [175°C]

TOASTED COCONUT CRISPS

1 fresh coconut	grated parmesan cheese
salt	

Pry coconut meat from husk and flake into thin strips with a potato peeler or sharp knife. Arrange on a large greased tray and sprinkle lightly with salt and parmesan. Toast in an oven at 325°F until golden brown, shaking occasionally to ensure even colouring. Cool and store in an air-tight jar. Serve as appetizers in place of potato crisps. [160°C]

Water Coconut Palm

See *Nipa palm* p. 130.

Coquito

Chilean palm tree. Its sap is tapped to make Palm honey, its edible seeds are eaten as sweetmeats and its fibre is used for rope. Another South American palm also from the West Coast is known as Coquito de San Juan or Ibappo. It has pineal leaves and its fruit is edible.

Date Palm

5 cm

The date palm, originally from Middle East and Western Asia but now grown in many warm climates has a highly nutritious fruit. Hard and soft dates are grown but the soft are more highly regarded. Fresh dates are about 2 inches long and have a yellow-red skin and a sweet, winey taste. In many places, only dried dates are available. The best are packed whole in long boxes. Poorer quality dates are stoned and compressed and sold by weight for use in cakes and puddings. See also *Jujubes* or Chinese 'dates'.

Use: raw as sweetmeat, in salads, fruit cups and as garnish
    stuffed—with cream cheese; or almonds; or candied
      fruit
    in cakes, sandwiches and puddings

FRESH DATES IN SYRUP

1 kg
2½ cups
315 g

2 lb fresh dates	few drops lemon juice
1 pint water	sufficient blanched
10 oz. sugar	almonds to equal
whole cloves	number of dates

Carefully peel dates and then boil in water until tender. Retain water but remove dates and drain and dry thoroughly. Push out stones with a steel rod or knitting needle. Into a saucepan place layers of sugar and dates, starting with a layer of sugar. Add one or two cloves to each layer. Stand overnight. Remove dates and shake off sugar. Add water in which dates were boiled to sugar and cloves and boil to reduce to a thick syrup. Stuff dates with almonds and boil gently in syrup for 10 minutes. Store in covered glass jars. Can be offered as sweetmeats at any time, or with cakes at afternoon tea.

Date Sugar Palm

Wild palm grown for its sweet sap, sometimes sold as a drink but usually made into sugar.

Deleb Palm

African variety with rich soft fruit, tasting like apricots. Arabs slice fruit then boil in water to extract a sweet syrup.

Down Palm or Gingerbread Tree

Palm of East Africa and Madagascar grown for its toddy or sap.

Guinea Palm

See *Oil Palm* below.

Hill Palm

See *Toddy Palm* opposite.

Ita Palm or Tree of Life

South American native whose fruit may be used to produce a flour when immature or saccharine when ripe.

Nipa or Water Coconut Palm

Low stemless variety growing in countries bordering the Indian Ocean including Indonesia, New Guinea, Queensland in Australia, and the Philippines and introduced to West Africa. Its sap or toddy is harvested for its sugar content.

Oil or Guinea Palm

Major source of palm oil but the kernels are also used for food. Grown in West and East Africa where natives use palm oil as much as Europeans use butter.

Palmyra Palm

Grown in Madagascar, Southern India, Burma and Indonesia as a source of sugar.

Patava Palm

Native of tropical America, grown for oils yielded by the pulp and kernel.

Sago Palm

Low, thick-set tree, native of Indonesia, growing in marshy regions. When the tree is about 15 years old, it is felled and its pith (the inside of the stem) is made into sago.

Sugar or Arenga Palm

Native of India, Indo-China (Viet-Nam), Japan and the Philippines. When 10 years old, trunks yield about 6 pints of sap or toddy for a period of two years. Sugar is extracted from the sap and the liquor arrack may be distilled from it. Female trees bear fruit but cannot be tapped.

Toddy or Hill Palm

Native of Bombay and tapped for toddy from the age of 15 to 25 years. When exhausted, trunk is felled and pith is made into a form of sago, used for bread, boiled into thick gruel, and a major staple food in the areas where it grows.

Tree of Life

See *Ita Palm* opposite.

Wax Palm

Grown in Brazil. The edible root is called a Carnauba.

Wine Palm

West African palm grown for its toddy or sap. Another variety is also grown in Brazil.

Yatay Palm

Palm tree of Central America with edible shoots and fruit.

Palm Cabbage: *Palmetto*

Very young tender terminal shoots or buds of cabbage palm (several species are used) sometimes available

15 cups

canned in oil, and highly seasoned as an *achar*, with saffron, ginger, pimento and allspice.

Preparation: remove from tin and drain oil in which they are packed. Place in glass jar and cover with olive oil.

Use: as cold entrée

Palm Hearts: *Ubod* (Philippines)

Hearts of tender shoots of certain types of palm tree.

Preparation: peel stalks completely and boil in salted water like asparagus, bound in bundles, in a deep saucepan, with a tight lid, and the tips above the water.

Use: hot with a white sauce
cold with vinaigrette or in any other manner asparagus is used
cooked hearts may also be sautéed in butter served au gratin

Pandanus: *Screw Pine*

Variety of tree akin to the bulrushes which have a large fruit forming into many nut-like segments.

Preparation: baked in coals by Aboriginals in Australia and eaten like *chestnuts*.

Paprika

See *Herbs and Spices* p. 79.

Parsley

See *Herbs and Spices* p. 79.

Hamburg Parsley

See *Herbs and Spices* p. 79.

Parsnip

Winter root vegetable with creamy white flesh and

131

tapering conical root. Distinctive flavour is sweet and somewhat aromatic. Originally of southern and central European origin, was widely used in folk remedies.

Preparation: as for *carrots* and *kohlrabi*.
    peeled then sliced in rounds or cut into fingers.

Use: boiled until tender then mashed with butter and salt
    and pepper
    fried in butter
    in soups and stews

CREAMED PARSNIPS

Time: 40 minutes
Serves: 7

6 parsnips, washed, peeled and cut in strips	freshly ground black pepper
2 oz. butter	1 tablespoon cream or top of milk
2 teaspoons sugar	

60 g

Cook parsnips in boiling salted water until tender (30 minutes approx.) Drain and pass through a sieve. Return to saucepan, add butter, pepper and sugar, whisk together over a low heat and when hot, add cream and serve.

FRIED PARSNIPS

Time: 30 minutes
Serves: 7

2 lb parsnips, washed, peeled, cut in strips and boiled until tender	1 egg, beaten breadcrumbs oil for frying
salt and pepper	

1 kg

Dry cooked parsnips in a towel, dust with salt and pepper, dip in egg then breadcrumbs and deep fry until golden brown. Drain and serve hot.

BAKED PARSNIPS AND APPLES

Time: 45 minutes approx.
Temperature: 350°F *175°C*
Serves: 4 as entrée

2 cups parsnips, boiled and mashed	1 teaspoon lemon juice ½ teaspoon nutmeg
1 cup cooking apple, cored and thinly sliced	breadcrumbs grilled bacon
1 tablespoon brown sugar	

Arrange layers of parsnip and apple slices in a small casserole dish, topping with a layer of apple. Sprinkle with brown sugar, lemon juice, nutmeg and breadcrumbs. Bake in oven at 350°F until breadcrumbs are browned. *175°C*
    Serve with grilled bacon.

Cow Parsnip

Common English weed whose leaves may be cooked like spinach. It has a flavour reminiscent of asparagus.

Passion Fruit: *Granadilla*

Fruit of a vine, originating in South America but now widely grown especially in northern Australia. The fruit is an elongated sphere with a skin which is first smooth and green and then becomes purple-brown and eventually wrinkled. Only when the skin is wrinkled and papery is the fruit at its ripest, though in warmer climates it is eaten earlier. The yellowish, aromatic seedy pulp is edible and has a refreshing piquant flavour. It is smaller but has more juice than the Giant Granadilla, see *Granadilla* p. 64.

Use: eat flesh raw, spooning flesh from cut halves
    add to fruit salad
    in jellies and cordials, ices

PASSION FRUIT PUNCH

Serves: 6–8

2 cups sugar	pulp of 12 fresh passion fruit
1 pint water	
1 dessertspoon citric acid	iced water to serve

Boil sugar and water to form a syrup and pour over

passion fruit pulp. Add citric acid and stir until ingredients are well mixed. Stand until cold, then strain and chill in refrigerator.

Serve with iced water to taste. If desired, vodka may also be added.

PASSION FRUIT PAVLOVA

Claimed to be Australia's one contribution to the desserts of the world.

Time: 2½ hours
Temperature: 275°F   135°C
Serves: 4–6

For meringue:	*For filling:*
whites of 4 eggs	1 cup passion fruit flesh
8 oz. castor sugar	and seeds 250 g
1 dessertspoon cornflour	Pale pink ice cream or
1 teaspoon vinegar	cream for topping
	crystallized cherries and
	angelica for decoration

To make meringue: Beat egg whites until very stiff and gradually add sugar, beating well until thoroughly blended. When mixture is crumbly, fold in cornflour and vinegar. Cut greaseproof paper to size to line a 7-inch [18 cm] cake tin. Hold paper under cold tap, shake off surplus water then line tin. Pour in meringue mixture and hollow in centre. Leave some paper projecting at each side to assist in removal. Bake in a very slow oven 275°F [135°C] until meringue is crisp and dry. For immediate use, the Pavlova should be crisp outside but like marshmallow within (1½ hours). For storing in an airtight container, it should be dried throughout (2 hours). Allow to cool and remove from tin, very carefully. Store until ready to serve.
Filling: Fill meringue case with passion fruit and top with pale pink ice cream or cream. Decorate with crystallized cherries and angelica.

PASSION FRUIT SKIN JAM

Quantity: About 1 pint   2½ cups

12 passion fruit skins	1 cup sugar to each cup of
juice of 1 lemon	pulp
3 pints water 7½ cups	

Place skins in a saucepan, add lemon juice and just cover them with water. Boil for 20 minutes until pulp of skins becomes puffy and soft enough to be easily removed with a spoon. Drain water from skins and save, scrape out pulp and add 1 cup warmed sugar to each cup of pulp. Mix pulp and sugar and replace in liquid in saucepan. Boil quickly until syrup jells when tested (about 45 minutes). Sterilize jars and pour warm jam into them.

PASSION FRUIT AND PINEAPPLE CREAM

Serves: 4–6

½ cup *canned* and crushed	1 tablespoon sugar
pineapple, fresh pine-	2 teaspoons lemon juice
apple prevents gelatine	2 teaspoons gelatine
from setting	¼ cup cold water
½ cup passion fruit pulp	½ pint cream, whipped

Drain pineapple and mix with passion fruit pulp, sugar and lemon juice. Stand 1 hour for flavours to mingle. Soften gelatine in cold water and then dissolve by placing cup in a bowl of hot water. Add dissolved gelatine to fruit mixture then gently fold in cream so that it is thoroughly mixed. Pour into mould and chill in refrigerator for 4 hours.

Serve on chilled plate.

Pawpaw: *Papaya*

Large angular and oblong tropical fruit, originally from South America but now grown widely. Pawpaws may grow to a weight of 20 lb. [9 kg] Thick skin is green to yellow-green and tender flesh is bright orange with a centre of small seeds. Juice and seeds have high enzyme content and are excellent as tenderizers for rubbing into flesh of meat, some time before cooking. If harvested from tree, pick 3 days before it is ripe, make fine razor slits through skin on each side and allow sap to run through them. Use after 3 days.

Preparation: cut in half and scoop out seeds

Serve: ripe—raw with lemon juice and sugar, and ginger
with pepper and salt
Green—baked
peeled and boiled then cut in small pieces and
served with a vinaigrette
also pickled and preserved

PAWPAW FRUIT SALAD

1 pawpaw
castor sugar

4 Chinese gooseberries
dry white wine

Cut pawpaw in half, scoop out seeds and peel skin. Cut flesh in cubes and place in a bowl. Sprinkle with sugar. Peel Chinese gooseberries, slice into rings, place in separate basin and sprinkle with sugar. Chill fruit.

To serve, combine both fruits in individual dishes and half fill with white wine.

PAWPAW SURPRISE

Serves: 4

1 ripe pawpaw
½ cup diced fresh fruit
and/or stoned cherries
1 dessertspoon gelatine

1 packet green jelly
crystals
sherry or creme de menthe

Slice away the top of the pawpaw and scoop out the seeds. Stone the cherries and dice fresh fruits in season. Make green jelly according to directions in packet, but add extra gelatine and water to the mixture; and add sherry or liqueur. Add fruit and cherries to jelly. Place pawpaw upright and pour liquid jelly and fruit into it. Allow to stand until jelly sets. Put aside any remaining jelly mixture to set.

Replace top on pawpaw, place on a platter, and around it use remaining jelly. Place in refrigerator and chill thoroughly.

Serve on a platter and cut in slices. Canned fruits may replace fresh fruits and their syrup should be mixed in jelly instead of water.

metric equivalent

PAWPAW APPETIZER

Serves: 4

1 pawpaw, peeled and
chopped into cubes
4 bananas, sliced
juice of 1 lemon

12 dates, sliced and
chopped
castor sugar
brandy

Mix fruits together and sprinkle with lemon juice, sugar and brandy. Chill and serve at beginning of meal.

PAWPAW LIQUEUR

4 cups sugar
1 cup lime or lemon juice

4 cups pawpaw pulp
1 cup rum

Add sugar and lime juice to pawpaw and whip into pulp. Stand for 2 days and place in a cloth bag and allow to drip into a bowl. Add rum to bowl, bottle and store.

PAWPAW JAM

1¼ cups

½ pint water
2 cups sugar
3 cups pawpaw, peeled
and diced
1 sprig of fresh green mint

1 teaspoon lime or lemon
juice
pinch of salt
sterilized jars with lids

Bring water and sugar to boil, add diced pawpaws and lime juice. Cook for 30 minutes and add mint and salt. Test for gel and when cool enough, place in prepared sterilized jars.

Peaches

Globular stone fruit with soft, plushy skin, often flushed deep pink to red or golden. Grown in many parts of the world but originally from China, peaches are now grown for the table, for cooking and for canning. The flesh of table peaches is white flushed with red around the stone. Canning peaches, such as Clingstone and Hale are larger and have a yellow or golden flesh.

Eat: some people eat the peach, including the skin, after
washing it. Others peel the skin, slice it in half
and remove the stone and eat it in slices.

Use: pies
    for preserving
    as fruit moulds and stuffed for dessert
    in jams, jellies and to flavour ice creams

PEACHES IN BRANDY

Time: 1½ hours

		metric equivalent
4 lb peaches, not quite ripe	2 sticks cinnamon, cut in	2 kg
1½ lb castor sugar	strips	750 g
1½ bottles brandy		

Slit peaches and remove stones, retaining shape of peaches as much as possible. Place layer of peaches in a wide-mouthed screw-top jar and cover with sugar and add a strip of cinnamon. Then add peaches, sugar and a cinnamon strip in layers finishing with sugar. Cover with brandy until there is half an inch above the top layer. Screw top on tightly then release half a turn. Place jars in large pan but rest jars on sponges. Jars must not touch metal bottom or sides of pan. Half fill pan with water, cover and slowly bring to boiling point. Simmer for 10 minutes, removing bottles to screw top tightly while cooking. Remove jars, cool and store until needed.

BEEF WITH PEACH SAUCE

The peach is said to have been brought from China to Persia and from there it spread through Europe. Certainly the Persians probably have a greater range of peach dishes than any other nation and this is one of their most succulent. Frequently peaches are used to flavour fowl or meat when combined with lemon and sugar, and this combination produces quite a delicious effect.

Time: allow 1½ hours
Serves: 4

		metric equivalent
4 tablespoons beef	2 oz. butter	60 g
dripping or butter	1 onion, finely chopped	
1 lb stewing steak cut into	1 tablespoon lemon juice	500 g
1 inch cubes (or 1 lb	2 oz butter	3 cm 60 g
lamb shank; or 3 lb	4 large fresh peaches, not	1·5 kg
chicken, also cubed)	ripe	
1 teaspoon salt	2 tablespoons lime and	

		metric equivalent
½ teaspoon white pepper	lemon juice (or lemon	
¼ teaspoon paprika	juice alone)	
1 chicken stock cube	4 oz. sugar	125 g
(crushed to powder) or	6 oz. water	¾ cup
1 teaspoon cinnamon	boiled rice to serve	
½ pint water		1¼ cups

Melt beef dripping or butter in a large heavy frying pan and sauté the steak (or lamb, or chicken) with the salt, pepper, paprika and crushed chicken cube, until browned. Add half a pint of water and simmer on low heat for 25 minutes.   1¼ cups

In another frying pan, melt butter and sauté onion until golden brown. Remove from heat, drain onions and place in a bowl. Add lemon juice and let this stand. Wash the peaches and remove fuzz with your fingers but do not skin. Cut them in half, remove seeds and slice. Melt butter in the second frying pan and sauté the peaches, until they are golden, turning once. Add onions to the meat and arrange the peaches over the meat and reduced sauce. Mix lime and lemon juice and sugar and add it to to the meat mixture. Then add 6 oz. water and cover the   ¾ cup heavy frying pan. Simmer over a low heat for 20 minutes. If preferred, cinnamon may replace the crushed chicken cube.

Serve with crisp boiled and buttered rice.

PEACH MELBA

Serves: 4–6

6 firm ripe peaches	1 cup fresh or frozen
½ teaspoon vanilla essence	raspberries and their
½ pint vanilla ice cream	juice

Peel peaches, cut in halves and remove stone. Rub raspberries and juice through a sieve and add vanilla to them. Into a clean frying pan, place peach halves and raspberry mixture and heat until peaches are soft but not broken. Remove peaches, drain and cool. On a serving platter, make a mound of ice cream. Around this place the peach halves, and over all, pour raspberry purée.

Pears

Common and popular fruit grown in most of the temperate regions of the world. The many hundreds of varieties can all be traced to three parent stocks. They are the common pear (*Pyrus comunis*) from which have been cultivated the dessert pears; the Chinese sand pear from which have come some hard decorative varieties, only edible when cooked; and the Snow pear which is grown solely for crushing and its juice used to make perry or pear cider. Pears vary from pear shaped to that of a calabash and their skin may range from pale green, golden yellow, russet brown to others flushed with red. Dessert pears are soft, sweet and juicy. Cooking pears are not acid but lack flavour and need to be cooked in red wine or syrup. They are usually smaller and very hard.

Preparation: cooking pears—peel, core, then simmer in oven whole, or in halves in a thin syrup with lemon rind until they turn reddish-brown.
dessert pears—eat with or without skin, when just ripe. If over-ripe, they deteriorate quickly. Ideal with a cheese board for dessert.

PEAR AND APRICOT FLAN

Serves: 4–6

6 dessert pears	1 cooked pastry flan case
2½ cups — 1 pint water into which has been mixed 2 teaspoons salt	(obtainable ready made in self-service stores)
1 teaspoon arrowroot	2 tablespoons apricot jam
150 ml — ¼ pint water	blanched almonds

Peel and core pears and place in salted water until needed. Drain and dry pears and arrange in flan case. Blend arrowroot with ¼ pint water and heat in saucepan. Mix in apricot jam. Bring slowly to boil, stirring to keep smooth and cook until thick and clear. Cool, then pour over pears. Decorate with almonds and chill. *(150 ml)*

BAKED PEARS IN CLARET

Serves: 4–6

6 pears, peeled and cored and cut in half	castor sugar
grated nutmeg	claret

175°C

Peel and core the pears and cut in half lengthways. Place in a casserole dish, sprinkle with grated nutmeg and castor sugar and cover with claret. Bake in oven at 350°F until pears are soft enough for a fork to pass through them easily. When cooked, rapidly boil away some of the juice and pour remainder over them as a glaze.

PEAR CONDÉ

Time: 40 minutes
Serves: 8

4 pears, peeled, halved and cored	*For glaze:*
2 oz. sugar (60 g)	5 oz. pear cooking syrup (150 ml)
5 oz. water (150 ml)	5 oz. water (150 ml)
2 oz. rice (60 g)	2 tablespoons raspberry jam
1 pint milk (2½ cups)	1 oz. sugar (30 g)
1 oz. sugar (30 g)	½ teaspoon gelatine
2 tablespoons cream	lemon juice
jam glaze	cochineal

Cook pears slowly in sugar and water until soft. Remove pears, drain and cool. Save the syrup. Wash rice and cook slowly in milk until tender but still crisp. Remove from heat and add 1 oz. sugar and cream. Pour rice equally into 8 dessert glasses and cool. Place half a pear on top of rice. *(30 g)*

To make glaze: Place 5 oz. of pear cooking syrup, water, jam, sugar, gelatine and lemon juice in a small saucepan. Bring to boil and simmer for 5 minutes. Strain and when cooked but not set, add a drop or two of cochineal. Pour over pears and chill them in refrigerator. *(150 ml)*

Anchovy Pear: *River Pear*

Fruit of a West Indian tree, inedible when raw.
Preparation: as for pickled *gherkin*.

Vegetable Pear: also known as *Brionne* (France); *Chayote* (Mexico); *Christophine; Choko* (Australia); *Cho-Cho* (Jamaica); *Custard Marrow; Xuxu* (Portugal); *Pepinella*

No vegetable appears to have so many individual names than this fruit of a climbing vine in the gourd family. Originally from Mexico, it is now widely grown in countries with tropical, subtropical and warm temperate climates. The fruit is up to 6 inches long, pear-shaped and with pale green, spiny and deeply ribbed skin. Beneath the thick skin, the flesh is firm, white and not too watery.   *15 cm*

Preparation: cut into quarters or lozenges under water to remove exudation, peel and remove central seeds. Boil in salted water until just tender but not mushy (about 20 minutes).

Use: toss in butter
serve with butter and grated parmesan
in a white sauce
chilled with seafoods
in salads
with lima beans, green peppers and tomatoes
in South America and the West Indies it is cooked as for *pumpkin* and made into soups, mashed, used in pies.

VEGETABLE PEAR AND CHEESE SANDWICHES

slices of gruyere cheese	melted butter	
1 lb vegetable pear cooked	breadcrumbs	*500 g*
and cut into thin slices	olive oil	

Place a slice of cheese between two slices of vegetable pear, brush with melted butter, dip in breadcrumbs and fry in olive oil until breadcrumbs are golden.
Serve as entrée or with savouries.

BRAISED VEGETABLE PEAR

Serves 4–6

1 lb vegetable pear, peeled and quartered	beef stock, made from stock cube but only half	*500 g*

metric equivalent

2 carrots, sliced	recommended quantity	
2 onions, sliced	of water	
bacon rinds	1 oz. butter	*30 g*

Blanch vegetable pear in boiling salted water. Place in buttered saucepan with sliced carrots, onions and bacon rinds. Cover vegetables with stock and cover with tight-fitting lid. When liquor is reduced to glaze, add some more stock, simmer. Drain vegetable pear and reduce liquid in saucepan. Add 1 oz. butter, strain and pour over vegetable pear.   *30 g*

VEGETABLE PEAR, TOMATOES AND ONIONS

Serves: 4

1 lb vegetable pear, peeled, quartered and blanched	3 tomatoes, peeled, seeded and coarsely chopped	*500 g*
1 oz. butter	clove of garlic, minced	*30 g*
1 tablespoon oil	cooked rice to serve	
½ cup chopped onions	chopped parsley	
bouquet garni		

Sauté vegetable pear in butter and oil with onions, tomatoes, bouquet garni and garlic in heavy saucepan with tight-fitting lid. When vegetable pears are tender, arrange on dish of hot crumbly rice, pour over other vegetables and sprinkle with freshly chopped parsley.

VEGETABLE PEAR MERINGUE

Serves: 6

4 large vegetable pears	1 lb breadcrumbs	*500 g*
10 cloves	3 eggs, separated	
juice of 2 lemons or limes	½ pint milk	*1¼ cups*
1 oz. butter	½ lb castor sugar	*30 g 250 g*
1 teaspoon grated nutmeg	few drops almond essence	

Prepare vegetable pears and boil with cloves until tender. Drain and mash the vegetable pears, adding lemon juice, butter, nutmeg and place in well buttered casserole dish. Cover with breadcrumbs. Beat 3 egg yolks with 1 egg white, add to milk and sugar and pour into casserole. Bake in oven at 375°F until browned. Beat 2 egg whites with 2 tablespoons sugar and almond essence until stiff.   *190°C*

Shape into spoonfuls and place on top of pie. Return to oven to allow meringue to cook and brown.

Peas

A climbing plant cultivated mainly for its seeds in most countries of the world. In some cases, the pods also are edible. There are many varieties but they can be reduced to three varieties for culinary use:

Edible Podded Peas; Sugar Peas, Tirabeques *(Spain)* **Pois Mangetout** *(France)*

Special variety of peas whose pods have no parchment lining. They are picked when the peas within the pods are very small.

Preparation: remove tip, tail and stringy spine and cook as for *kidney beans*. When cooked, drain and add butter and eat pods intact.

Use: cut in half, parboil and use as filling for omelette in sweet and sour chinese dishes

FRIED TIRABEQUES

2 cm Simmer gently in half an inch of water for 5–6 minutes. Drain. Dip in an egg and flour batter or in egg and flour separately, then fry in hot olive oil until crisp. In some parts of Spain lard is considered to impart a better flavour to the tirabeques.

Shelling Peas: *Green Peas* or *Garden Peas* (*Pisum sativum*)

As the name suggests, these are grown for the peas alone which must be extracted from the pods (shelling). For best use peas should be picked young and small. At this stage, they are tender, sweet and delicious. When older, they become tough and have far less flavour. Also obtainable deep frozen or canned.

Preparation: always shell peas just before cooking. Standing in water kills their flavour. Wash in a
3 cm colander under a cold tap. Place in 1 inch of

salted boiling water to which a teaspoon of sugar and a sprig of mint have been added. Cover and bring to boil, reduce heat and simmer until tender (8–12 minutes). Drain then serve hot dotted with butter and seasoned with salt and pepper; or cool and serve in a salad dressing on their own, or add to other cooked vegetables in a salad.

Use: with roast duck, roast lamb
freshly boiled green peas served with freshly boiled tiny white or tree onions
garnish freshly cooked peas with crisp bits of bacon

GREEN PEAS FRANCAISE

Serves: 4–6

125 g	4 oz. butter	large leaves of lettuce,
	2 cups of peas, freshly shelled	washed and not dried

Melt butter in a thick saucepan, add the peas and cover with lettuce leaves. Do not add any water. Cook slowly over a low heat until peas are just tender.

MACEDOINE OF VEGETABLES

		1 turnip	few cauliflower fleurettes
125 g	3¾ cups	4 oz. carrots	1½ pints water with
		few runner beans	½ teaspoon salt
250 g		8 oz. shelled peas	parsley, chopped
250 g		8 oz. potatoes, cut into serving sizes	butter

Peel and dice all vegetables. In boiling salted water first boil the turnip, then add carrots, runner beans, peas, cauliflower and finally the potatoes so that all will be cooked at the same time. Strain, saving stock if needed for soup. Place in serving dish, sprinkle with chopped parsley and dot with butter.

Serve separately or on the same platter as any meat dish.

Split Peas; Dried or Fried Peas, Pease

Dried peas, particularly valuable for their protein, especially when green peas are not available. Both green and yellow varieties are available.

Preparation: soak overnight, boil until tender in water to which a small *bouquet garnet* and an onion have been added.

Use: in soups and stews
     mashed into a purée

PEASE PUDDING

		metric equivalent
1 lb split peas	butter	500 g
2 lb boiled pork, cut in cubes with water saved	salt and pepper	1 kg

Soak peas overnight, place in a cloth and boil for 1½ hours or until tender in water from boiling pork. Drain, place in bowl and mash with butter, salt and pepper. Put peas back into cloth and boil with pork for half an hour.

Asparagus Pea

See p. 10.

Chick Peas: *Gram Peas*, *Garbanzos* (*Cicer arietinum*)

Native plant of western Asia and southern Europe, now extensively grown in Mediterranean countries. Its seeds or 'peas' are used fresh or dried, mostly in soups and stews or roasted as a coffee substitute. The finest variety is the white chick pea grown in Spain. In India the chick pea is known as the *gram* but should not be confused with green gram which is the *mung bean*.

CHICK PEA AND SILVER BEET SOUP

Time: 2 hours
Serves: 6

		metric equivalent
½ lb dried chick peas	1 tablespoon paprika	250 g
4 pints salted water	1½ lb silver beet or 2 lb spinach	6 cups
1 bayleaf		750 g or 1 kg
1 onion, skinned but whole	2 cloves garlic	
1 tomato	1 tablespoon olive oil	
6 cloves garlic	2 tablespoons white wine or wine vinegar	
1 sprig parsley		

Soak chick peas overnight in cold water to which a little salt has been added. When swollen, wash and drain well. Place soaked peas into 4 pints of tepid salted water and add bayleaf, onion, tomato, 6 cloves garlic (whole), parsley and paprika. Heat to boiling point and allow to simmer, for 1 hour, adding hot water to maintain water level. Add silver beet (well washed) or spinach and simmer for another 20 minutes. Remove from heat and extract onion and tomato. Pound together with two uncooked cloves of garlic and pass through sieve. Grind about 20 cooked peas in mortar and mix with 1 tablespoon olive oil and sieved onion, tomato and garlic. Mix with a little of soup and pour back into soup. Simmer 10 minutes more. Before serving, add 2 tablespoons wine or wine vinegar.

(metric equivalent: 6 cups)

Cow Peas

See *Herbs and Spices* p. 79.

Gungo Peas

Common variety of peas used in Jamaica, either green or dried.

Use: as for *green peas* or *split peas*

Chinese Snow Peas

An oriental form of peas, used particularly by Chinese and Indonesians and renowned for their very delicate texture and subtle flavour. May be available from Chinese stores in temperate zones, either in dried or deep frozen form. Both pods and peas are edible.

Use: as with normal peas but take care not to overcook.

SNOW PEAS WITH PRAWNS

Serves: 4

1 lb shrimp or prawns	1 tablespoon dry sherry
1 onion, finely chopped	8 oz. whole fresh snow
2 tablespoons oil	peas
(preferably peanut)	2 oz. crisp fried onion
2 tablespoons soya sauce	flakes or dehydrated
salt and pepper to taste	onion flakes

250 g appears beside "1 onion, finely chopped" and *60 g* beside "2 tablespoons soya sauce".

Shell prawns and split, cutting halfway through. Clean and dry them. Fry onion in hot oil for 2 minutes. Add prawns, soya sauce, salt and pepper and sherry and cook for 10 minutes. One minute before serving, add fresh snow peas and stir into the mixture.

Serve hot, topped with onion flakes.

Pea Sprouts

Grown from green mung peas, they can be grown in a little water at any time of the year and are rich in vitamin C. The shoots are white with olive-green hoods. See also *bean sprouts*.

To grow: soak 1 cup dried mung peas (or dried green peas) in water for 2–3 days. When sprouts appear, spread peas evenly between two layers of blotting paper in a deep basin. Place in a dark warm place, and water every day. Use when sprouts are 1 inch long and plump.

Preparation: stir sprouts in dish of cold water so that green shells or hoods float to the surface and can be skimmed away. Then trim sprouts from roots.

Use: when cooking, do not overcook. They should always be crisp.

3 cm appears in the margin beside "long and plump."

BRAISED PORK WITH PEA SPROUTS

Serves: 4–6

1 lb pea sprouts	1 tablespoon soya sauce
½ lb pork fillet (tenderloin)	1 teaspoon sugar
cut in very thin strips	1 teaspoon salt
peanut oil	4 oz. cup beef stock (from
2 tablespoons dry sherry	stock cube)
or saki	

500 g and *250 g* appear in the margin beside "1 lb pea sprouts" and "½ lb pork fillet"; *½ cup* beside "peanut oil".

Wash pea sprouts and remove shells and trim roots. Drain. Sauté pork strips in hot oil until lightly browned. (If preferred, pork may first be marinaded in the sherry, soya sauce, sugar and salt for a short while.) Add pea sprouts, sherry, soya sauce, sugar, salt and stock. Stir and cover and cook for 2 minutes only.

Pennyroyal

See *Herbs and Spices* p. 79.

Pepino

Yellow fruits of a South American plant, cultivated in Chile. The small fruits have a pleasant acid and refreshing flavour.

Pepper

Black Pepper

Capsicum or Sweet Pepper

Hot South American Pepper

Pimentos

Red or Cayenne Pepper

See *Herbs and Spices* p. 79.

Persimmon: *Virginia Date Plum* (U.S.A.) *Black Sapota* (Mexico) *Kaki* (Japan)

Fruit of tree, originally from Japan, now widely grown in many parts of the world. Resembling a tomato in appearance, the fruit is round, smooth skinned and changing from yellow to red as it ripens. The texture of the flesh is not unlike a tomato's and the flavour is tart unless the fruit is kept until spongy and soft. Then its tanin content is reduced and develops its distinctive sweet flavour. In Asia, persimmons are also dried and sold as 'date plums'. The Mexican Black Sapota is almost seedless, dark fleshed and pleasant tasting. The Japanese Kaki is also grown in France.

Eat: raw; slit leathery skin and peel back like petals

without removing stem. Then suck the sweet sub-acid pulp.

Use: in compotes
jams
for flavouring ices
in preserves

PERSIMMON AND GRAPEFRUIT ENTRÉE

Serves: 2

1 persimmon, cut in half	½ grapefruit, cut in	
sprinkling of sugar	segments (or canned	
sprigs of fresh mint	segments)	

Remove persimmon pulp, mix with grapefruit, sprinkle with sugar and spoon into 2 cocktail glasses. Top with sprig of young fresh mint, refrigerate and serve icy cold.

PERSIMMON AND PINEAPPLE ENTRÉE

Serves: 4

1 × 8 oz. can crushed	4 persimmons	250 g
pineapple	kirsch	
1 teaspoon lemon juice		

Pass pineapple through a fine sieve, add lemon juice and chill in refrigerator. Cut hole in persimmons around the stalk and scoop out pulp without breaking skins. Sprinkle kirsch inside skins and steep for 1 hour in refrigerator. Sieve persimmon pulp and mix well with chilled pineapple. Fill persimmon skins with mixture and serve.

PORK WITH PERSIMMON SAUCE

½ lb bean sprouts	12 oz. persimmons	250 g	375 g
3 oz. carrots	1 teaspoon salt	90 g	
3 dried mushrooms	⅔ tablespoon sugar		
4 tablespoons vinegar	monosodium glutamate		
½ lb pork	(optional)	250 g	

Cook bean sprouts in boiling salted water until tender and drain. Cut carrots into 1½ inch long strips, sprinkle with salt and stand until softened. Squeeze out excess liquid. Soften mushrooms in water and cut in strips. Mix

vegetables together with 1 tablespoon vinegar then drain surplus liquid. Cut pork into slices, 2 inches thick and sprinkle lightly with salt. Boil in fresh water until tender. Peel and remove seeds from persimmons. Grate flesh in a bowl and with the pulp, mix remaining vinegar, 1 teaspoon salt, sugar and MSG. Mix vegetables, pork and dressing together and serve.

Pigweed (*Amaranthus* spp.)

Annual weed with hard shiny red, white or black edible seeds, cultivated in tropical Africa, India and Ceylon. They are important articles of food for hill tribes in India, in South Africa among the Zulus and for natives in Portuguese East Africa. In some places, young leaves, shoots and young flower heads are boiled in salted water and used as green vegetables or mixed with maize meal and boiled until a thick paste is obtained. Young leaves are also dried for use when fresh vegetables are not obtainable. The term 'pigweed' is also used for other weeds including goosefoot (*Chenopodium bonushenricus*) and the *purslanes* (*Portulaca* spp.) see p. 166.

Pindo

Edible fruit of a South American tree.

Pineapple: *Sugar Loaf; Ananas; Pina; Abacaxi*

Native plant of tropical America, now widely grown in warm climates. Its orange fruit is somewhat like a very large pine cone, up to 12 inches long and topped with a crest of small, often prickly leaves. It is rich in sweet juice which has a high content of citric and malic acids. Pineapple juice is said to help the digestion and should be drunk at the end of a meal. Its flesh is golden but on some varieties, white. The flavour is distinctive but said by some to contain hints of strawberry, apple and peach. It may be available fresh and always in canned forms.

31 cm

Eat: raw, crushed for juice
in many forms of cooking including desserts, jams, cakes and drinks

Preparation: remove top and thick skin and cut in slices or other conveniently sized pieces.

Note: Never add fresh pineapple to gelatine because it prevents it setting. However, canned pineapple may be used.

PINEAPPLE FRUIT LOAF

Serves: 6

1 pineapple	castor sugar
1 punnet fresh	sprigs of mint to garnish
strawberries, picked	2 tablespoons brandy
washed and dried	

Cut top off pineapple and cut and scoop out flesh. Cut flesh in cubes and mix with strawberries. Refill pineapple case with mixture, sprinkle with castor sugar and replace top. Serve remaining fruit around base of pineapple. Chill in refrigerator and serve with sprigs of fresh mint and sprinkled with brandy.

PINEAPPLE WITH HAM

Pineapple goes particularly well with ham. It may be used in the following ways:

pineapple slices sautéed in ham fat or butter and served on slices of hot or cold ham;

when baking a ham, rub surface with dry mustard, ground cloves and brown sugar. Place pineapple rings on the ham and sprinkle them with brown sugar;

when baking ham, 1 hour before removing from oven, glaze with brown sugar and a cup of pineapple juice.

PINEAPPLE SAUCE

2 cups pineapple juice	4 tablespoons brown sugar
$\frac{3}{4}$ cup ham stock	1 tablespoon cornflour

Heat juice, stock and sugar just to boiling point, thicken with cornflour and simmer a few minutes.
Serve with baked ham or tongue.

PINEAPPLE DUCK

Time: $1\frac{1}{2}$ hours
Serves: 4

metric equivalent

2·5 kg	1 duck, 5 lb weight
	4 cups cold water
2 cm	2 teaspoons salt
	3 tablespoons duck fat
	$\frac{1}{2}$ clove garlic, crushed
	1 cup duck broth
	1 cup pineapple pieces, diced

1 capsicum, skinned, seeded and cut into 1 inch squares
2 tablespoons cornflour
$\frac{1}{4}$ cup cold water
1 tablespoon lemon juice
1 teaspoon soya sauce
hot boiled rice to serve

Cut duck into quarters and place in large saucepan with neck, giblets, 4 cups water and 2 teaspoons salt. Cover and cook gently until tender (about 45–55 minutes). Remove duck, drain liquid and skim fat. Remove skin and cut meat into sticks about 2 inches long and $\frac{1}{2}$ inch square cross section. Put duck fat into a large frying pan, add garlic and cook 2 minutes over low heat. Remove garlic and add duck meat, increasing heat and browning on all sides. Add duck broth, pineapple and capsicum and mix well. Mix cornflour and $\frac{1}{4}$ cup water, add lemon juice, soya sauce and add to broth. Cook, stirring until sauce thickens.
Serve with hot boiled rice.

5 cm

See recipes for *Breast of chicken with lychee and pineapple* p. 98.
Persimmon and pineapple entree p. 141.
Passionfruit and pineapple cream p. 133.

Piquillin

Edible fruit of a South American tree, more frequently used to make *arrobe*, a syrup and a fermented wine which is distilled into a fiery brandy.

Pitanga: *Surinam*, *Cayenne* or *Florida Cherry*

Fruit of Brazilian myrtle tree, at first green and then becoming yellow and eventually becoming scarlet or crimson.

Use: fresh, when green
   in jelly as for *medlars*

Plantain (*Musa cavendishii?*)

Fruit of the banana family but growing to a larger size
and with a firmer, more fibrous flesh. Should be cooked
before eating. For methods of use, apply any methods for
cooking *bananas*.

Preparation: peel and boil and serve whole with meat, in
   a sauce
   mash well, form into round balls and steam, serve
   dotted with butter.

PLANTAIN STEW

Serves: 6–8

10 green plantains, peeled and washed	2 tomatoes, finely diced
2 onions, medium sized and finely chopped	1 teaspoon salt
	1 oz. butter 30 g

Place plantains, tomatoes, onions and salt in a saucepan.
Add sufficient water to cover. Simmer until soft. Drain
surplus water. Add 1 oz. butter and keep warm until   30 g
ready to serve.

Plantain (*Plantago major*)

English weed related to hartshorn usually considered
objectionable in paths and lawns. Its young leaves may
be used in green salads like corn salad. Canaries eat
plantain seeds.

Plums

Stone fruit, harvested in late summer or early autumn.
Both eating and cooking varieties are available. Varieties
include:

Bullace

Wild form of Damascus plum, unsuitable for eating raw
but useful in jams and jellies.

Use: like *Damsons*

Cherry Plum

Bright red fruit, about the size of a cherry or slightly
larger but with a stone shaped like a plum. Used for
cooking.

Chickasaw Plum: Mountain Cherry

Native plum of the southern states of the U.S.A. The
fruit, though edible, is small and of low quality.

Chinese or Japanese Plum

Large yellow or pale red plum grown in China. Fruit is
very juicy.

Damsons and Damascenes: Shropshire, Black Jack Damsons

Small round plums, with deep blue skin and greenish
flesh. They are believed to de derived from the native
plum of Damascus and are closely related to sloes.
Damascenes are a smaller and rounder variety of
Damsons.

Use: damsons can be eaten raw but are not recommended
   cook in tarts, puddings, pickles, preserves, etc.

Greengage

Dark green variety of plum with golden flesh. Flavour is
scented and sweet and with round stone, not oval as in
plums. They are considered the sweetest and most
aromatic of all plums.

Eat: raw

Use: in tarts
   puddings
   jams
   and preserves

GREENGAGE SPONGE

Time: 1½ hours
190°C   Temperature: 375°F
Serves: 6

For filling:
500 g 90 g   1 lb greengages, stoned
90 g   2 tablespoons water
125 g   4 oz. sugar
125 g

For sponge:
3 oz. butter
3 oz. sugar
2 eggs
4 oz. self-raising flour

To make filling: Place fruit and water in bottom of pie-dish and sprinkle with sugar.

To make sponge: Cream butter and sugar until soft and aerated, fold in eggs and whisk into mixture, then gradually whisk in flour. Spread over fruit. Bake in oven 190°C at 375°F for about 1 hour, reducing heat after 35–40 minutes if top is browning too quickly.

Mirabelle

Small round yellow, sweet-scented, similar to a cherry plum which is bright red. Best for cooking.

Eat: dessert varieties, wipe skin with damp cloth and eat raw or cut in half to remove stone first.

Use: in desserts
 fruit salads
 jam
 pickles
 pies

Natal Plum: Amatungula; Carissa

Red fruit from a spiny South African shrub, varying in size from that of an olive to a damson, with refreshing acid taste.

Use: fresh
 stewed and preserved (then similar to cranberry jelly)

Sand Cherry

Small, sweet fruit of a small shrub in the plum family, cultivated on the western plains of the U.S.A.

Sand Plum

Thick-skinned variety of plum cultivated in the southern states of the U.S.A.

Victoria

Large, oval with red and yellow skin and fine flavour. Good for dessert, cooking, jam and bottling.

PLUM PIE

Time: 40 minutes
205°C   Temperature: 400°F
Serves: 6

500 g 250 g   1 lb plums   ½ lb frozen short pastry
155 g   5 oz. sugar

Wipe fruit and remove stones. Place half fruit in pie dish add all the sugar then remainder of fruit, packing down firmly. Do not add any water. Roll pastry to size larger than the pie dish. Cut a strip round the pastry. Wet edges of pie dish and lay strip on, with cut edge to inside of pie dish. Roll pastry a little thinner, wet edges of strip and place pastry on top. Trim and mark the edges. Place pie dish in oven and bake for 40 minutes. When pastry is pale-golden colour, make two slits on either side to allow steam to escape. Reduce heat and cook until fruit is tender. Serve hot or cold with thick cream.

PLUM AND PEANUT PIE

Serves: 6

750 g   1½ lb plums   grated rind ½ lemon
500 g   1 cup sugar   1 lb frozen short pastry
250 g 60 g   ½ lb peanuts   2 oz. melted butter
2 teaspoons ground   1 egg, beaten lightly
 cinnamon

1 cm   Wash and stone plums, cut into ¼ inch thick slices. Sprinkle with half the sugar. Combine nuts, remaining sugar, cinnamon and lemon rind. Roll part of dough thinly on lightly-floured board and line cake tin (8 inch 20 cm diameter tin, 2 inches deep). Arrange half the plums on 5 cm pastry, cover with half the nut mixture and sprinkle with

half the melted butter. Cover with a layer of pastry and then a layer of plums, nut mixture, melted butter and another layer of pastry. Seal pastry by folding top crust under bottom crust and flute edge. Brush top pastry with beaten egg and bake in oven pre-heated to 375°F for 1 hour.

190°C

Chinese Apricot Plum

A Chinese species, with fruit similar to an apricot or a small nectarine, first introduced to Europe in 1867. Today, grown chiefly in the U.S.A. where flavour of hybrids has been considerably improved.

Use: As *nectarines*
     or *plums*

Coco(a)-Plum: *Icaque; Icaco* (Cuba)

West African tree, also grown in Central America with fruit resembling a Victoria plum. Its flesh is white and taste insipid.

Eat: raw or dried like prunes

Use: to make jams and preserves

Guinea Plum

Fruit of a large West African tree. Similar to a plum, in both size and colour, it lacks the flavour and acidity of true plums.

Australian Native Plum: *Bush Apple; Black Apple; Wild Plum; Rose Apple*

Large plum-shaped fruit of a native Australian tree *Syderoxylon australe.*

To eat: raw

Pokeweed: *Poake; Poakan*

Native shrub of North America, picked as a vegetable when its leafy shoots are 6 to 8 inches long. Their flavour combines those of asparagus and spinach. Pokeweed may be forced like sea-kale.

15–20 cm

Preparation: when forced, like *sea-kale;* pick young shoots with leaves attached, tie in small bundles and rapidly boil in *unsalted* water for 10 minutes. Drain and serve with an egg and cream sauce.
Use: as above
served cold in a vinaigrette

Pomegranate

Originally from North Africa, the pomegranate tree has been taken to many parts of the world and thrives particularly well in the warmer parts of Australia and in California. As its name suggests, the pomegranate is like an apple with grains. Its skin is rough and reddish brown. It is filled with large seeds embedded in red pulp. The flavour is tart but delicious and the juice is used to make the syrup known as grenadine. As often happens, when a fruit is taken from its place of origin, techniques of using it become forgotten and in Persia, for example, pomegranates are used in soups, sauces and desserts. In the Middle East, even the skin is used to prepare a dye for wool and rugs.
Eat: peel skin and eat flesh and seeds with sugar or with salt.
To drink juice: squeeze the fruit within the thick skin. Then make a small hole in the skin and suck the juice out.
Use: seeds—as garnish in salads, to add colour and interest to poultry or meat dishes, or in puddings or sprinkled over ice cream, or in compotes

POMEGRANATE SOUP

½ lb minced steak
1 onion, grated
¼ teaspoon cinnamon
¼ teaspoon salt
¼ teaspoon pepper
8 cups water
½ cup rice
2 teaspoons salt
1 cup chopped spinach
1 cup chopped parsley
½ cup chopped chives

1½ cups pomegranate seeds 250 g
  or 1 cup pomegranate
  juice from one fresh
  pomegranate
⅓ cup sugar
1 tablespoon dried or
  chopped fresh mint
¼ teaspoon cinnamon
¼ teaspoon pepper
salt
1 tablespoon lemon juice

4 cm

Mix together meat, onion and cinnamon, salt and pepper, and form into 1½ inch diameter meat balls. Place water into a heavy saucepan and cook rice with salt for 15 minutes. Add spinach, parsley and chives and cook a further 15 minutes. Add meat balls, pomegranate seeds (or juice) and sugar to the ingredients in the saucepan and simmer 20 minutes. Mix mint, powdered or crushed, cinnamon and pepper together and add to soup just before cooking is finished. Taste soup and if needed, add salt and lemon juice. This soup may be kept in a refrigerator for several days and the flavour improves with storage.

CHICKEN IN POMEGRANATE SAUCE

1·5 kg   185 g

3 lb chicken, quartered	6 oz. butter
1 teaspoon salt	¾ cup pomegranate seeds,
pepper to taste	or pulp
1 teaspoon paprika	15–20 dried apricots
4 tablespoons oil	2 tablespoons lemon juice
1 cup water	½ cup sugar
1 onion, finely chopped	boiled rice to serve

Season the chicken with salt, pepper and paprika, then sauté in oil until golden. Add water and simmer for 30 minutes. In another pan, sauté onion in 3 oz. butter until golden. Then add pomegranate and sauté 5 minutes more. Wash apricots and sauté them in 3oz. butter separately for 5 minutes. Add onions, pomegranates and apricots to chicken and mix well. Mix lemon juice and sugar and add to chicken mixture. Simmer 20 minutes and if necessary, thin sauce with a little water.

90 g

90 g

   Serve with crumbly boiled rice.

Alternative: in place of apricots and paprika, use 2 tablespoons tomato purée, 2 cups finely chopped walnuts and cinnamon. Use pomegranate juice or syrup instead of pulp and/ or seeds.

Poppy Leaves

Very young leaves of the field poppy are edible if harvested before the plant flowers. They have a nutty flavour.

Use: cook as for *nettles* p. 78.

Poppy Seeds

See *Herbs and Spices* p. 80.

Potatoes

Edible tubers of a plant, originally growing wild in the mountains of Peru and Chile and brought to Europe in the sixteenth century. Their popularity is due, not only their value as a food but also to their versatility in all forms of cooking. Potatoes are rich in potassium but have less than half the carbohydrates of bread. Different varieties have different qualities. Floury potatoes are good for baking and mashing, slightly waxy for chips and roasting and very waxy for salads.

Preparation: wash away soil and dust, and remove skins.

Use: baked in their skins
     peeled and baked
     fried
     boiled
     or steamed

Boiled

In their jackets: wash away all dirt then place in saucepan of salted boiling water. Cook until tender. Drain, then return potatoes to hot saucepan with lid on. Keep warm for 20 minutes, then peel.
     Serve: In halves with butter and chopped parsley.

Peeled and mashed: Wash away dirt, then peel and cut into similar sizes. Place into boiling salted water until tender but not mushy. Drain, mash and add butter, milk and pepper to taste and blend into a smooth cream.
     Serve dotted with butter.

Mashed variation: Add chopped ham and green sweet peppers.

Baked

205°C

In their jackets: Wash skins clean of dirt, place on a greased steel tray or rack and bake in oven at 400°F until tender.
     Serve cut in half with butter.

Peeled: Wash and peel, place in greased baking dish with roast and cook in oven until tender and golden brown. If in hurry, first place peeled potatoes, cut in similar sizes, in cold salted water and bring to boil and cook 5 minutes. Then place in oven to brown and complete cooking at 425°F.

215°C

Deep Fried

First wash and peel then cut to desired shape and cook in deep oil until golden. Drain, keep warm and serve.

Matchsticks

Cut as long and fine as matches, then fry.

Cubed

Cut into 1 inch cubes, then cook in oil or boil gently in water.

3 cm

Crisp or French Fried

Cut in circles, about $\frac{1}{16}$ to $\frac{1}{8}$ inch thick, then fry.

·5 cm

Chips

Cut lengthways with cross section about $\frac{1}{2}$ inch square, then fry in oil or dripping.

Sautéed

Wash and peel, slice, salt, and sauté in butter (or olive oil) with onions, finely chopped bacon and sprinkled with chopped parsley; or sauté slices and at last moment add 1 tablespoon each of chopped parsley and garlic.

Stuffed

Bake in jackets in oven until tender. Cut in half, scoop out $\frac{2}{3}$ of flesh and rub through sieve. Mix with one of following and then refill the jackets and complete as suggested:

Poached oysters and mushrooms and serve with white wine sauce

two thirds its weight of braised chopped cabbage, sprinkled with cheese, dot with butter and brown in oven or under grill

sliced chicken livers and mushrooms, sautéed in butter and served with juice from pan to which glass of white wine has been added and reduced by half

spinach sautéed in butter and served with cheese sauce

with canned tuna;

with asparagus tips;

chicken

minced meat

Potato Balls with Cheese

$\frac{1}{2}$ lb mashed potato	1 medium onion, finely chopped	250 g
1 tablespoon grated parmesan cheese	2 egg yolks	
sprig parsley, finely chopped	breadcrumbs oil for frying	

Mix together potato, parmesan, parsley, onion and egg. Mix well and make into balls of 1$\frac{1}{2}$ inch diameter. Roll in breadcrumbs and deep fry in oil or form into fancy shapes and brown in oven at 375°F.

4 cm

190°C

POTATO SALAD WITH ASPARAGUS TIPS

Time: $\frac{1}{2}$ hour plus cooling
Serves: 4

2 cups cooked potatoes, cold and diced	3 tablespoons vinaigrette dressing or mayonnaise
1 tablespoon spring onions, chopped	lettuce leaves, washed, dried and crisp
1 cup cooked peas (fresh, canned or deep frozen)	4 eggs, hard boiled, peeled and sliced
1 large tin asparagus tips	parsley to garnish

Mix potato cubes with spring onions and peas. Toss gently in vinaigrette or mayonnaise. Line dish with lettuce leaves, cover with asparagus tips, towards outside edge, tips facing outwards. Heap potato salad in centre. Garnish with egg slices and parsley.

See recipe for *Celeriac and Potato Purée* p. 40.

Sweet Potato: *Long* or *Spanish Potato; Kumara*
(New Zealand); *Peruvian Skirret* (Obsolete);
Batata

Climbing plant, related to morning glory (*Convolvulus*),
with edible tubers somewhat resembling elongated
potatoes. It is originally a native of South and central
America and possibly some South Pacific islands but is
now grown in many countries where there is a warm
climate. The cooked tuber tastes sweet and resembles an
artichoke. Today, many varieties of sweet potato are
cultivated and in some areas, young leaves are also
eaten. The tubers have a pale brown, grey, pink or purple
skin and the flesh colour varies from cream to dark
yellow and orange.

Preparation: some advocate boiling sweet potatoes but
it is generally considered that they should only be
baked, or cut in slices and fried in oil. In Japan,
they are sliced, dried in the sun until brittle and
then stored.

Use: as vegetable with roast meats
preserved in syrup
in jam
peeled and grated before cooking in a pudding
roasted, mashed and served with mashed boiled
haricot beans and dotted with butter

SPICED SWEET POTATOES

Time: 1 hour
175°C Temperature: 350°F
Serves: 4

500 g 1 lb sweet potatoes, peeled brown sugar
and sliced   freshly ground black
rashers of bacon   pepper
halved pineapple rings 2 teaspoons celery seed

Arrange sweet potato slices in a buttered casserole dish.
Top with bacon rashers and pineapple rings, sprinkle
with brown sugar, pepper and celery seed and bake in
175°C oven at 350°F until tender (about 45 minutes).
Serve with baked veal and other meats.

SWEET POTATO DESSERT

Time: 1 hour
175°C Temperature: 350°F
Serves: 4

4 large sweet potatoes golden syrup
3 egg yolks, beaten   3 egg whites beaten stiff
2 tablespoons ground   with 1 tablespoon sugar
almonds   cinnamon

Bake sweet potatoes in oven. When cooked, remove
skins and pass flesh through a sieve. Mix with beaten egg
yolks and almonds, mould to form a ring and place in a
buttered casserole dish. Paint with golden syrup. Beat egg
whites stiff with sugar and place on top of syrup.
175°C Sprinkle with cinnamon and bake in oven at 350°F for
15–20 minutes until meringue is slightly browned.
May be served hot or cold, but is better cold.

SWEET POTATO KEBABS

Serves: 3

2 medium sized sweet 1 small can pineapple
potatoes   slices
60 g 6 rashers of bacon   2 oz. butter

Wash potatoes and bake in oven until just tender. Peel
and cut into inch-thick slices. On kebab skewers, arrange
alternate potato slices, quarter pineapple slices, and
pieces of bacon and dabs of butter. Place skewers on edge
of baking dish, pour pineapple syrup over them and bake
in oven for 15 minutes, basting every 5 minutes.

Evening Primrose

Bienneal plant, native of Peru, whose tender and fleshy
roots are edible.

Use: may be cooked like *parsnips*

Pulassan: *Capulassan*

Fruit of tree, native to the Malaysia-Indonesia
archipelago, about the size of a plum. The thick skin has
a deep-pink pebbly surface. There is a single seed to which

edible pulp is attached. The flavour is similar to mangosteen but is less juicy and sweeter than rambutan.

Use: raw

Pumpkin

metric equivalent

Large, flattened, and round gourds of the squash family, with yellow flowers. Ground growing and usually segmented, weighing from 15 to 200 lb. Generally with thick skins and capable of being stored. Flesh is yellow or orange and the flavour rather sweet.

6·7 kg–90 kg

Preparation: peel and cut into sections.

Use: boiled, baked or roasted
mashed with potatoes
in pies
in soups

Giraumont

West Indian pumpkin with sweet and delicate flesh and a musky flavour.

Eat: raw in salads as *cucumber*
Cook: as *pumpkin*

PUMPKIN OMELETTE

Time: 5 minutes
Serves: 4

2 cups cooked pumpkin   3 eggs
¼ cup milk   butter for frying
salt and pepper

Boil pumpkin, strain then mash well and mix with milk, salt and pepper. Beat eggs and mix with pumpkin mixture. Fry in butter, fold and serve hot.

PUMPKIN PIE

Serves: 4

3 eggs, separated   ½ teaspoon each ginger,
1 cup sugar   nutmeg and cinnamon
1½ cups pumpkin pulp   ¼ cup water
½ cup milk   baked pie case
½ teaspoon salt   whipped cream
1 tablespoon gelatine

Beat egg yolks with ½ cup sugar. Add pumpkin, milk and seasonings. Cook in double boiler, stirring until it thickens. Add gelatine which has been soaked in water for 5 minutes. Stir until gelatine is dissolved and cool. Beat egg whites stiff with ½ cup sugar. When gelatine begins to thicken, fold in egg whites beaten stiff with sugar, pour into pie case and garnish with whipped cream.

Chill and serve.

149

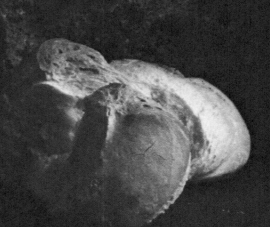

QUINCE

Q

Quamash: *Camass*

North American plant whose bulbs were a staple of the native Indian tribes on the West Coast.

Quandong: *Native Peach*

Edible stone fruit of a native Australian tree, related to sandalwood. Its shape and size are similar to a peach and its stone holds a kernel which is known as a quandong nut. Many people consider the nut the best part of the fruit.

Quinces

Fruit of small trees or shrubs, natives to the Western Mediterranean, the Caucasus and Iran. The fruit may be either round or an irregular pear shaped yellow gold with a grey bloom, and a yellow flesh which turns pink when cooked. Anyone who has ever tasted a raw quince will remember the exquisite torture of the mouth appearing to desiccate and wrinkle under the stringent action of its acid juice. In Europe, quinces have been relegated to jam making or for use in jellies or purées. In Iran, however, housewives stuff quinces in much the same way as the Italians stuff capsicums and baby marrows (zucchini). In this savoury dish, the true taste of quince is evident in a quite unique sweet-and-sour savoury dish.

Preparation: wash quinces but do not peel. Cut thin slices from stem of each and put aside. Remove pulp with a small teaspoon and make a cavity large enough to contain the stuffing.

Use: in jams and jellies
small piece added to apple pie
stuffed

QUINCE PASTE

750 g — 1½ lb quinces   sugar

Wash quinces, cut in quarters, remove seeds but do not peel. Steam until soft then pass through a sieve. Add equivalent weight of sugar to remaining pulp and mix well. Cook in a heavy saucepan, stirring frequently until

2 cm — the paste begins to candy. Place paste into ¾ inch deep tins and cool. Dry in the sun for several days or place in warm oven, after roasting is finished and the oven turned off. When dry, store in tins and serve in squares as a sweetmeat with strong black coffee.

BEEF WITH QUINCES

Time: 2½ hours
Serves: 6

1·5 kg — 3 lb brisket of beef, cut into 1 inch cubes / 4 large quinces, peeled, cored and cut into thick slices
2 onions, finely chopped
2 tablespoons beef dripping / 1 tablespoon sugar / 1 tablespoon flour
2 cups water / 2 tablespoons water
salt and pepper / boiled rice to serve

Sauté beef and onions in dripping until onions are soft and beef is browned. Add 2 cups of water and bring to boil. Season with salt and pepper and simmer for about 1 hour, or until meat is half cooked. Add quinces and if necessary, more water to just cover them. Sprinkle with sugar, cover tightly and simmer for another hour, until meat is very tender and quinces are soft.

Remove lid and reduce liquid to a cupful. Combine flour and cold water and stir into liquid. Cook for 5 minutes.

Serve meat in centre of platter and surround with quince slices. Pour gravy over meat. Serve with boiled rice.

QUINCE JELLY

Time: 1 hour

2 kg / 6¼ cups — 4 lb quinces / rind and juice of 2 oranges
2½ pints water / sugar

Peel and core the quinces then cut in slices. Place in saucepan with water, orange rind and juice and simmer for 35 minutes. Strain through muslin and measure the liquid. Add 14 oz. sugar for every pint, boil rapidly for 10–15 minutes, and test to set. When correct, pour into a warm jug and then into heated jars. Cover when cold.

435 g — 2½ cups

SAUTÉED QUINCES AND BEEF

Time: 1¾ hours
Serves: 4

		metric equivalent
2 large quinces	½ teaspoon pepper	
3 oz. butter	½ teaspoon cinnamon	90 g
4 tablespoons oil	pinch grated nutmeg	
1 lb stewing steak or	2 cups water	500 g
round steak cut into	3 tablespoons lemon juice	
1 inch cubes	2 teaspoons sugar	3 cm
1 onion, finely chopped	⅓ cup split peas	
1 teaspoon salt	buttered rice to serve	

Wash and core the quinces, cut in slices then sauté in butter. Put oil in heavy saucepan and sauté meat, onion and seasoning until meat is browned all over. Add water, lemon juice and sugar to saucepan and simmer 30 minutes. Add split peas and simmer a further 25 minutes. About 15 minutes before serving, add sautéed quinces to the meat mixture and simmer for 15 minutes.
    Serve with crumbly buttered rice.

STUFFED QUINCES

Serves: 4–6

6 quinces	1 teaspoon salt	
¼ cup split peas	pinch pepper	
1½ cups water	½ teaspoon cinnamon	
1 onion, finely chopped	¾ cup water	
2 oz. butter	⅓ cup wine vinegar	60 g
1 lb minced steak	½ cup sugar	500 g

Wash quinces but do not peel. Thinly slice the top from each quince and save. Remove the pulp and make a cavity large enough for the stuffing. Cook split peas in water for 30 minutes or until tender and drain. Sauté onion in butter, drain and set aside. Then sauté meat until thoroughly cooked. When cool, thoroughly mix peas, onions, meat, salt, pepper and cinnamon. Spoon this mixture into each of the quinces, replace the tops, and place them side by side upright in a saucepan. Pour water to depth of 1 inch. Cover pan and heat. When at boiling point, simmer gently until quinces are tender (about 30 minutes). Mix vinegar and sugar in another saucepan

3 cm

and boil for 5 minutes. Just before quinces are ready to remove, baste them with the vinegar/sugar and simmer the quinces another 15 minutes. Serve, pouring over remaining vinegar/sugar sauce.

Japanese Quince

Ornamental shrub with clusters of red flowers bearing ovoid yellow-green berries. They contain a rich aromatic lemon flavoured juice.

Use: in jellies and preserves
    ice cream

Quinoa

South American grass, cultivated in the Andes for its edible leaves. In Peru, its seeds are used in soups and cakes, and in brewing.

Preparation: leaves should be boiled twice, in different waters, to reduce their acrid taste.

Use: as for *spinach*

153

R

Radishes

Relatives of mustard and originally cultivated in China, many varieties of this pungent root are now grown. Some are white and others red, their shapes range from spherical to long 'icicles'. Spanish black radishes are much larger and Japanese radishes are 3 feet long and 4 inches in diameter (see also *Daikon*). They are at their best when young, especially if grown quickly. Otherwise, they tend to become woody.

90 cm/10 cm

Use: raw as an appetizer
    tender leaves sometimes cooked with butter and salt like *spinach*
    winter radishes (the larger kind) may be pickled in brine
    Japanese radishes are boiled like *potatoes*
    Black radishes: peel, cut into slices, dust with salt and stand 30 minutes, wash and serve.

RADISHES IN CREAM

Serves: 4 as side dish

1 large bunch of radishes (about 1 lb weight without tops)	salted water, boiling butter 1½ cups cream

Peel or scrape radishes, blanch in salted water for 5 minutes. Sauté in a little butter, turning, until tender. Heat cream in double saucepan and reduce by one third, but do not boil. Place radishes in a deep dish and pour cream over them.

RADISHES IN MEAT STOCK

Serves: 4

1 bunch radishes salt water	1 beef cube dissolved in half the recommended quantity of water

Peel or scrape radishes, blanch in salted water for 5 minutes. When tender, place meat stock, or juice from roast, into a saucepan and boil and reduce. When it is thick and brown, place radishes in it and simmer gently for a few minutes.

RADISH TOP FRICASSEE

Serves: 4

30 g	leaves of 2 bunches of radishes	1 oz. butter ¼ teaspoon salt
2½ cups	1 pint of water with 1 teaspoon salt, boiled 2 boiled eggs	pinch pepper 2 tablespoons milk top

Cut tops from radishes and remove all withered ones. Cook radish leaves in boiling water until they are tender. Boil eggs in water for 10 minutes. Drain, saving the stock to add to a soup.

Chop radish tops roughly, replace in saucepan with butter, salt and pepper. Peel and chop hard-boiled eggs and add to radish tops. Sauté a minute or two then add top of milk. Stir gently until hot, but do not simmer and boil. Serve hot.

Rambutan

Fruit from Indonesian tree, related to the lychee and the pulassan but covered with soft, curled tentacle-like hairs or spines, giving it an external similarity to a chestnut casing. Fruits grow in clusters and each is about 2 inches long with ½ inch thick outer flesh. Outer skin is crimson to greenish-orange-yellow. It encloses a white translucent flesh adhering to a flattened and pointed seed. Flavour resembles grapes.

5 cm
2 cm

Use: tear away leathery outer cover to expose raw flesh
    add to tropical fruit salad

Rampion

European weed, cultivated for its long edible fleshy roots.

Cook: as for *salsify*.

Rape

See *Herbs and Spices* p. 80.

Raspberry

See *Berries* p. 27.

Ravigote

See *Herbs and Spices* p. 80.

Rest Harrow: *Ground Furze*

European wild plant whose young shoots may be pickled in brine or eaten green in salads.

Rhubarb

Plant with tuberous roots, thick juicy red stems and large coarse leaves. Originally growing wild in Asia, the Chinese used dried rhubarb roots as a medicine 2,000 years ago. Rhubarb stalks are best when young and pink, the leaves however, contain oxalic acid and are poisonous.

Preparation: cut off leaves, wash and stew stalks or make into jam.

Use: stewed—simmer stalks in syrup, cool and serve with cream;

baked—cut in 4 inch lengths; place in casserole   10 cm
sprinkled heavily with brown sugar, add no water,
and bake in oven at 350°F until tender.   175°C

STEWED RHUBARB WITH CARDAMOMS

Serves: 4

1 lb young rhubarb	honey to taste	500 g
water to cover	2 teaspoons cornflour	
1 teaspoon cardamom seeds	mixed in a little cold water	

Wash and cut rhubarb stalks into 4 inch lengths, just   10 cm
cover with water, add cardamoms and honey and simmer until soft. Rub through a sieve then return to pan, add cornflour and water and heat until thick and clear.
Variations: after stewing or baking rhubarb (see above) add:

sliced and sugared fresh strawberries (or bake with rhubarb)

½ cup shelled pecan nuts, unsalted, while rhubarb is being baked.

RHUBARB PUNCH

Quantity: about 1 pint   2½ cups
Time: 30 minutes

1½ lb rhubarb	1 tablespoon lemon juice	750 g	
¼ pint water	5 oz. rum	150 ml	150 ml
¼ lb sugar	5 oz. brandy or whisky	125 g	150 ml
½ teaspoon nutmeg			

Prepare rhubarb, chop and cook in water until quite soft. Place other ingredients in a punch bowl or large jug, and strain rhubarb juice into them. Punch may be served hot or cold with slices of lemon and sprigs of mint.
See recipe for *Fig and Rhubarb Jelly* p. 59.

Rocket

See *Herbs and Spices* p. 80.

Sea Rocket

Coastal weed whose young leaves may be used in green salads.

Rose Hips

See *Herbs and Spices* p. 80.

Rosemary

See *Herbs and Spices* p. 81.

Rose Water

See *Herbs and Spices* p. 81.

Rozella: *Roselle*

Fruit of hibiscus plant, originally from the East Indies, with many different uses.

Use: flowers, seed pods and young stems can all be used for jams and jellies;

flowers—in pies and tarts

leaves—as a pot-herb for flavouring soups, stews, curries and salads

Rue

See *Herbs and Spices* p. 81.

Rutabagas

See *Turnips* p. 177.

Saffron

See *Herbs and Spices* p. 81.

Sage

See *Herbs and Spices* p. 81.

Salads

Cold dish of raw or cooked vegetables or made from a variety of fresh fruits. Green salads of raw vegetables may be served with meat, poultry or game, either as an accompaniment, as a side dish, or immediately afterwards as a separate course. They may also be served with cheese. Other salads may be served as hors d'oeuvres. Vegetable salads are usually served with a dressing (see *Salad dressing*).

Vegetable Salads

To make a good salad, always:

Use only crisp lettuce and other greens. Wash in cold water, dry well with a tea towel then place in refrigerator crisper for several hours.

Try to serve salads from a wooden bowl. To enhance the flavour, rub bowl with a cut clove of garlic before using.

Dressing may be tossed with the salad or served separately. If tossed, never add until just before serving or salad will lose its crispness.

To enhance a salad, try
   dipping edges of lettuce leaves in paprika;
   decorate with Chinese gooseberries, or feijoas or
   Cape gooseberries;

Good salads should not have too large a variety of ingredients. If desired serve two or more smaller salads, each with a distinctive flavour. Selective use of herbs (see p. 70) such as lemon, thyme, mint and marjoram may be used in small quantities to give only the slightest distinctive flavour, yet elusive enough to be indefinable; nasturtium flowers and calendula petals are good for decoration. They have a distinct flavour and are edible; chestnuts, boiled for 20 minutes and then shelled, skinned and chopped, also enhance a salad.
Never cut a lettuce leaf—always tear leaves with hands.

SALAD INGREDIENTS

Green salads	*Dressing*
Burnet	Vinaigrette
Corn salad or lamb's lettuce	Vinaigrette
Cress	Vinaigrette
Dandelion	Hot bacon fat and vinegar
Endive, chicory and escarole	Mustard or Remoulade sauce or anchovy dressing
Lettuce	Vinaigrette
Purslane	Vinaigrette
Rampion	Vinaigrette
Salsify, stems and tender leaves	Cream sauce
Samphire	Vinaigrette
Spring turnip leaves	Vinaigrette
Watercress	Vinaigrette

Vinaigrette dressing for green salads: use three parts of olive oil to one of wine vinegar or lemon juice, salt and pepper, made freshly just before using.

Preparation of a green salad: wash greens in several waters, then freshen by soaking a few minutes in iced water, dry in a clean towel, and place them in the refrigerator.
To remain crisp, never 'toss' (i.e. mix, using wooden fork and spoon) until the last minute.

Salad Herbs

Many flavourings may be added to green salads to give them new zest or flavour. Finely chopped fresh herbs are best including chervil, fresh dill, parsley in very small quantities, sweet basil and tarragon. For garnishing and a different taste, add sliced mushrooms, or blanched almonds, strips of red or green capsicum, strips or shreds of carrot.

160

Cooked Vegetable Salads

Cooked vegetable	Sauce
Artichoke tubers, diced	Vinaigrette
Chinese artichokes	Vinaigrette and hard boiled eggs, sliced
Asparagus tips—mayonnaise with pimento and chopped parsley	Vinaigrette with green pepper slices
Beans, dried haricot—vinaigrette sauce poured over them hot and then allowed to chill	Vinaigrette with chopped onion
Beans, broad	Vinaigrette with savoury
Beetroot	Chopped chives, parsley and sour cream or mustard
Broccoli, single fleurettes	Vinaigrette
Brussels sprouts, tiny	Vinaigrette
Cabbage, red, white or green, sliced	Vinaigrette
Cardoons, cooked and diced	Mustard
Cauliflower, in single fleurettes	Vinaigrette
Celeriac, sliced in strips	Mustard
Egg plant, slices blanched in salt water	Mustard
Jerusalem artichoke hearts	Mayonnaise or Vinaigrette
Lentils, boiled and drained	Vinaigrette
Leeks	Vinaigrette
Marrows, baby	Vinaigrette or tomato juice
Parsnips	Vinaigrette or mayonnaise
Potatoes, boiled and diced	Mayonnaise and chopped parsley or spring onions
Peas, green with vinaigrette poured over when they are hot and then cooled and chilled	Vinaigrette
Salsify	Mayonnaise
Spinach leaves, blanched lightly	Vinaigrette
Sweet potatoes, baked and diced	Vinaigrette

Raw Vegetable Salads

Use only young fresh vegetables, where possible, straight from the garden.

Raw vegetable	Dressing
Artichoke hearts, when very small	Vinaigrette
Avocado	Vinaigrette—3 parts oil, 1 part vinegar
Cabbage, green heart cut in thin strips	Mustard sauce
Cabbage, red	Vinaigrette with a few caraway seeds
Cucumber in thin slices, marinaded for one or two hours in the dressing before use	In spiced vinegar, vinaigrette or fresh cream
Carrots, whole baby	Horseradish or cream
Celery, cut like matches	Anchovy dressing or mustard or Remoulade sauce, with paprika sprinkled on it
Fennel, shredded	Vinaigrette
Leeks, green parts of young ones	Vinaigrette
Mushrooms, baby, sliced. Marinade in vinaigrette 30 minutes before using	Vinaigrette
Radish	Without sauce
Soya bean shoots	Mustard sauce
Tomatoes	Vinaigrette of 2 parts oil and 2 parts vinegar with chopped fresh basil added.

Specific Vegetable Combinations

Vegetable	arranged on	garnished with	dressing
Asparagus	watercress	green capsicum strips	vinaigrette
Asparagus	lettuce	slices of hard boiled egg	green mayonnaise
Beetroot sliced or diced	sliced onion	orange segments	vinaigrette with fresh tarragon
Cauliflower whole almost undercooked	watercress or lettuce	chopped parsley sprinkled with paprika	vinaigrette
Cucumber peeled and thinly sliced		chopped dill in sour cream 1 hour before serving	
Orange segments	cucumber, diced		$\frac{1}{4}$ pint sour cream, 1 tablespoon chopped mint, salt, pepper, 1 clove garlic crushed, 1 teaspoon sugar, blended together
Spinach cooked		blanched almonds	curry sauce
Tomatoes peeled and sliced	thin slices of avocado	finely chopped onion	vinaigrette
Tomatoes sliced	chilled cooked asparagus spears	hard boiled egg	vinaigrette served separately

To make a substantial supper, add a few other ingredients to a basic green dressed salad.

General Vegetable Combinations

Fresh peas, whole string beans, shredded raw carrot, sliced beetroot, garnished with tomato and rings of green capsicum

cooked asparagus tips, raw cauliflower buds, cooked carrot slices, sliced tomatoes, garnished with hard boiled eggs and pimento strips

thin strips of raw baby marrows, tomato slices, thin onion slices, cooked asparagus tips, sliced baby mushrooms, garnished with capsicum rings and watercress.

Meats and Eggs

Variations: strips of cold ham, cold chicken and Gruyère cheese or strips of cold tongue, Gruyère cheese and hard boiled egg;

cold turkey slices, hard boiled egg and asparagus

cold cooked dried haricot beans (any colour or type but red kidney beans are prettiest), artichoke hearts and grated parmesan

cold chicken and blanched almonds

crabmeat and thin slices of avocado

peeled segments of grapefruit and sliced avocado

beetroot, onions and hard boiled egg

cooked or tinned green peas, grated raw carrots, and sliced hard boiled eggs.

Classic Salads

ANTIPASTO SALAD

250 g   125 g   1 lettuce broken; with 8 oz. sliced salami; 4 oz. black olives; 1 small can artichoke hearts, halved; whole radishes; tomato wedges arranged on top; dressed with vinaigrette to which has been added finely chopped garlic, finely chopped chives and tarragon.

CAESAR SALAD

2 small lettuce, torn apart, ½ inch cubes bread browned in butter and garlic; crisp bacon bits; chopped parsley and grated parmesan; with mustard cream sauce.

CSALAMADE

2 cups green cabbages, finely shredded; chopped green capsicum; tomatoes and shallots and onion rings tossed in vinaigrette, with sour cream added.

GAZPACHO

1 onion, 1 cucumber, 6 peeled tomatoes, all sliced thinly; arrange in alternate layers, sprinkle with dry breadcrumbs, pour over vinaigrette to which chopped garlic has been added.

MIMOSA SALAD

Lettuce, endive, young green spinach tossed in vinaigrette sprinkled with 2 hard boiled egg yolks, pressed through a sieve.

NICOISE SALAD

Lettuce torn and sprinkled with fresh dressing; topped with finely chopped onion; small can tuna, drained; 2 hard boiled eggs, halved; 1 small can anchovy fillets; 12 black olives; all topped with french dressing.

POTATO SALAD

1 lb diced hot potatoes; 2 teaspoons chopped onion; 3 teaspoons chopped parsley; all tossed in mayonnaise then chilled.

500 g

RUSSIAN SALAD

1 pickled herring, or cubed cooked chicken; 1 beetroot, chopped; 3 cooked potatoes and diced cooked turnips, 2 cooked carrots, cubed; 1 raw apple diced; ½ small cucumber, diced; 1 sour pickled gherkin, sliced; 2 hard boiled eggs, sliced; dressed with vinaigrette, dry mustard and a little sugar.

WALDORF SALAD

3 apples, cored, cubed but with skin; juice of 2 lemons; 6 sticks of celery, sliced; 2 oz. chopped walnuts; all tossed together in mayonnaise; lettuce leaves to line bowl.

Salad Dressings

There are a multitude of salad dressings and a variety are given here. However, the four basic dressings are mayonnaise, mustard cream, Remoulade and vinaigrette which are included.

ANCHOVY

To a vinaigrette of 2 parts oil, 2 parts vinegar, and freshly ground pepper, add 2 anchovy fillets, unsalted and put through a sieve. Allow to stand in the bottom of the salad bowl before adding vegetables or greens and toss at the last moment.

CREAM SAUCE

Mix 4 tablespoons fresh cream with 1 tablespoon wine vinegar or lemon juice, season with salt and cayenne pepper.

CURRY

Cook 1 tablespoon onion, finely chopped in 1 tablespoon olive oil. Add 1 teaspoon (or more if preferred) curry powder, 1 teaspoon lemon juice, salt and pepper and a little crushed garlic. Cook together, and when blended and onions are transparent, remove and cool. When ready to use, add 2 teaspoons olive oil.

MAYONNAISE

Serves: 6

3 egg yolks, raw	1 tablespoon lemon juice
1 teaspoon salt	(or wine vinegar)
white pepper to taste	⅔–1 pint olive oil

2–2½ cups

French or English mustard may be added if desired

Place egg yolks, free from any white, into a bowl and

sprinkle with salt and pepper and a few drops of lemon juice. Whisk these ingredients lightly. Add the oil, a drop at a time to start with then in a trickle, beating constantly with a whisk or wooden spoon (but NOT an egg beater). Gradually blend all the oil into the mayonnaise, thinning by adding a few drops of lemon juice when necessary. When satisfactory, beat in 2 to 3 tablespoons boiling water. This preserves the texture and prevents it curdling. To ensure a mayonnaise is successful, remember

1 cup
  no more than 8 oz. oil to each egg yolk
  use oil at room temperature or slightly warmed in cold weather
  add oil by drops and only increase to a trickle when the sauce begins to thicken.

Variations: Anchovy Mayonnaise—add anchovy paste, tarragon vinegar, chopped shallots, garlic salt and finely chopped onion
Caper Mayonnaise—add chopped capers
Curry Mayonnaise—add curry powder, half quantity dry English mustard, Worcestershire sauce, and lemon juice
Cucumber Mayonnaise—add sour cream and diced cucumber and season with black pepper
Green Mayonnaise—add finely chopped parsley, or spinach, or chives, or tarragon, or chervil (or combinations of two or more) to mayonnaise and add a little garlic
Red Mayonnaise—add a little tomato purée and some finely chopped fresh or dried basil or oregano.

MUSTARD CREAM

2 tablespoons English mustard (French if a milder version is preferred)   4 tablespoons fresh cream
lemon juice
salt and pepper

Mix mustard with cream until thoroughly blended. Add only a few drops of lemon juice and season with salt and pepper.

REMOULADE

3 hard boiled egg yolks   1 tablespoon lemon juice (or wine vinegar)
475 ml
15 oz. olive oil
salt and pepper

Sieve or crush egg yolks and blend with oil and lemon juice as for mayonnaise. Season to taste.

RUSSIAN DRESSING

Add chili sauce, finely chopped hard boiled egg, chopped onion, parsley and olives.

SWEET AND SOUR

Combine in a jar one cup olive oil, 1 cup white vinegar, $\frac{1}{2}$ cup sugar, $\frac{1}{4}$ cup minced chives, $\frac{1}{4}$ cup minced celery, 2 tablespoons minced capsicum, 2 teaspoons dry English mustard, 1 tablespoon Worcestershire sauce, 2 teaspoons salt and pinch pepper. Store at least 24 hours to ensure aromas and flavours blend and shake well before using.

TARTARE SAUCE

Mayonnaise to which is added finely chopped fresh tarragon, parsley and chives, capers and chopped pickled gherkins (sour) and shallots;
Mayonnaise to which is added finely chopped green onion, dill pickle and parsley plus a little grated horseradish.

VINAIGRETTE

Place 1 part oil in a bowl and to it slowly add 3 parts of vinegar, whisking all the time so that it emulsifies. Season with salt and pepper.

Variations: Add crushed clove of garlic
  Add sieved anchovy
  Add chopped and fried onion first mixed with curry powder and crushed garlic in frying pan
  Add fried minced onion and paprika
  Add 2 sieved tomatoes, reduced to half their original quantity by cooking
  Add 1 tablespoon honey with 1 cup vinaigrette
  Add crumbled gorgonzola cheese

VINEYARD DRESSING

Wipe salad bowl with crushed garlic and sprinkle with salt. Into mixing bowl, mix 3 tablespoons olive oil and 1 cup yoghurt. Add 2 tablespoons claret and ½ teaspoon tabasco sauce. Pour over salad and sprinkle with paprika.

Fruit Salads

Contrasting flavours are the main aim when devising and making a fruit salad, and from the practical viewpoint, this should generally be made from the fruit available at the time. Wherever possible, both bitter and sweet fruits should be used. The discreet addition of liqueur to a fruit salad can often provide a subtle difference.

Many different combinations of fruit may be used to make a good fruit salad. They include fresh, tinned or frozen:

pineapple, peaches, apricots, plums, pears, lemon juice, grated fresh apple, oranges, passionfruit, bananas, pawpaw, Chinese gooseberries
strawberries, pineapple, peaches, watermelon and grapes
guavas (cooked), figs, passion fruit, pears, pawpaw (or melon), bananas, orange, Chinese gooseberries

To adjust the taste of a fruit salad, add sugar to sweeten or lemon juice to make tart.

For variety, boil 12 large sprigs of mint with 1 cup water and ¾ cup sugar. Boil 5 minutes, strain and cool then pour over fruit.

'OUT OF THIS WORLD' FRUIT AND VEGETABLE SALAD

1 bunch salsify, or canned heart of palm (canned from Chinese food shops)
water chestnuts (canned from Chinese food shops)
1 medium thick slice pawpaw
1 medium thick slice watermelon
2 slices pineapple, fresh or canned
2 oranges, in segments, membrane removed
2 mangoes, diced (fresh or canned)
2 grapefruit, in segments, membrane removed
½ red capsicum, seeded and finely chopped

metric equivalent

6 ackees, boiled with vinegar and salt (canned or optional)
8 champignon de paris (button mushrooms)
2 onions, finely chopped
1 avocado, cut in cubes
2 small carrots, diced
corn from 2 corn cobs, boiled in fresh water until tender
½ green capsicum, seeded and finely chopped
1 cucumber, diced
1 large tomato, diced
2 small turnips, diced
½ lb fresh green peas, boiled — 250 g
salted peanuts
parsley
capers

For lime dressing:
½ teaspoon sugar
¼ teaspoon salt
few drops chili sauce
paprika
1½ tablespoons lime (or lemon) juice
3 oz. olive oil — 100 ml

Place all ingredients in a glass jar with a screw top, tighten lid and shake vigorously to blend.

For coconut cream dressing:
milk from inside of 1 coconut
pinch powdered ginger
pinch grated nutmeg
pinch paprika
pinch salt
pinch black pepper
½ teaspoon sugar
pinch garlic salt
pinch dry English mustard
sprig of parsley, finely chopped
dash Angostura bitters

Put all together in a bowl and mix well.

After preparing dressings, drain every fruit and vegetable containing juices. Mix firm ingredients together and toss in lime dressing. Add softer ingredients carefully, then pour over the coconut cream dressing. Toss salad again, allowing both dressings to mingle and ingredients to be well mixed. Grind peanuts and chop parsley. Add capers, chopped and sprinkle all on top of the salad. Chill in refrigerator and serve.

As in every salad, quantities of ingredients may be varied. This Jamaican recipe was devised by Mrs Turmeta Patterson for the 1969 Culinary Arts Festival in Kingston, Jamaica. It is recommended that this be prepared, in larger quantities, for an important occasion. The variety and combinations of fruits, vegetables and dressings is mouth watering.

TROPICAL FRUIT SALAD WITH MANGO SAUCE

1 slice watermelon, 1 inch thick	*For mango sauce:*
¼ pawpaw	1 cup tinned (or fresh) mango purée
2 slices pineapple, fresh or tinned	1 tablespoon vinegar
2 mangoes, fresh or canned	1 teaspoon dry English mustard
grapes, washed and pitted	pinch salt
1 carrot	pinch pepper
1 tomato	½ tablespoon peanut oil
leaves of lettuce	

Dice all ingredients and allow to drain. Place in a wooden salad bowl and mix well.

To make sauce: combine sauce ingredients and cook for 15 minutes. Pour over the salad while sauce is still hot, allow to cool then chill in refrigerator.

Salmonberry

See *Berries* p. 27.

Salsify or Oyster Plant

European vegetable also grown in the U.S.A. Two types are generally used, the white and the black (*scorzonera*), the latter are larger and reputed to be the best. The plant is a variety of the wild-plant known as Goat's Beard and is cultivated for its long, tapering root which is delicately flavoured and reminiscent of oysters or asparagus. Shoots of young plants can be eaten raw in salads or prepared as for *spinach*.

Preparation: scrub roots well, dip into water containing a few drops of lemon juice or vinegar to prevent discolouring, then boil in salted water until tender (about 45–50 minutes). Drain, rub or peel away the skin and serve hot with melted butter.

Use: boiled
  creamed
  in béchamel or mornay sauce
  with veal
  and in fritters

FRIED SALSIFY CAKES

Time: 30 minutes
Serves: 4

500 g	1 lb salsify, prepared as above	juice ½ lemon
		1 egg, beaten
30 g	1 oz. butter	breadcrumbs
	top of milk	oil for frying
	salt and cayenne	

Mince or pound the cooked and skinned salsify, mix with butter and top of the milk, season to taste and add lemon juice. Thoroughly mix then chill in refrigerator to firm the mixture. Form into flat cakes, dip in egg, then breadcrumbs and fry until golden brown.

Goat's Beard

Wild salsify, with roots coarser than those of salsify but can be prepared in same manner.

Salt

See *Herbs and Spices* p. 81.

Samphire: *See Fennel* (*Crithmum maritimum*)*; also refers to* Inula crithmoides [*Golden Samphire*, *Glasswort*, *Saltwort* or *Prickly Samphire* and the *French St. Peter's Cress*]

A salty, green fleshy plant, growing wild on coastal marshes, sand-dunes and cliffs in Europe. Eaten mostly in salads but can be cooked in butter or cream in its own juices, or pickled as for *gherkins* in brine or vinegar.

Sea Sandwort: *Sea Purslane; Notchweed*

Coastal weed of northern hemisphere, often pickled like samphire or treated as for *sauerkraut* (see p. 35). See also *Orach* p. 123.

Sapodilla: *Naseberry Plums* (West Indies); *Sawos Manila* (Indonesia); *Zapota; Sapote; Mamey* or *Mammee Apple* (Mexico)

Edible fruit of a large evergreen tree, originally from the West Indies and Mexico and now grown in West Africa, India and the Malay archipelago. Fruit is about the size of a lemon, 3–6 inches long, with grey to russet brown rough rind. The delicious reddish-yellow flesh has a flavour akin to apricots. However it does not preserve and can only be eaten when fully ripe. If immature, it contains tannin and a milky latex.

Use: remove skin, extract hard, shiny black seeds and eat flesh.

5–15 cm

SAPODILLA WINE

8 ripe sapodillas	¼ lb prunes	125 g
2 pints hot water	slice of orange	5 cups
1 lb castor sugar	½ cake yeast	500 g
¼ lb raisins		125 g

Cut sapodillas and pour hot water over them. Add sugar and other ingredients. Mix yeast with a little sugar and add to mixture. Place in a corked jar and tie down cork. Store for 1 month then strain and bottle. Store in a cool place.

White Sapota

Casimiroa edulis, a tree of Central America and Mexico grown for its round, pulpy and edible fruit.

Sauce Alone

See *Herbs and Spices* p. 81.

Savoury

See *Herbs and Spices* p. 81.

Sea Buckthorn

See *Berries* p. 25.

Sea-Kale: *Sea-Kale Beet; Sea-Kail; Sea-Cole*

Renowned for its subtle flavour, sea-kale grows wild in parts of England but is usually forced and blanched for market. The 6 to 8 inch stems are pure white and topped with grey-green tips. It may be served as a separate course like *asparagus*.

15–20 cm

Preparation: wash and tie in bundles, trim black roots and steam in salted water for about 50 minutes, until tender. Drain well and serve with melted butter or hollandaise sauce
simmer gently in vegetable stock until tender. If overcooked, it becomes hard
parboil bundle for 5 or 10 minutes, remove and drain, place in casserole dish, cover with a cheese sauce and bake in hot oven until golden brown.

Green tops: cut from stalks and tear into small pieces. Serve in vinaigrette which has chopped chives and fresh tarragon added.

SEA-KALE CROQUETTES

Serves: 4

1 bunch sea-kale, boiled in a little salted water, drained and chopped finely	4 thick slices bread, softened in milk
	1 clove garlic, crushed
	1 onion, finely minced
½ lb minced steak	1 egg yolk
salt and pepper	oil for frying

250 g

Mix sea-kale, minced steak, bread and seasoning together, bind with yolk of egg and fry in a little oil. Mixture may also be used to stuff savoury pancakes, or ravioli.

Sea-Oxeye

Fleshy plant growing in sandy coastal areas.

Use: pickled in vinegar as a condiment, see *Samphire*.

Seaweeds

Edible seaweeds and their products are used extensively in Japanese and Chinese cookery and are rich in vitamins and minerals. They are also found in many other parts of the world and deserve to be used more often. They may be collected live or obtained dried in sheets from stores specializing in oriental products. Varieties include:

Agar-Agar (*Eucheuma spinose; Gelidium japonicum; Gracilaria lichenoides*)

Name given to certain red seaweeds from Asia from which various gelatinous substances are obtained. They are also known as Ceylon Moss, Chinese Isinglass, Japanese Agar, Mousse de Japan. In Asia, it is used extensively in soups and jellies. Chinese swallows use this seaweed to make their nests from which bird's nest soup is prepared.

Alga Mar (*Durvillea antarctica*)

Edible seaweed from Chile, prized for its qualities and exported to the U.S.A.

Badderlocks: Murlin; Henware; Honeyware (*Alaria esculenta*)

Edible seaweed gathered in the Faroe Islands and off the most northerly coasts of the British Isles.

Carrag(h)een: Irish Sea Moss; Iberian Moss; Pearl Moss; Sea Moss (*Chondrus crispus*)

Dark purple, green or brown branching cartilaginous edible seaweed common on many coasts of northern Europe and North America. It is prepared by thorough washing to remove salt and then hung to dry and be washed in the rain. When bleached to a creamy white by the sun and dried, it is known as Irish Moss. It is a valued food for children and invalids.

Use: gently stew in milk to make jellies and blancmanges.

Dulse: Dillisk; Dillesk (*Rhodymenia palmata*)

Reddish brown edible seaweed, gathered from some parts of Scotland, the west coast of Eire and the northern coasts of the Mediterranean.

Hai Tai

Popular edible seaweed, used widely in the Asian region. It grows among other seaweeds in separate strands fixed to rocks on the ocean bed and has to be selected from these and then brought to the surface. In Japan, women harvest Hai Tai off the island of Quel-part.

Hair Seaweed; Sea Wrack; Rock Weed (*Fucus* spp.)

Species of membraneous or filamentous seaweed known as *Faht Choy* in Chinese cookery where it is used in savouries and vegetable dishes, often as a condiment. It is said that in hard times, this seaweed is also eaten by inhabitants of Iceland, Faroe Islands, Scotland, Norway, Denmark and North America. In Scotland, the young stems of tangle or *sea lettuce* are sometimes eaten as a salad, however it is an acquired taste.

Lettuce Laver: Green Laver (*Ulva latissima, Ulva lactuca*)

Seaweed with bright green and crinkly fronds, not unlike a curly lettuce.

Red or *Purple Laver: Slouk* (Scotland); *Stoke* (Ireland) (*Porphyra vulgaris*)

Filmy, reddish purple seaweed, frequently seen on the coasts of South Wales and Cornwall. Its fronds are rich in iodine and make a good pickle. It is produced commercially in Japan and sold as *Asakusanori* for use in soup, as a vegetable, or raw in salads. In Chinese cookery it is known as *Jee Choy* and is used mostly in soups.

Redware: Tangle (*Porphyra laciniata*); *Sweet Tangle* (*Laminaica saccharina*)

Edible seaweed, related to laver (see above) found in Orkneys and Scotland.

Sargasso (*Sargassum* spp.)

Edible seaweeds used in salads in Spain.

Preparation: wash then bring to boil, reduce heat and simmer until tender. Beat into a pulp, add a little salt then heat again with lemon juice. Season with pepper and a knob of butter.

Use: as vegetable with meat; served on hot toast
with mutton, serve laver as above but with squeeze
of juice from a Seville orange
mix pulp with vinegar or lemon juice and a few
drops of olive oil and pepper. Serve cold as hors
d'oeuvre or savoury—its flavour suggests a
mixture of olives and oysters
mix pulp with oatmeal and fry in flat cakes for
breakfast

SEAWEED SOUP

Serves: 8

¼ lb purple laver (obtained dried from Chinese shops)	4 oz. ham, diced	125 g	125 g
	1 teaspoon soya sauce		
2 pints soup stock (made from stock cube to flavour desired)	1 teaspoon monosodium glutamate (optional) chopped chives	5 cups	

Soak laver in warm water for 10 minutes. Rinse several
times until cleaned of all sand. Squeeze dry. Heat soup
stock and add ham. Boil for 5 minutes then add seaweed.
Boil for another 5 minutes then add soya sauce, MSG.
Serve garnished with chopped chives.

Sesame Seeds

See *Herbs and Spices* p. 81.

Silver Weed

Common weed of the Hebrides Islands, north of Britain,
whose roots may be eaten as for *parsnips*.

Simsim (Africa)

See *Herbs and Spices* p. 82.

Skirret

Chinese plant with bunch of edible swollen roots, similar
to those on dahlias.

Preparation and cooking: as for *salsify*.

Sloe

Fruit of the wild blackthorn tree of Europe, mostly used
in the manufacture of gin. The fruit resembles a dark blue
plum but is smaller, harder and very sour. It is inedible
raw. In the U.S.A., this name is applied to the fruits of
various wild plums which may be used as *damsons*,
usually combined with apples.

Use: cook with elderberries to make jelly.

SLOE AND APPLE JELLY

3 lb sloes	3 lb sugar	1·5 kg	1·5 kg
5 lb apples		2·5 kg	

Place sloes in a 7 lb preserving jar, stand in the centre of a
saucepan of cold water with cloth wrapped around
bottom and sides of jar. Bring to boil and cook until juice
of sloes is released. Drain juice (about 1 pint) and fill jar
with 1 pint water and sloes. Cook again and strain juice
which should be about 1½ pints and save.

Place peel and cores of apples in a preserving dish,
cover with cold water and cook until they are soft. Strain
to give about 2 pints of juice. Add first extracted sloe
juice and apple juice in a saucepan with sugar. Bring to
the boil and skim then boil for 45 minutes. Test for gel
then cool and pour into jars and cover (quantity about 2
pints). Second extract of sloe juice and stewed and sieved
flesh of apples may be mixed together to form a purée. To
this add ½ lb sugar to each 1 lb of purée, and boil until it
forms a gel—30 to 45 minutes.

The purée may be used as a preserve, in pies, or poured
over cakes, or served with custard or with fresh cream.

Metric equivalents in right column: 3·5 kg; 2½ cups; 2½ cups; 3¾ cups; 5 cups; 5 cups; 250 g 500 g

Snake Root

An alpine grass whose young leaves are prepared as for
spinach. Its name comes from the roots which grow into
one another in a serpentine manner.

Solomon's Seal

Decorative member of the wild lilies whose young shoots
may be prepared and eaten like asparagus.

Sorrel

See *Herbs and Spices* p. 82.

Southernwood: *Lad's Love*

Plant related to tarragon and used finely chopped in salads when fresh.

Cook: as for *spinach*.

Sow Thistle: *Milkweed* (U.S.A.)

Plants of the *Sonchus* group with somewhat leathery leaves. Tender leaves may be used raw in salads and have flavour of both lettuce and endive.

Preparation: roots as for *salsify*
leaves boiled in salt water and then treated as for *spinach*.

Spearmint

See *Herbs and Spices* p. 82.

Spignel

See *Herbs and Spices* p. 82.

Spiked Rampion

Wild *Campanula*, common in Switzerland where it is used in salads, and also in England where it is rarely used.

Spikenhead

See *Herbs and Spices* p. 82.

Spinach: *Calaloo* (Jamaica)

Delicate leaf vegetable with a distinctive flavour and a dark green appearance when cooked. It originated in Persia.

Preparation and cooking: strip leaves, wash several times in cold water, remove any yellow or damaged leaves. Drain thoroughly and place in bottom of a thick saucepan *without any water*. Add 2 oz. of butter for

60 g

250 g

each pound of raw spinach leaves, season with salt and black pepper and simmer gently, stirring constantly until spinach is soft and tender. Allow $\frac{1}{2}$ lb raw leaves for each serving.

Use: blanched as a salad
raw young leaves, well washed, in a salad

SPINACH AND MUSHROOM ENTRÉE

Time: 20 minutes
Serves: 4

1 lb spinach, cooked	1 tablespoon onion,
4 oz. mushrooms	minced
butter for frying	grated parmesan cheese
4 slices toast, buttered	parsley to garnish
salt and pepper	

500 g
125 g

After cooking spinach keep hot. Peel and chop the mushrooms and fry in a minimum of butter. Place a layer of spinach on the toast, then add a layer of mushrooms, sprinkle with onion and season with salt and pepper and then a little parmesan cheese. Place under the grill for a few minutes and serve garnished with parlsey.

FLORENTINE SPINACH

Serves: 6

1 bunch spinach cooked in	1 cup milk
butter	1$\frac{1}{2}$ cups grated cheddar
salt	cheese
3 oz. butter	paprika for garnish
3 tablespoons flour	

90 g

Wash and cook spinach as described under Preparation above. Drain and chop, saving any liquid remaining. Melt 2 oz. butter, stir in flour and cook 1 minute. Add milk gradually and cook as it thickens. Add any spinach liquid. When smooth, add cheese and stir until melted. Place spinach in hot serving dish, pour the sauce over it, dot with remaining butter and sprinkle with paprika. Place under grill to brown.

60 g

Giant Mexican Spinach

Leaves of a shrub growing to height of 7 feet, often yielding 2 to 3 lb from a plant. Leaves are 7–9 inches long and should be prepared as for *spinach*.

metric equivalent

2 m
1–1·5 kg
18–23 cm

New Zealand Spinach: *Ice Plant*

Unrelated to the true spinach (*Spinacea oleracea*) New Zealand 'spinach' (*Tetragonia expansa*) is related to the redroot pigweed, an Indian plant. For practical purposes, New Zealand spinach is often grown to harvest in summer when its leaves remain crisp while true spinach tends to wilt.

Squash

Originally an American term for various edible and ornamental gourds including *pumpkin* and *zucchini* (see *baby marrows*). Varieties include the American Hubbard and acorn or Danish squashes, and in Australia, the scalloped squash, the long necked yellow squash and custard marrows, Winter squashes, (originally from Argentina) including hubbard, green and acorn have a very hard rind and will keep well. They should be baked or steamed with seeds removed. Summer squashes which grow on low bushes mature quickly and should be picked when soft and cooked soon afterwards.

Preparation: for baking—do not remove rind. Cut in half, remove seeds, brush interior with melted butter, and bake in oven at 350°F for 45–50 minutes until tender. Season with salt, pepper and more butter

175°C

for steaming—remove rind with a sharp knife, cut flesh into 4 inch squares, or cut in quarters. Place in perforated steaming pan over hot water and steam until tender (30–45 minutes). Season with salt and pepper and melted butter.

11 cm

boiled summer squash—should be sliced and cooked in a very little boiling salted water until tender (10–15 minutes). Drain and season with salt, pepper and lots of melted butter

Use: baked in pies
      sautéed
      boiled
      and steamed

metric equivalent

SWEET SQUASH FOR BREAKFAST

Serves: 6

3–4 lb banana or other type of squash	1 lb brown sugar	1·5–2 kg	500 g
	2 oz. water		¼ cup

Wipe the squash skin, cut into quarters and remove seeds. Pack brown sugar on top of each piece and place in a pan which has a tight lid. Add water to pan, cover and simmer until squash is tender. Scoop cooked squash into a cereal bowl, pour syrup over the squash, add milk and eat for breakfast.

CANDIED SQUASH

Serves: 4

1 Danish squash (also called Acorn or Table Queen)	2 tablespoons dark corn syrup	
4 oz. butter	¼ teaspoon nutmeg	
½ cup brown sugar	2 tablespoons water	125 g

Boil whole squash in deep saucepan for 15 minutes. Drain, split; remove seeds. Peel and cut into chunks. Melt butter in heavy frying pan and stir in sugar, syrup, nutmeg, water add squash. Toss well, cover and simmer for 10 minutes. Remove lid and simmer uncovered 5 minutes or until tender.

Stonecrops

Ornamental plants, often used in rock gardens, whose young leaves may be used in green salads. Varieties include white, crooked yellow and orpine stonecrops.

Use: in salads
      pickled

Strawberry

See *Berries* p. 27.

Strawberry Tomato: *Tomato Strawberry; Chinese Lantern; Barbados Gooseberry; Winter* or *Ground Cherry; Coqueret*

Yellow fruit of the Mexican shrub *Physalis alkengi,* now cultivated in Mediterranean regions. Fruit looks like a small yellow tomato.

Use: see *Cape Gooseberry.*

Succory

See *Endive* p. 55.

Sumac

See *Herbs and Spices* p. 82.

Sunflower (*Helianthus* sp.)

This herbaceous plant is used for various purposes in different places. In France, it is grown for its tuberous roots which taste similar to, but milder than, Jerusalem artichokes. They are prepared and used as for *salsify* and *Chinese artichokes.*
In Russia and China, sunflower seeds are eaten and are said to be rich in vitamin E, and reputedly good for counteracting sterility. In Peru, the seeds are crushed to make sunflower oil.

Susumber

See *Berries* p. 27.

T

Tamarind: *Assam; Asem* (Indonesia)

Fruit of tree grown in tropical Asia and West Indies and used as condiment because of its acrid flavour. The fruit is shelled and its pulp is dark brown but more fibrous than a date. Where mentioned in recipes, lemon juice may be used as a substitute but this does not give the same sour-sweet flavour. Dried tamarind (*amyli*) is made in India and may be obtained from shops specializing in ingredients for curries and other spices.

Preparation: shell fruit before use

Use: fresh fruit in curries
　　for making chutneys
　　infused with water to make curry sauce
　　In India, leaves and flowers are also eaten and the
　　seeds ground and used to make cakes.

TAMARIND JUICE

Soak 2 tablespoons shelled tamarinds in a cup of water for 30 minutes. Stir until the flesh dissolves. Will keep several days in the refrigerator. It is used as an additive to curries.

TAMARIND SYRUP

metric equivalent		
125 g	¼ cup	4 oz. sugar
1 cup		8 oz. water

2 oz. tamarind juice

Put all ingredients into a saucepan and bring to the boil. Lower heat and simmer for 40 minutes. Pour mixture through a sieve and cool the resulting syrup.

To serve, pour 1½ to 2 tablespoons in a glass and add crushed ice and water to make a refreshing beverage. In Indonesia, this is called *Setrup Asem*.

TAMARIND FRIED FISH

Preparation: 45 minutes
Serves: 6

metric equivalent		
½ cup		4 oz. tamarind juice (see above) or lemon juice
250 g		salt to taste
1 kg		2 lb white fleshed fish, in fillets

peanut oil for frying
½ lb long-grained rice, boiled and crumbly (kept hot)

Mix tamarind juice and salt and rub into all sides of fish fillets. Let them stand for 20 minutes then fry in hot (but not boiling) oil for 5 minutes only on each side, turning only once. Drain and serve on hot plates with crumbly boiled rice.

TAMARIND CHUTNEY

metric equivalent			
125 g	30 g	4 oz. mature green tamarinds	1 oz. chili
15 g	30 g	½ oz. English mustard powder	¼ teaspoon salt
	125 g		1 oz. garlic cloves, crushed
30 g		1 oz. green ginger	4 oz. castor sugar

Slice tamarinds lengthways, remove seeds. Then pound all ingredients in a mortar until smooth. Bottle and store.

Tangerine: *Mandarine; Satsuma; China Orange* (Malaysia)

Small, flat loose-skinned variety of oranges, originally from China and smaller than most oranges. Their juice is very sweet.

China Oranges

Very large tangerines from Malaysia. See also *Clementine*.

Naartje

Native tangerine of South Africa, probably the best citrus fruit of the area.

Use: fresh, as a dessert, in fruit salads
　　crystallized
　　in jellies

Tangle Berry

See *Berries* p. 27.

Tansy

See *Herbs and Spices* p. 82.

Tara: *Tara Fern*

New Zealand fern with swollen roots which Maoris eat boiled or baked and then ground.

Use: as for *yams*.

Taro: *Egyptian Ginger; Dasheen; Old Coco Yam*

Edible tubers of the coco yam, a plant of the arum family, widely cultivated in the Pacific area. The leaves, when small and young, are shredded and prepared as for *spinach*.

Preparation: peel tubers then steam or boil until tender.

Use: boiled and mashed in soups.

Poi

Poi, staple food of Hawaiian natives, is taro peeled, steamed or boiled then pounded to a paste. It is allowed to ferment for two or three days then eaten.

DUCK BRAISED WITH TARO

Serves: 4–6

3 lb duckling, jointed and chopped into 3 inch pieces	8 oz. stock (from duck's heart, gizzard, neck and feet)	1·5 kg 8 cm	1 cup
peanut oil	1 lb taro, peeled and cut into 1 inch cubes fried in deep fat until golden brown (sweet potatoes may be used as an alternative)	500 g 2 cm	
2 tablespoons soya sauce			
2 tablespoons sherry			
1 teaspoon fresh green ginger root, minced			
salt and pepper			

Brown duck in deep oil, then pour away as much oil as possible. Add soya sauce, sherry and ginger. Season with salt and pepper and add stock. Cover and simmer 30 minutes. Add taro and simmer 10 minutes more.

Tarragon

See *Herbs and Spices* p. 83.

Tasi

Fruit of South American *Araujia* tree, eaten roasted.

Thimbleberry

See *Berries* p. 27.

Thyme

See *Herbs and Spices* p. 83.

Lemon Thyme

See *Herbs and Spices* p. 83.

Tomato or **Love Apple**

Originally from Peru and related to the potato, there are now many varieties, with red or yellow fruit which may be round, oval or pear shaped. Originally, in Europe, tomatoes were fried in oil with salt and pepper or else boiled with salt and spice to form a sauce for other foods. They are obtainable fresh, preserved in bottles or cans, canned as purée, and as tomato juice, excellent when mixed with vodka, salt and pepper and a dash of Worcestershire sauce.

Preparation: to skin tomatoes, the following methods may be used
like a capsicum, hold pierced on a fork over a low flame until the skin wrinkles and can be peeled off
drop in boiling water for 2 minutes, remove, peel and cool
rub surface of tomato with back of a knife to loosen skin from flesh. Slit and carefully remove skin.

Use: raw—as hors d'oeuvre, in sandwiches and salads mixed with other vegetables or on their own.

TOMATO ASPIC

Serves: 4–6 as side dish

4 cups canned or fresh tomato juice	½ teaspoon Worcestershire sauce
2 tablespoons castor sugar	2 tablespoons gelatine in ½ cup hot water
1 onion, minced	
1 teaspoon salt	slices of tomatoes
2 tablespoons lemon juice	1 hard boiled egg, sliced
1 teaspoon oregano	lettuce leaves

Heat tomato juice, sugar, onion and seasonings together until they are simmering, add dissolved gelatine and strain through a sieve. Pour into wet moulds, cool and refrigerate. If desired, when jelly is half set, slices of tomato and hard boiled eggs may be placed in the jelly. When set, turn out mould on bed of lettuce and top the aspic with slices of tomato and hard boiled egg.

TOMATO EGGS

175°C Temperature: 350°F
Serves: 6

6 large tomatoes	salt and pepper
oregano or basil	parmesan cheese, grated
6 raw eggs	rashers of bacon, fried

175°C Cut tops off tomatoes and scoop enough from centres to hold one raw egg. Then sprinkle a little oregano or basil inside. Break egg into hole and sprinkle with salt and pepper and grated parmesan. Place in oven at 350°F until egg is set.
   Serve as an entrée with a rasher of bacon skewered around tomato.

Variations: Instead of eggs, stuff with
   1 cup crabmeat, $\frac{2}{3}$ cup dry breadcrumbs, 2 well beaten eggs, 2 tablespoons chopped chives, $\frac{1}{2}$ teaspoon salt, pinch dry mustard
   1 cup chopped mushrooms sautéed in 3 tablespoons butter, combined with $\frac{1}{2}$ cup cooked buttered rice, 1 tablespoon finely chopped onion, 1 teaspoon Worcestershire sauce, $\frac{1}{2}$ teaspoon salt, 1 tablespoon chopped parsley

250 g Sauté together in butter, $\frac{1}{2}$ lb minced steak, 1 tablespoon uncooked rice, $\frac{1}{2}$ teaspoon chopped mint, $\frac{1}{2}$ teaspoon chopped fresh dill, salt and pepper until rice is cooked. Cool, stuff tomatoes, add butter and water to a saucepan, place tomatoes in layers, fit a tight lid and simmer for 30 minutes or until tomatoes are tender.

INDONESIAN TOMATO SAMBAL

Serves: 3

2 cloves garlic	3 fresh red chilis, seeded
1 small piece tamarind	and cut in strips
1 small onion, finely	2 leeks
chopped	salt
peanut oil	1 tablespoon brown sugar
500 g 1 lb fresh tomatoes	$\frac{1}{2}$ cup coconut cream

Crush garlic and tamarind and fry with onion in oil. Add chilis, and one by one, the tomatoes and leeks, frying each vegetable for a few minutes. Season with salt and sugar, add coconut cream, bring to boil, reduce heat and simmer 10 minutes.

TOMATO SAUCE

1¼ cups Quantity: $\frac{1}{2}$ pint

2 onions, chopped	1 teaspoon dill seeds,
1 carrot, chopped	pounded
1 stick celery, chopped	bay leaf
1 clove garlic	salt and pepper to taste
butter to sauté	1 teaspoon lemon juice
750 g 1½ lb tomatoes	1 teaspoon sugar

Sauté onions, carrot, celery and garlic in hot butter. Add pounded dill seeds and when vegetables begin to soften, add tomatoes, bay leaf and season to taste. Simmer for 45 minutes, put through a sieve, add more seasoning if required and add lemon juice and sugar and mix well together.

DEVILLED TOMATOES

Serves: 4–6 for supper

6 tomatoes, cut in halves	salt and pepper
oil	1 teaspoon English
60 g 2 oz. butter	mustard powder
2 tablespoons castor sugar,	1 egg
crushed to powder	1 tablespoon vinegar
1 hard boiled egg yolk	

Fry tomato halves lightly in oil. Beat butter with sugar

and hard boiled egg yolk and season with salt and pepper. Add mustard, raw egg and vinegar and whisk together into a smooth cream. Cook in a double boiler until it thickens, stirring continuously. Pour over the tomatoes and serve as an entreé.

See recipe for *Vegetable Pears, Tomatoes and Onions* p. 137.

Strawberry Tomato
See p. 172.

Tree Tomato
Large South American shrub, *Cyphomandra betacea*, with red-brown egg-shaped, juicy fruit. It lacks any significant flavour.

Topepo
Fruit resembling a tomato but said to be a hybrid between the true tomato and the red capsicum.

Turmeric
See *Herbs and Spices* p. 83.

Turnips and Rutabagas: including *Swede Turnips*
Winter root vegetables, still growing wild in eastern Europe and Siberia, most palatable when gathered young. Turnip flesh is white and the tops are leafy. Swede turnips have a yellow flesh, are firmer and less watery than turnips and grow to a much larger size. Their flavour is milder.

Preparation: young turnip tops—as with *spinach* after removing stalks from older leaves
roots—wash, peel, cut into pieces or cubes and boil in salted water until tender (about 30 minutes)

Use: like haricot beans, turnips will absorb large quantities of fat and are traditionally served with fatty meats such as mutton and duck
Spring turnips are an excellent accompaniment to duckling
they may be served in cheese sauce
mashed with butter and seasoned black pepper
in soups and stews

GLACÉ TURNIPS

metric equivalent

Serves: 4–6

| 1 lb small whole turnips, peeled | castor sugar butter | 500 g |

Boil or steam baby turnips in salted water for 10–15 minutes, or until nearly tender. Drain and put into a small fireproof buttered dish. Sprinkle with castor sugar, and brush them with melted butter and add 2 or 3 tablespoons of the water in which the turnips were cooked. Place dish on a very low heat until sauce browns and becomes sticky. Watch to ensure it does not burn. Spoon this glaze over the turnips and serve in same dish.

PICKLED TURNIPS

Serve as condiment

1 lb turnips, young and small	1 cup vinegar	500 g
2 cups water	2 teaspoons salt	
1 beetroot	4 garlic cloves	

Wash turnips and cut slice from top of each. Slice lengthways into $\frac{1}{4}$ inch slices, to within half an inch of the bottom but do not separate them. Soak in water overnight and discard this water. Wash in morning and place in glass jar with beetroot. Mix the 2 cups of water, the vinegar, salt and garlic cloves, heat together to boiling point and pour over the turnips. When cool, store in a sealed jar. They may be eaten after 3 days.

7 mm

UVWXYZ

Udo

See *Herbs and Spices* p. 83.

Ugli (England): *Tangelo* (U.S.A.)

Citrus fruit with a loose skin like the tangerine but much larger and more irregular in shape—a hybrid between a grapefruit and an orange.

Use: raw as a dessert fruit when peeled
    in fruit salads
    to flavour iced drinks

Unicorn Plant

Creeper from Brazil producing many ovoid fruits, distinguished by a curved or hooked point at one end. They are gathered when small and preserved as with *capers* in vinegar.

Vanilla

See *Herbs and Spices* p. 83.

Vegetable Pear

See p. 137.

Vine Leaves

See *Grapes* p. 66.

Wampi

Yellow marble-sized citrus fruit of Thailand with flavour variously described as resembling grapes or gooseberries.

Use: in jam
    in cool drinks

Water Chestnut

See p. 43.

Watercress

A member of the nasturtium family, growing wild in Europe, found in slow running shallow water. It tastes rather bitter and peppery. Varieties include Winter Cress or Rocket Salad of the U.S.A.
Preparation: wash in cold water, remove thicker stems and yellowed leaves.

Use: raw—in salads, to garnish grilled and roast meats
    in herb stuffing
    chopped and added to mashed potatoes
    cook—blanch in salt water, drain and dry then simmer in butter as for spinach
    after simmering—add fresh cream or juice of roast beef;
    puréed: sieve and add to quarter its volume of potatoes, mix and add butter.

WATERCRESS AND EGG TART

Time: 25 minutes
220°C   Temperature: 430°F
Serves: 4

250 g

8 oz packet prepared short pastry	6 tablespoons watercress, chopped
4 eggs	salt and pepper
1 tablespoon spring onions, chopped	milk

Line a tart plate with half the pastry. Beat the eggs together and to them add chopped onion, watercress, salt and pepper. Pour over the pastry. Then cover with remaining pastry, moistening edges and then crimping together. Brush top with a little milk and bake in hot oven until top is golden brown.
    Serve hot or cold with a freshly tossed French salad.

Water Lily

See p. 96.

Red or True Whortleberry

See *Berries* p. 27.

Wineberry

See *Berries* p. 27.

Wood Sorrel

See *Herbs and Spices* p. 82.

Ximenia

Small tropical African plant with edible fruit, called mountain plums or wild limes.

Yam: *Indian Potato*

Large or very large vines of a tropical creeper (*Dioscorea*) originally from China but now growing wild in Asia and on islands in the Pacific Ocean and cultivated in West Africa and the West Indies. Tubers of the Asiatic or Chinese yam grow two to three feet long and weigh 30–40 lb. Some South Pacific varieties reach 100 lb weight and 8 feet length. Yams, when cooked, taste more like potatoes than sweet potatoes. Their skin is pinky or brown and the flesh white. In each locality, yams are often given individual common names but there are about 12 species.

60–92 cm
13–18 kg
44 kg
2·5 m

Preparation: peel and place in cold water to which some lemon juice or vinegar has been added. Boil in salted water with lemon juice until soft.

Use: baked
boiled
fried

BOILED YAMS IN CHEESE SAUCE

Serves: 4–6

1 lb yams, boiled and kept hot	8 oz. milk	500 g 1 cup
For sauce:	4 oz. grated parmesan cheese	125 g
2 oz. butter	salt and pepper	60 g
2 tablespoons plain flour	cayenne pepper	

To make sauce: Melt butter and mix in flour to form a paste and cook until golden brown. Add milk, stirring constantly, then the cheese and the salt and pepper. If mixture is too thick, thin with water or chicken broth. Pour over yams and sprinkle with cayenne.

YAM AND HARICOTS

Serves: 4–6

1 cup haricot beans (any type)	4 cups water
1 lb yam, prepared and boiled until soft	butter and milk
	salt and pepper to taste

500 g

Soak beans overnight. Boil them in 4 cups of hot water until tender. Drain and add to yam. Mash together adding butter and milk to make the purée smooth and creamy. Season to taste with salt and pepper.

YAM SOUFFLE

Serves: 6

4 large yams	2 tablespoons brown sugar
5 oz. butter	2 eggs, beaten
½ teaspoon salt	2 tablespoons white wine
¼ teaspoon pepper	½ teaspoon cinnamon

155 g

Bake yams in foil at 450°F for about 1 hour or until they can be pierced by a thin steel skewer. Remove skins, and mash with 4 oz. butter. Add salt, pepper, sugar, eggs, and wine and beat until fluffy. Pour into a buttered casserole dish and sprinkle with cinnamon. Dot with 1 oz. butter and bake in oven at 350°F for 30 minutes.

230°C

125 g

30 g
175°C

Yam or Manioc Beans

Tropical climbing plant with edible turnip-like roots and edible pods.

Preparation: roots—wash and add finely sliced and uncooked to salads
'Beans' or pods—boil as for *green beans*.

Note: widely grown the following names are used for this particular plant or its relatives:

AJIPA BEAN *Pachyrhizus ahippa*

GIRI-GIRI (Nigeria) *Sphenostylis stenocarpia*

GOA BEAN (India) *P. tuberosus*

SHORT-PODDED YAM BEAN *P. erosus*

STARCH BEAN *P. tuberosus*

YAM BEAN *P. tuberosus*

Yarrow

See *Herbs and Spices* p. 83.

Yautias: *New Coco Yam* (Africa)

Corms and tubers of taro-like plant, native of Americas but now used as food in South America and Africa.

Youngberry

See *Berries* p. 27.

Yuzo

See *Grapefruit* p. 65.

Zapallito

See p. 64.

Zibet

See p. 122.

Zucchini

See *Marrows* p. 102.

A

Abacaxi 141–2
Abbevillea 56
Abiu 2
Acacia 2
Acoub 2
Achojcha 2
Ackee 2
Aduwa 50
Adzuki 17
African Cucumber 106
Agar-Agar 168
Agi 3, **72**
Aguacate 10
Aguay 3, **24**
Aguncate 3
Aji **72**
Ajipa Bean 182
Akee 2
Alecost 3, **72**
Alectryon 3
Alga Mar 168
Algaroba Bean 21
Alisander 3, **72**
Alleluia 82
Allgood 78
Alliara 3, **72**
Alligator Apple 5
Alligator Pear 10
Allspice 3, **72**
Almonds 3, **114–15**
Almonds, Earth 44, 118
Almonds, Java 121
Almonds, Javanese 115, 117
Almonds, Pili 117
Amaranth 3
Amatungula 144
Amazombe 3
Ambarella 4
American Cherries 43
American Cress 46
Ananas 141–2
Anchovy Pear 4, 136
Angelica 4, **72**
Anise 4, **72**
Apio 7
Apples 4–6
Apple, Balsam 106
Apple, Belle 65
Apple Berry, Baked **25**
Apple, Golden 65
Apple, Tomato 175–7

Apricot 6–7
Apricot Plum, Chinese 145
Arachichu 7
Arbute 7, **24**
Arenga Palm 128, **131**
Arracacha 7
Arracacia 7
Arrowhead 8
Artichokes 8–9
Artichokes, Globe 37
Asem 174
Asparagus 9–10
Asparagus Bean 18
Asparagus Broccoli 29
Asparagus Bush 10
Asparagus Pea 10, 139
Assam 174
Aubergine 10, **54**
Australian Bean 21
Australian Native Plum 145
Avocado 10
Awarra Palm 128
Aya 44
Azarole 11

B

Baby Marrows 102
Badderlocks 168
Badian 14
Bael 14
Baked Apple Berry **25**
Balm 14, **72**
Balsam Apple 106
Balsam Pear 106
Bamboo Shoots 14
Bamia 120
Bananas 14–15
Bangi 15
Bank Cress 46
Bannet 15, **72**
Baobab 107
Barbados Cherries 25, 43
Barbados Gooseberries 36, 172
Barbardine 64
Barbarine 15, 103
Barberry 15, **24**
Barberry, Blue **24**
Barcelona Nut 116
Basela 15
Baselle 15
Basil 15, **72**
Bay Leaf 15, **72**

Beans 15–22, 71
Beans, Manioc 181
Bean Sprouts 21
Beans, Yam 181
Beautiful Beans 18
Bee Balm **72**
Beech Nuts 115
Beet 22
Beet, See-Kale 41–2, 167
Beet, Silver 22
Beet Spinach 22
Beetroot 22, 71
Beet, White 41–2
Belgian Endive 75
Belle Apple 65
Belle Isle Cress 46
Bell Peppers **73**
Bengal Quince 14
Berberry **24**
Berberry, Black **24**
Bergamot 23, **72**
Berries 23–8
Betel Palm 128
Bilberry **24**, 28
Bilimbi 28
Bilva 28
Bird's Foot Bean 18
Bistort 28
Bitter Melon 106
Black Apple 145
Black Bean 20, 21
Black Berberry **24**
Blackberry **24**, 28
Black Bryony 31
Black Cap **24**, 28
Black Cap Berry **27**
Black Currants **25**
Black-Eyed Bean 18
Black-Eyed Pea 79
Black Gram Beans 20
Black Jack Damsons 143
Black Pepper 79, 140
Black Sapota 140–1
Black Soya Beans, Fermented 21
Blaeberry **24**
Blue Barberry **24**
Blueberry **24**, 28
Boboa 101
Bog Strawberry **25**
Bok Choy 36
Bonavist Bean 19

Bonne Damme 123
Borage 28, **72**
Borecole 91
Bottle Gourd 37, **64**
Bouquet Garni 28, **73**
Boysenberry **24**, 28
Bracken 59
Braganza 28, **35**
Brazil Cherry 62
Brazil Nuts 115
Breadfruit **28–9**
Brinjal 54
Brinjal, Hairy 29, 54, **103**
Brionne 137
Broad Beans 15–16
Broccoli 29–30, 71
Broccoli, Asparagus 29
Broome, Yellow 30, **73**
Brown Dutch Bean 18
Brown Onions 122
Brush Apple 6, 56
Brussels Sprouts 30, 71
Buchu 31
Bucku 31
Bucksthorn Plantain 70
Buckthorn, Sea **25**, 31
Buffalo Berry **25**, 31
Buffalo Currants **25**
Bulbous Chervil **43**
Bullace 31, **143**
Bullace Plums 143
Bullock's Heart Apple 6
Burdock 31
Burma Beans 19
Burnet 31, **73**
Bush Apple 145
Butter Beans 17, 18
Butter Beans, Madagascar 19
Butter Nuts 118
Button Onions 122

C

Cabbage 34–6, 71
Cabbage, Celery 41
Cabbage Turnip 91
Cactus 36
Caimito 2
Cajun Beans 19
Calabash 37, **64**
Calabash, Sweet 65
Calabrese 29
Calafate Berry **24**

Calaloo **170–1**
Calalu 37
Camambu **25**, 37
Camass 152
Canavalis Gotani 17
Canistel 37
Cantaloup 104
Cantaloup (U.S.A.) 105
Cape Gooseberry **62**
Cape Kidney Bean, Marbled 19
Capers 37, **73**
Capsicum 37, 71, **73**, **79**, 140
Capulassan 148
Capulin 42
Carachis 117
Carambola **28**
Caraway 37, **73**
Cardamom 37, **73**
Cardoon 37
Caribbean Cabbage 36
Carissa 144
Carnauba Palm 128
Carob Bean 21
Caroube Bean 21
Carrag(h)een 168
Carrots **37–8**, 71
Casaba 104
Cashew 38, 115
Cashew Nut 38, **115**
Cashew Pear 38
Cassava **38–9**
Cassia Bark 73
Catjang 10
Catmint 39, **73**
Catnip **73**
Cauliflower **39–40**, 71
Cayenne 40, **73**
Cayenne Cherry 142
Cayenne Pepper **79**, 140
Celeriac **40**
Celery Cabbage **35**, 41
Celery **41**, 71
Celery Seeds 41, **74**
Celery, Turnip-Rooted **40**, 41
Ceriman 107
Chanar 41
Chanra 41
Chard **41–2**
Chard, Swiss 41–2
Charentais 104
Chartres Beans 19

Chayote 137
Checker Berry **27**
Cherimoya 6
Cherries **42–3**
Cherry, Barbados **25**
Cherry, Brazil 62
Cherry, Cayenne 142
Cherry, Cornelian **25**, 45
Cherry, Florida 142
Cherry, Ground 62, 172
Cherry, Mountain 143
Cherry Plum 143
Cherry, Sand 144
Cherry, Surinam 56, 142
Cherry, Winter 172
Chervil 43, **74**
Chervil, Bulbous **43**
Chestnut 43, **115–16**
Chestnut, Water **43**, 180
Chevriers Beans 19
Chickasaw Plum 143
Chickling Vetch 44
Chick Peas **139**
Chickweed 44
Chicory 44, **55**
Chicory, Endive and **55–6**, 75–6
Chicory Endive **75**
Chilean Nut 116
Chile Hazel 116
Chile Powder 44, 73, **74**
Chili Hazel 116
Chili Powder 44, 73, **74**
Chilis 44, **74**
Chilis, Red 44, **74**
China Beans 19
China Pea **79**
China Orange 174
Chinese Amaranth 3
Chinese Apricot Plum 7, 145
Chinese Artichokes **8**
Chinese Bean 20
Chinese Cabbage 36
Chinese Dates 91
Chinese Five Spices **74**
Chinese Gooseberry **63**
Chinese Lantern 172
Chinese Mustard 111
Chinese Mustard Cabbage 110
Chinese Mustard Greens 110
Chinese Olives 121
Chinese Parsley 75

Chinese Plum 143
Chinese Snow Peas **139–40**
Chinese Winter Melon **103–4**
Choan-Choy 110
Cho-Cho 137
Choko 137
Chorogi 8
Chinois 48
Chives 74, **122**
Christophine 137
Chrysanthemum Flowers 44
Chufa 44
Cinnamon 44, **74**
Ciruela 107
Citrange 44
Citron 44
Citron Melon 104
Citrus Peel **44–5**
Civet Beans 19
Clary 45, **74**
Clementine 45
Cloudberry **25**, 45
Cloves 45, 56, **74**
Cob Nuts 116
Cob Nuts, Jamaican 117
Cock's Claw 86
Coco(a)-Plum 45, **145**
Coco Beans 17
Coconuts 45, 116, **128**
Coconut Palm 128–9
Coconut Palm, Water 129
Coco Yam, New 182
Coco Yam, Old 175
Colewarts 91
Collards 36, 45, 91
Colocasia 45, **74**
Comfrey 45, **74**
Congo Beans 19
Coquerot 172
Coquito 129
Coriander 45, **75**
Cormandel Gooseberry **28**
Cornel **25**, 45
Cornelian Cherry **25**, 45
Corn-on-the-cob 45–6
Corn Salad **45**
Corossal 5
Costmary 72
Coucouzelle 102
Courgeron 102
Courgette 102

Couvé Tronchuda 35
Cowberry **25**
Cow Parsnip 132
Cow Peas **79**, 139
Cowslip 46, **75**
Crab Apple 5
Crakeberry **25**
Cranberry **25**, 46
Cream Nuts 115
Cress **46**
Cress, American 46
Cress, Bank 46
Cress, Belle Isle 46
Cress, Indian 114
Cress, Cand 46
Cress, Meadow 46
Cress, Mexican 114
Cress, Upland 46
Crin-Crin 46
Crinkleroot 46
Crowberry **25**, 47
Cuban Bean 18
Cucumbers **47**, 64, 71
Cucumber Snake 48
Cumin 48, **75**
Cummin 75
Cumquat 48
Curcuma 48, **75**
Curly Endive 75
Currants **25**, 48
Curry Powder 48, **75**
Custard Apple 5, 6
Custard Marrow 137

D Dahlia 50
Daikon 50
Damascenes 143
Damascus Plum 143
Damson Plums 143
Dandelion 50
Darwin Berry **24**
Dasheen 175
Daso 60
Date Plum 130
Dates 50, **128**
Dates, Chinese 91
Dates, Dessert 50
Date Sugar Palm 130
Deleb Palm 130
Dessert Date 50
Devil-in-the-bush 78

Dewberry **26**, 51
Dhal 95
Dhanya 75
Dill 51, **75**
Dillesk 168
Dillisk 168
Dishcloth Gourd 64
Doan Choy 110
Doan-Gwa 103–4
Dock 51, **75**
Dog's Mercury 78
Doliches Sesquipedalis 18
Down Palm 130
Dragon's Eye 97
Dried Peas 139
Drum-head Cabbage 34
Dulse 168
Durian 51
Dutch Bean, Brown 18
Dutch Beans 19
Dutch Cabbage, White 34

E *Earth Almond* 44, 118
Earth Nut 117
Edible Podded Peas 138
Eggplant 54–5, 71
Egyptian Bean 19
Egyptian Ginger 175
Egyptian Melon 104
Elder 55, **75**
Elderberry **26**, 55
Endive 75
Endive and Chicory 55–6, 75–6
England Berry **24**
Escarol 76
Escarole 55, 56
Eugenia and minor
  myrtaceous fruits 56
Evening Primrose 148

F *Fabriama* 60
Fan-Kot 91
Fat Hen 123
Feijoa 56, **58**
Fennel **58**, 76
Fennel Flower 78
Fenugreek 59, **76**
Fermented Black Soya Beans 21
Fermented Mustard Greens 110
Fern Shoots 59
Fern, Tara 174

Fiddle Heads 59
Field Beans 16
Field Garden Beans 17
Figs 59
Filberts 116
Fines Herbes 76
Fine Herbs 59, **76**
Flageolets 18
Flageolets **19**
Flava Beans 15
Florida Cherry 142
Flowers 59–60
Foxberry **25**
Fra-Fra 60
French Artichokes 8
French Beans 17
French Spinach 123
French St Peter's Cress 166
Fried Peas 139
Fruit, Miraculous **26**, 107
Fura-Fura 60

G *Garbanzos* 139
Garden Peas 138
Garlic 62, **76**
Garlic Mustard 62, **76**
Geranium Leaves, Scented **77**
Geranium Leaves 62, **77**
Gherkin 62
Giant Granadilla 64
Giant Mexican Spinach 171
Ginger 62, **77**
Ginger, Egyptian 175
Gingerbread Tree 130
Gingko Nuts 116
Giraumont **149**
Giri-Giri 182
Glasswort Samphire 166
Globe Artichokes 8, 37
Goa Beans 17, 182
Goat's Beard 166
Gobo 31
Golden Apple 65
Golden Currants **25**
Golden Gram Bean 19
Golden Hog 4
Golden Samphire 166
Good-King-Henry 78
Gooseberry **26**, 62
Gooseberry, Barbados **36**, 172
Gooseberry, Cape **62**

Gooseberry, Chinese **63**
Gooseberry, Cormandel **28**
Gooseberry, Grosela **67**
Gooseberry, Otaheiti 64, **67**
Goosefoot 78, 94
Goumi **26**, 64
Gourd 64
Gourd, Bottle 37, **64**
Gouriilos **55**, 64, 76
Goy Choy 110
Gram Peas 139
Granadilla 64, 132–3
Granadilla, Giant 64
Granadilla, Sweet 65
Granadilla, Yellow 65
Grapefruit 65–6
Grape Leaves 66–7
Grape Pear **27**, 104
Grapes **66**–7
Grapes, Riverside **26**, 66
Grass Pea 44
Great Burdock **31**
Green Beans 17
Green Cabbage 34
Green Gram Bean 19
Green Laver 168
Green Lima Beans 16
Green Onions 122
Green Peas 138
Greengage Plums 143–4
Grenadilla 64
Grosela Gooseberry **67**
Ground Cherry 62, 172
Ground Furze 157
Ground Nut 117
Grumichana 67
Guabiyu 56, **67**
Guarana 67
Guava 68
Guiana Nuts 118
Guinea Palm 130
Guinea Plum 145
Gumbo 120
Gum Jum 96
Gungo Peas 139

H Hackberry **26**, 70
Hair Seaweed 168
Hairy Brinjal 29, 54, **103**
Hairy Melon 103
Hai Tai 168

Haldi 83
Hamburg Parsley 70, **79**, 131
Hard-Headed Cabbage 34
Haricot Beans, Dried 17–18
Haricot Beans, Fresh 18
Haricot Beans, Fresh White 18
Haricots Blancs Frais 18
Haricots Verts 17
Harm-choy 110
Hartshorn 70
Hazelnuts 116
Hedge Mustard 46, 90
Henware 168
Herbs and Spices 70–86
Herbs and Spices and
  Matching Vegetables 71
Hickory Nut 116
Hill Palm 130, 131
Himalayan Berry **24**
Hondapara 86
Honeydew Melon 105
Honey Dew Melon 104
Honey Tree 86
Honeyware 168
Hop Shoots 86
Horse Beans 15, 17
Horseradish **77**, 86
Hot South American Pepper 74, **79**,
  140
Huckleberry **26**, 87
Huckleberry, Worts **24**
Huevo De Gallo 87
Hurt Berry **24**
Husk Tomato 62
Hyacinth Bean 19
Hyssop **77**

I *Ibas* 90
Iberian Moss 168
Icaco 145
Icaque 145
Ice Plant 171
Igbá Jay 56
Igba Purú 90
Ilama 6
Imbu 90
India Bean 20
Indian Corn 45–6
Indian Cress 114
Indian Currants **25**
Indian Custard Apple 6

187

Indian Lettuce 96
Indian Potato 181
Indian Sorrel 78
Indian Spinach 15
Indian Tree Lettuce 96
Inga 90
Irish Sea Moss 168
Isiqwashumbe 90
Italian Marrows 102
Italian Squash 102
Ita Palm 130
Izibo 90

J Jaboticaba 90
Jack Beans 17
Jack-by-the-hedge **72**
Jackfruit 90–1
Jamaica Cherry 43
Jamaica Honeysuckle 65
Jamaican Cob Nut 117
Jamaican Pepper **72**
Jamberberry 62
Jamblow 58, **91**
Jambu 56, **91**
Japanese Artichokes 8
Japanese Beans 19
Japanese Medlar 97
Japanese Plum 143
Japanese Quince 153
Japanese Radish 50
Japanese Raisin Tree 86
Java Almonds 121
Javanese Almond 115, 117
Java Plum ·56, **91**
Javan Haricot Beans 19
Javril, Sweet **77**
Jeera 75
Jersey Cudweed 48
Jerusalem Artichokes 9
Jerusalem Melon 104, 105
Jew's Mallow 46
Jigger Nuts 115
Jacote 107
Jook Sun 14
Jujube 91
Juneberry **27**
Jungli Amba 4
Juniper **77**

K Kaffir Orange 124
Kaki 140–1

Kale 91
Kamachile 91
Kamanchile 91
Kangaroo Apple 6
Kidney Beans 17
Kidney Beans, Red 19
Kiu-Ts'ai 77
Kiwi Fruit **63**
Knepe 100
Knot Root 8
Kohlrabi 91
Kotenashi Beans 19
Kuchay **77**
Kudzu 91
Kumara 148
Kumquat 48
Kuruba 65

L Lablab Bean 19
Lablab Vulgaris 19
Lad's Love 170
Lady's Fingers 14, 120
Lady's Smock 46
Lamb's Lettuce 45
Lamb's Quarters 94
Land Cress 46
Langsat 101
Lanzone 101
Laver, Purple 168
Laver, Red 168
Lawton Berry **26**, 94
Leaf Mustard 111
Leechee 98
Leeks **94**
Lemon, Water 65
Lemons 94–5
Lemon Thyme **83**, 95, 175
Lentils 95
Lettuce 96
Lettuce, Indian 96
Lettuce, Lamb's 45
Lettuce Laver 168
Lichee 98
Lily, Tiger 96
Lily, Water **96–7**, 180
Lima Bean 19
Lima Bean, Mottled 19
Lime 97
Lime, Spanish 100
Litchi 98
Locust Bean 21

Loganberry **26**, 97
Longan 97
Long Potato 148
Loofah Gourd 64
Loose-Headed Cabbage 34
Loquat 97
Lotus 97–8
Lovage **77**, 98
Love Apple 6, **175–7**
Lucoma 2
Lungan 97
Lychees 98

M Macadamia Nut 117
Mace **77**, 100
Macora 56, **100**
Macore 56, **100**
Madagascar Butter Bean 19
Magellan Berry **24**
Mahura 28
Maize 45–6
Malabar Nightshade 15
Malanga 37
Malay Apple 6, 56
Mallow 100
Malpighia Glabra 43
Mamey Apple 166–7
Mammee Apple 166–7
Mamoncillo 100
Mandarine 174
Manduvira 100
Mangaba 100
Mangabeira 100
Mangel 100
Mangel-Wurzel 100
Mangistan 101
Mangoes 100–1
Mangold 100
Mangold-Wurzel 100
Mangosteen 101
Manioc 38–9
Manioc Beans 21, 181
Marbled Cape Kidney Bean 19
Marjoram, Sweet **78**, 101
Marrows 64, **101–3**
Marrows, Custard 137
Marrows, Vegetable 64, **101–3**
Masha **78**, 104
Mastuerzo 104
Mat Beans 17
Meadow Cress 46

Mealies 45–6
Medlars 104
Melilot **78**, 104
Melloco 104
Melon de Malabar 106
Melon, Hairy 103
Melons 64, **104–6**
Mercury **78**, 106
Mexican Cress 114
Mexican Spinach 123
Mexican Spinach, Giant 171
Milfoil **78**, 106
Milkweed 170
Mint **78**, 107
Mint, Sweet 78
Mirabelle Plums 144
Miraculous Fruit **26**, 107
Missouri Currants **25**
Mistol 107
Moelle de Chicoree **55**, 76, 107
Mombin, Red 107
Monkey Apple 5, 6
Monkey Bread 107
Monkey Nut 117
Monkey Puzzle Nut 117
Monstera Deliciosa 107
Moreton Bay Chestnut Bean 21
Moringa 107
Massberry **25**
Moss, Iberian 168
Moss, Irish Sea 168
Moss, Pearl 168
Moss, Sea 168
Moth Beans 17
Mottled Lima Bean 19
Mountain Apple 6, 56
Mountain Cherry 143
Mountain Spinach 123
Mugwort **78**, 107
Mulberry, **26**, 107
Mung Bean 19
Murlin 168
Mushrooms 71, 107–10
Musk Melon 105
Mustard **78**, 110
Mustard Cabbage, Chinese 110
Mustard Greens, Chinese 110
Mustard Greens, Fermented 110
Mustard Greens, Salted 110
Mustard, Hedge 46, **90**
Mustard Leaf 111

Muy-Choy 110
Myrtaceous Fruits 111
Myrtaceous fruits, minor 56
Myrtle **78**, 111

N

Naartje 174
Nangka 114
Nangkaboom 114
Narcissus Bulbs 114
Naseberry Plums 166–7
Nasturtium **114**
Nasturtiums, Tuberous-rooted 114
Natal Plum 144
Native Peach 152
Native Plum, Australian 145
Navy Bean 19
Nebraska Currant **25**
Nectarine 114
Neopolitan Medlar 11
Nepal Berry **24**
Nettle **78**, 114
Newberry **26**, 114
New Coco Yam 182
New Zealand Spinach 171
Nigella **78**, 114
Niggertoe Nuts 115
Nightshade, Malabar 15
Nipa 130
Nopal 36–7
Normandy Berry **24**
Notchweed 166
Nutmeg **79**, 114
Nutmeg Kernel 77
Nutmeg Melon 105
Nuts 114–18

O

Oca 120
Occa 120
Ohia 6
Ohia Apple 56
Oil Palm 130
Okaplant 120
Okra 120–1
Old Coco Yam 175
Olives 121
Olluco 122
Onion Pickled 110
Onions *and their relatives* 122–3
Orach 123
Orache 123
Oranges **123–4**

Oranges, China 174
Oregano **79**, 124
Ortanique 124
Otaheite Apple 4
Otaheite Plum 4
Otaheiti Gooseberry 64, **67**
Otenashi Beans 19
Oudo 83
Oxeye, Sea- 167
Oysternut 117
Oyster Plant 125, **166**

P

Pacuri 125
Palm Cabbage 36, **131**
Palmetto 131
Palm Hearts 131
Palms 128–31
Palmyra Palm 130
Pamplemouse 65
Pandanus 131
Papaya 133–4
Paprika 73, **79**, 131
Paradise Nuts 118
Parchita 65
Parsley **79**, 131
Parsley, Chinese 75
Parsley, Hamburg 70, **79**, 131
Parsley, Turnip Rooted 79
Parsnip **131–2**
Parsnip, Cow 132
Partridgeberry **25**
Passion Fruit 64, 65, **132–3**
Patava Palm 130
Pawpaw 133–4
Pea Bean 18
Pea, Black-eyed 79
Peaches 134–5
Pea, China 79
Pea, Cow **79**
Peanut 117
Pear, Balsam 106
Pear, Cashew 38
Pear, Grape **27**, 104
Pearl Moss 168
Pears 136–8
Pear, Sugar **27**
Pear, Sweet **27**, 104
Pear, vegetable **137**, 180
Peas 71, **138–40**
Pease 139
Pea Sprouts 140

Pea, White-eyed **79**
Pecan Nuts 117
Penny Royal **79**, 140
Pepinella 137
Pepino 140
Pepper **79**, 140
Pepper, Black 79
Pepper, Cayenne 79
Pepper, Red 79
Peppers, Bell 73
Peppers, Hot South American 74
Peppers, Spanish 80
Peppers, Sweet 73, 80
Pera de Compos 56
Perpetual Spinach 22
Persian Melon 105
Persimmon **140–1**
Peruvian Custard Apple 6
Peruvian Skirret 148
Pe-tsai 36
Pigeon Peas 19
Pignoli 117
Pigweed 94, **141**
Pili Almond 117
Pimentos **79**, 80, 140
Pimientos 80
Pina 141–2
Pindo 141
Pineapple 141–2
Pine Nuts 117
Pinon 117
Pino Nut 117
Pinto Beans 19
Piquillin 142
Pistachio Nuts 118
Pitanga 142
Pitomba 56
Plaintain (Banana) 14, 143
Plaintain Weed 143
Plum, Coco(a) 45, **145**
Plum, Java 56, **91**
Plums **143–5**
Plum, Spanish 107
Poakan 145
Poake 145
Poi 174
Pois Mangetout 138
Poivrons **73**
Pokeweed 145
Pomegranate **145–6**
Pomelo 65

Pomme d'or 65
Poor Man's Beans 17
Poppy Leaves 146
Poppy Seeds **80**, 146
Portugal Cabbage 35
Potato 71, 146–8
Potatoes 60
Potato, Indian 181
Potato, Sweet 148
Preserving Melon 105
Prickly Samphire 166
Prickly West Indian Custard Apple 6
Primrose, Evening 148
Pulassan 148
Pumpkin 64, **149**
Pumpkin, Siamese 106
Purple Laver 168
Purslane 80
Pussley 80

Q

Quamash 152
Quandong 152
Queensland Nut 117, 118
Quenette 100
Quimbombo 120
Quinces **152–3**
Quinoa 153

R

Rabbit Berry **25**
Radishes **156**
Radish, Japanese 50
Rambutan 156
Rampion 156
Rangoon Beans 19
Rape 80, 156
Raspberry **27**, 156
Ravigote 80, 157
Red Cabbage 34
Red Chilis 44, **74**
Red Currants **25**
Rest Harrow 157
Red-Inside-Snow 110
Red Kidney Beans 19
Red Laver 168
Red Mombin 107
Red Pepper **79**, 140
Red Pimento, Dwarf 72
Redware 168
Red Whortleberry **27**, 180
Rhubarb 157
Rice Beans 17

River Pear 136
Riverside Grapes **26**, 66
Rocambole 122
Rocket **80**, 157
Rock Medlar **27**, 104
Rock Melon 105
Rock Weed 168
Rose Apple 6, 56, 145
Rose Hips **80**, 157
Roselle 157
Rosemary **81**, 157
Rose Water **81**, 157
Round Gourds 64
Rozella 157
Rue **81**, 157
Runner Beans 18
Rush Nut 44
Rutanagas 157, **177**

S   *Sabre Beans* 17
Saffron **81**, 160
Sage **81**, 160
Sago Palm 131
Sagu 38–9
Salad, Corn **45**
Salad Fruits 165–6
Salad Vegetables 161–4
Salmonberry **27**, 166
Salsify 166
Salt **81**, 166
Salted Mustard Greens 110
Saltwort Samphire 166
Samphire 166
Sand Cherry 43, **144**
Sand Leek 122
Sand Plum 144
Santol 101
Santul 101
Sapodilla 166–7
Sapota, White 167
Sapucaia Nut 118
Sargasso 168–9
Satsuma 174
Sauce Alone 76, **81**, 167
Savory 81
Savoury **81**, 167
Savoy Cabbage 34
Savoy Medlar **27**, 104
Sawos Manila 166–7
Scallions 122
Scaly Apple 6

Scandinavian Berry **24**
Scarlet Runner Beans 18
Scotch Beans 15
Screw Pine 131
Sea Buckthorn **25**, 31, 167
Sea-cole 167
Sea-Kail 167
Sea Kale 167
Sea-Kale Beet 167
Sea Moss 168
Sea Oxeye 167
Sea Purslane 123, 166
Sea Rocket 157
Sea Sandwort 166
Seaweeds **167–9**
Sea Wrack 168
See Fennel 166
See-Kale Beet 41–2
Service Berry 27
Sesame Seeds **81**, 82, 169
Sewt-Lay-Hoan 110
Shadeberry **27**
Shaddock 65
Shallots 122
Shell Beans 15
Shelling Peas 138
Shepherd's Purse 45
Short-Podded Yam Bean 182
Shropshire Damsons 143
Siamese Pumpkin 106
Sibby Beans 19
Sieva Beans 19
Silver Beet 22
Silver Skin Onions 122
Silver Weed 169
Sim Sim **82**, 169
Skirret 169
Sloe 169
Slouk 168
Small Onions 122
Snake Beans 17
Snake Cucumber 48
Snake Root 169
Snake Squash 64
Snap Beans 17
Snow Peas, Chinese 139–40
Soja Beans 19
Solomon's Seal 169
Soncoya 6
Sorrel **82**, 170
Sorrell, Wood **82**, 181

Souari 118
Sour Grass 82
Soursop 6
Sour-Sour 78
Southernwood 170
Sow Thistle 170
Soya Beans 18, **19–20**
Soy Beans 19
Spanish Chestnut 115–16
Spanish Honeydew Melon 105
Spanish Lime 100
Spanish Onions 122
Spanish Peppers 80
Spanish Plum 107
Spanish Potato 148
Spanish Watermelon 105
Spearmint **82**, 170
Spices and Herbs 70, 86
Spignel **82**, 170
Spiked Rampion 170
Spikenard 82
Spikenhead **82**, 170
Spinach 71, **170–1**
Spinach, Beet 22
Spinach, French 123
Spinach, Mexican 123
Spinach, Mountain 123
Spinach, Perpetual 22
Spinach, Strawberry 41–2
Spinach, Wild 78
Split Peas 139
Spondias 4
Sprouts, Brussels **30**
Spring Cabbage 34
Spring Greens 91
Spring Onions 122
Squash 64, 101, **171**
Squash, Italian 102
Squash, Snake 64
Star Apple 6
Starch Bean 182
Star of the Earth 70
Stick Beans 18
Stinging Nettle 78
Stoke 168
Stonecrops 171
Stone Leeks 122
Strawberry **27**, 172
Strawberry, Bog **25**
Strawberry Spinach 41–2
Strawberry Tomato 62, **172**, 177

Strawberry, Tree **24**
String Beans 17
Succory **55**, 76, 172
Sugar Apple 6
Sugarberry **26**
Sugar Loaf 141–2
Sugar Palm 131
Sugar Pear **27**
Sugar Peas 138
Sumac **82**, 172
Sunflower 172
Surinam Cherry 43, 56, **142**
Susumber **27**, 172
Swarri Nuts 118
Swede Turnips 177
Sweet Calabash 65
Sweet Cicely 44
Sweet Corn 45–6
Sweet Cup 65
Sweet Granadilla 65
Sweet Javril **77**
Sweet Marjoram **78**, 101
Sweet Mint 78
Sweet Pear **27**, 104
Sweet Peppers **73**, 80
Sweet Potato 148
Sweetsop 6
Sweet Tangle 168
Swiss Chard 41–2
Sword Beans 17
Syboes 122

T   *Tallow Gourd* 64
Tamarind 174
Tangelo 180
Tangerine 174
Tangle 168
Tangle Berry **27**, 174
Tansy **82**, 174
Tara 174
Tara Fern 174
Taro 175
Tarragon **83**, 175
Tasi 175
Thimbleberry **27**, 175
Thistle, Sow 170
Thyme **83**, 175
Thyme, Lemon **83**, 95, 175
Tiger lilies 96
Tiger Nut 44, **118**
Tirabeques 138

Toddy Palm   131
Tomatillo   62
Tomato   71
Tomato Apple   175–7
Tomato, Husk   62
Tomato, Strawberry   62, **172**, 177
Tongan Beans   17
Tonka Bean   19
Topepo   177
Tree of Life   130, 131
Tree Onions   122
Tree Strawberry   **24**
Tree Tomato   177
Tropical Fruit Salad Plant   107
True Artichokes   8
True Whortleberry   **27**, 180
T'sao   91
Turmeric   **83**, 177
Turnip   71, **177**
Turnip, Cabbage   91
Turnip-rooted Celery   **40**, 41
Turnip-rooted Parsley   79

U   Ubajay   56
Ubod   131
Udo   **83**, 180
Ugli   28, **180**
Unicorn Plant   180
Upland Cress   46
Urd Beans   20

V   Vanilla   **83**, 180
Vegetable Marrow   101–3
Vegetable Pear   **137**, 180
Velvet Bean   20
Victoria Plum   144
Vigna Catjung   18
Vine Leaves   66–**7**, 180
Virginia Date Palm   140–1

W   Walnuts   118
Wampi   180
Water Caltrop   43
Water Chestnut   **43**, 180
Water Coconut Palm   129, 130
Watercress   **180**
Water Lemon   65
Water Lily   96–**7**, 180
Watermelon   105
Wattle Blossoms   2

Wax Beans   17
Wax Gourd   64
Wax Plum   131
Wax Pod Beans   17
Weed, Silver   169
Whinberry   **24**
Whitebeam Berry   **27**
White Beet   41–2
White Cabbage   36
White Currants   **25**
White Dutch Cabbage   34
White-Eyed Pea   79
White Gourd   64
White Haricot Beans, Fresh   18
White Mustard   110
White Onions   122
White Sapota   167
Whortleberry   **24**
Whortleberry, Red   **27**, 180
Whortleberry, True   **27**, 180
Wild Cherry   42
Wild Plum   145
Wild Salisfy   166
Wild Spinach   78
Windsor Beans   15
Wineberry   **27**, 181
Wine Plum   131
Winged Pea   10
Winter Cherry   172
Winter Cress   80
Winter Melon   104
Winter Melon, Chinese   103–4
Winter Vegetable   110
Wong-Nga-Bok   35
Wood Sorrel   **82**, 181
Worts Huckleberry   **24**

X   Ximenia   181
Xuxu   137

Y   Yam   181
Yam Beans   181
Yam, New Coco   182
Yam, Old Coco   175
Yardlong Bean   10
Yarrow   **83**, 182
Yatay Palm   131
Yauta   37
Yautias   182
Yellow Berry   25

Yellow Broome   30, **73**
Yellow Granadilla   65
Yellow Mombin   4
Youngberry   **27**, 182
Yuca   38–9
Yuzu   **65**, 66, 182

Z   Zapallito   **64**, 182
Zapota   166–7
Zibet   **122**, 182
Zucchetti   102
Zucchini   **102**, 182
Zulu Nut   44

191

Ackee Float 3
Ackee Pies 3
Ackee Sawfish 2
Almond Soup—Spanish 115
Amberella and Chicken 4
Anchovy Salad Dressing 163
Apples, Carrots and Cheese 38
Apple and Cream Cheese Tart 5
Apple and Horseradish Salad 5
Apples and Parsnips, Baked 132
Apple and Sloe Jelly 169
Apple Rings, Fried 5
Apricots in Brandy 7
Apricots and Lamb Chops 5
Apricot Pudding Cake 7
Artichokes—Globe, Fried 8
Artichokes—Globe, Stuffed 8
Artichokes—Jerusalem, Curried 9
Asparagus and Orange Casserole 123
Asparagus Tips with Potato Salad 147
Avocado Dip 10
Avocado—Malaysian Dessert 10
Avocado Soup 11

Baby Marrow Pancakes 103
Baby Marrows—sautéed 102;
  sautéed with cheese 103
Bacon with Broad Beans 16
Baked Beans, Barbecued 21
Baked Beans, Canadian 20
Baked Belgian Endive 56
Baked Cauliflower 40
Baked Celery and Mushrooms 41
Baked Nectarines 114
Baked Parsnips and Apples 132
Baked Pears in Claret 136
Bamboo Shoots Braised with Chicken Breasts 14
Banana Bread 14
Bananas and Cheese Schnitzels 15
Banana with Haricot Beans 15
Barbecue Baked Beans 21
Basic Vegetable Stock 58-9
Beef, canned, salad 20
Beef and Bitter Melon Braised 106
Beef and Burdock 31
Beef with Coconut Butter 129
Beef with Peach Sauce 135
Beef with Quinces 152
Beetroot in Aspic 22
Beetroot—Borsch 23

Belgian Endive—Baked 56
With Cheese and Ham 56
With Cream 55
Berry Cheese 28
Beurre d'escargot 109
Bigarade Sauce 123
Bitter Melon and Braised Beef 106
Bitter-Sweet Haricot Beans 20
Black Soya Beans—Cantonese Lobster 21
Boiled Yams in Cheese Sauce 181
Borsch 23
Braised Beef and Bitter Melon 106
Braised Chicken with Mushrooms and Tiger Lilies
  96
Braised Duck with Olives 121
Braised Fennel 58
Braised Pork in Orange Sauce 124
Braised Pork with Pea Sprouts 140
Braised Vegetable Pear 137
Breast of Chicken with Lychee and Pineapple 98
Breadfruit and Bulls Testicles 29
Breadfruit Fritters 29
Breadfruit and Liver 29
Broad Beans with Bacon 16
Broad Beans in Poulette Sauce 16
Broccoli in Butter Sauce 30
Broccoli, Italian Style 30
Broccoli, puréed 30
Brussels Sprouts and Chestnuts 30
Bulls Testicles and Breadfruit 29
Burdock and Beef 31

Cabbage—cole slaw 35;
  fruit slaw 35
Cabbage Hearts with Crab Meat Sauce 36
Cabbage, red—with apples 34;
  with caraway seeds and allspice 34
Cabbage, Salted with Steamed Minced Pork 111
Cabbage—Sauerkraut 35
Cactus—Nopal Leaves—sautéed 37;
  scrambled 37
Canadian Baked Beans 20
Candied Peel 44
Candied Squash 171
Canned Bean Salad 20
Cantonese Lobster 21
Cape Gooseberry Compote 63
Cape Gooseberries, Glacé in Caramel 62
Capsicum Purée 84
Capsicum, Stuffed 84

Carrots, Apples and Cheese   38
Carrots marinated   38
Carrots and Onions, Sautéed   38
Carrot Purée with Rice   38
Cashew Nut—Velouté Sauce   115
Cauliflower—Baked   40; Fried   39
Cauliflower and Lettuce Soup   39
Celery Cabbage, Creamed   35
Celery Baked with Mushrooms   41
Celery, Chinese, Sautéed   41
Celery, Cooked, Salad   41
Celeriac, Mushrooms and Cheese   40
Celeriac and Potato Purée   40
Cheese, Baby Marrows Sautéed with   103
Cheese—Berry   28
Cheese, Carrots and Apples   38
Cheese, Celeriac and Mushrooms   40
Cheese and Ham with Belgian Endive   56
Cheese—Parmesan Mushrooms   110
   Eggplant Parmesan   55
Cheese and Vegetable Pear Sandwiches   137
Cheesecake, Grapefruit   65
Cherries with Claret   42
Cherry Fritters   42
Cherries Jubilee   42
Chervil and Sorrel Soup   86
Chestnuts and Brussels Sprouts   30
Chestnut and Veal Pudding   116
Chicken and Ambarella   4
Chicken, Braised with Tiger Lilies and Mushrooms   96
Chicken Breasts with Braised Bamboo Shoots   14
Chicken in Coconut Halves   128
Chicken and Hairy Melon Soup   103
Chicken Livers and Mushrooms   109
Chicken in Pomegranate Sauce   146
Chick Pea and Silver Beet Soup   139
Chili Con Carne   20
Chinese or White Cabbage for Cabbage Hearts
   with Crabmeat Sauce   36
Chinese or White Cabbage Soup   36
Chinese Gooseberry Dessert   63
Chinese Gooseberry Fruit Salad   63
Chinese Gooseberry Trifle   63
Chinese Sautéed Celery   41
Chocolate Macaroons   129
Chocolate Orange Peel   45
Chutney—Mango   101; Tamarind   174
Cloudberries, Berry Cheese   28
Coconut Butter   128
Coconut Butter—Beef with   129

Coconut Cream   129
Coconut Crisps, Toasted   129
Coconut Halves, Chicken in   128
Coconut and Pineapple Sauce   129
Cold Stewed Okra with Coriander   120
Cole Slaw   35
Cooked Celery Salad   41
Court Bouillon for Vegetables   58–9
Crab Apple Jelly   5
Creamed Celery Cabbage   35
Creamed Parsnips   132
Cream Sauce Salad Dressing   163
Crystallized Flowers   59
Csalamade   163
Cucumber Soup   47
Cucumber with Kidney Soup   47
Cucumber, Stuffed and Baked   47
Curried Jerusalem Artichokes   9
Curry Powder, Homemade   84
Curry Salad Dressing   163

Dandelion Purée   50
Dandelion Salad   50
Dates, Fresh, in Syrup   130
Devilled Tomatoes   176
Dip—Mango   101
   Pimento Cream   85
   Stuffed Olives   121
Duck Braised with Olives   121
Duck Braised with Taro   175
Duck with Pineapple   142

Eggplant Creole   55
Eggplant—Mousaka I   54
   Mousaka II   54
Eggplant and Okra   120
Eggplant Parmesan   55
Eggs and Sorrel Purée   86
Egg and Water Cress Tart   180
Endive, Belgian—Baked   56
   With Cream   55
   With Ham and Cheese   56

Feijoa Fruit Salad   58
Fennel Braised   58
Fig and Rhubarb Jelly   59
Fish Cakes and Lentils   95
Florentine Spinach   170
Flowers, Crystallized   59
French Pre-Cooked Vegetables   (xiii)
Fried Apple Rings   5

Fried Cauliflower   39
Fried Globe Artichokes   8
Fried Okra Rings   120
Fried Onion Rings   123
Fried Parsnips   132
Fried Salsify Cakes   166
Fritters—Breadfruit   29
    Cherry   42
    Leek   94
    Wattle   2
Fresh Dates in Syrup   130
Fruit Salads   165
Fruit Salad—Chinese Gooseberry   63
    Feijoa   58
    Pawpaw   134
    Tropical, with Mango Sauce   166
Fruit Slaw   35
Fruit and Vegetable Salad   165

Garlic Butter   85
Garlic Soup   85
Garlic Toast   85
Gazpacho   163
Gherkins, Pickled   62
Gingko Nut Sweetmeats   116
Glacé Cape Gooseberries in Caramel   62
Glacé Turnips   177
Globe Artichokes, Fried   8
Grapefruit Cheesecake   65
Grapefruit Jelly   65
Grapefruit and Persimmon Entrée   141
Grapefruit and Prawn Cocktail   66
Grape Leaves, Stuffed   67
Grapes and Spatchcocks   66
Greengage Sponge   144
Green Lima Beans—Succotash   16
Green Peas Francaise   138
Grilled Mushrooms   108
Guava Custard Pie   68

Hairy Melon and Chicken Soup   103
Half Orange Skins   45
Ham and Cheese with Belgian Endive   56
Ham and Winter Melon Broth   103
Haricot Beans with Banana   15
Haricot Beans, Bitter-sweet   20
Herbs and Spices—Matching Vegetables   71
    Recommended Uses & Preparation   70–83
Home Made Curry Powder   84
Horseradish and Apple Salad   5

Iced Melon Soup   105
Indonesian Tomato Sambal   176

Jackfruit Soup   90
Jam—Passion Fruit Skin   133
    Pawpaw   134
Jelly—Crab Apple   5
    Fig and Rhubarb   59
    Grapefruit   65
    Medlar   104
    Quince   152
    Sloe and Apple   169
Jerusalem Artichokes, Curried   9

Kidneys, Bacon and Mushrooms   109
Kidney Soup with Cucumber   47
Kohlrabi sautéed with Pork   91

Lamb Chops and Apricots   5
Leek Fritters   94
Leek Soup   94
Lemon Meringue Pie   95
Lemon Peel, Candied   44
Lentil Curry   95
Lentils and Fish Cakes   95
Lettuce and Cauliflower Soup   39
Lettuce, Sautéed   96
Lettuce Soup   96
Lime Julep   97
Liver and Breadfruit   29
Lotus Root or Stem Soup   97
Lotus Roots, Stuffed   98
Lychee and Pineapple with Breast of Chicken   98

Macedoine of Vegetables   138
Maitre d'hotel butter   109
Mango Chutney   101
    Dip   101
    Mousse   100
Mangoes Royale   101
Mango Sherbert   100
Marinated Carrots   38
Marrow Pie   102
Marrow, Stuffed   102
Malaysian Avocado Dessert   10
Mayonnaise   163
Medlar Jelly   104
Melon Soup, Iced   105
Melon Surprise   105
Mimosa Salad   163
Mint Syrup for Flavouring Watermelon   106

Mirepoix 85
Mousaka I 54
  II 54
Mushrooms, Celeriac and Cheese 40
Mushrooms and Celery, Baked 41
Mushrooms and Chicken Livers 109
Mushrooms in Greek Sauce 108
Mushrooms, Grilled 108
Mushrooms, Kidneys and Bacon 109
Mushrooms Parmesan 110
Mushrooms Sautéed 108
Mushroom and Spinach Entrée 170
Mushroom Stalk Purée 108
Mushrooms, Stuffed 110
Mustard Cream Salad Dressing 164
Mustard Greens Soup 110

Nectarines, Baked 114
Nicoise Salad 163
Nopal Leaves—Sautéed 37
  Scrambled 37

Okra, Cold, Stewed with Coriander 120
Okra and Eggplant 120
Okra Rings, Fried 120
Olives with Braised Duck 121
Olives, Stuffed for Dip 121
Onions, Pickled 123
Onion Rings, Fried 123
Orange and Asparagus Casserole 123
Orange Bigarade Sauce 123
Orange Peel, Candied 44
Orange Peel, Chocolate 44
Orange Sauce, Pork Braised in 124
Orange Segments in Spiced Claret 124
Orange Skins—Half 45
Orange, Veal a l'orange 124
'Out of this world' Fruit and Vegetable Salad 165

Parsnips and Apples, Baked 132
Parsnips—Creamed 132
  Fried 132
Passion Fruit Pavlova 133
Passion Fruit and Pineapple Cream 133
Passion Fruit Punch 132
Passion Fruit Skin Jam 133
Pawpaw—Appetizer 134
  Jam 134
  Fruit Salad 134
  Liqueur 134
  Surprise 134

Peaches in Brandy 135
Peach Melba 135
Peach Sauce with Beef 135
Peanut Crisps 117
Peanut and Plum Pie 144
Peanut Sauce 117
Peas, Green, Francaise 138
Pea Sprouts with Braised Pork 140
Pear and Apricot Flan 136
Pears Baked in Claret 136
Pear Condé 136
Pease Pudding 139
Peel, Candied 44
Persimmon and Grapefruit Entrée 141
Persimmon and Pineapple Entrée 141
Persimmon Sauce with Pork 141
Pickled Gherkins 62
Pickled Onions 123
Pickled Turnips 177
Pickled Walnuts 118
Pies—Ackee 3
  Guava Custard 68
  Lemon Meringue 95
  Marrow 102
  Plum 144
  Plum and Peanut 144
  Pumpkin 149
Pimento Cream Dip 85
Pineapple and Coconut Sauce 129
Pineapple Duck 142
Pineapple Fruit Loaf 142
Pineapple with Ham 142
Pineapple and Passion Fruit Cream 133
Pineapple and Persimmon Entrée 141
Pineapple Sauce 142
Plantain Stew 143
Plum, Greengage Sponge 144
Plum Pie 144
Plum and Peanut Pie 144
Pomegranate Sauce for Chicken 146
Pomegranate Soup 145
Pork—Braised in Orange Sauce 124
  Braised with Pea Sprouts 140
  Minced and Steamed with Salted Cabbage 111
  With Persimmon Sauce 141
Pork and Salted Mustard Greens 111
Pork and Water Chestnut Dumplings 43
Potatoes—
  Boiled 146
  Baked 146
  Chips 147

Cubed   147
Deep Fried   147
French Fried   147
Matchsticks   147
Sautéed   147
Stuffed   147
Potato Balls with Cheese   147
Potato and Celeriac Purée   40, 147
Potato Salad   163
Potato Salad with Asparagus Tips   147
Prawn and Grapefruit Cocktail   66
Pumpkin Omelette   149
Pumpkin Pie   149

Quince Jelly   152
Quince Paste   152
Quinces Sautéed with Beef   153
Quinces, Stuffed   153

Radishes in Cream   156
Radishes in Meat Stock   156
Radish Top Fricassée   156
Raspberries—Berry Cheese   28
Red Cabbage—With Apples   34
    With Caraway Seeds and Allspice   34
Red Kidney Bean—Chili Con Carne   20
Remoulade Salad Dressing   164
Rhubarb and Fig Jelly   59
Rhubarb Punch   157
Rhubarb Stewed with Cardamoms   157
Rice with Carrot Purée   38
Russian Salad   163
Russian Salad Dressing   164

Sage Claret   85
Salad—
    Antipasto   162
    Caesar   163
    Canned Bean   20
    Cooked Celery   41
    Csalamade   163
    Dandelion   50
    Gazpacho   163
    Horseradish and Apple   5
    Meat and Eggs   162
    Mimosa   163
    Nicoise   163
    Potato   163
    Russian   163
    Vegetable Salads   160–1
    Waldorf   163

Salad Dressings   163–5
Salad Dressing—Anchovy   163
    Cream Sauce   163
    Curry   163
    Mayonnaise   163–4
    Mustard Cream   164
    Pimento Cream   85
    Remoulade   164
    Russian Dressing   164
    Sweet and Sour   164
    Tartare Sauce   164
    Vinaigrette   164
    Vineyard Dressing   165
Salisfy Cakes, Fried   166
Salted Mustard Greens and Pork   111
Sapodilla Wine   167
Sauces—
    Butter   30
    Cheese   181
    Coconut and pineapple   129
    Crab Meat   36
    Mango   166
    Orange   124
    Orange bigarade   123
    Peach   135
    Persimmon   141
    Pineapple   142
    Pineapple and coconut   129
    Pomegranate   145
    Poulette   16
    Tomato   176
Sauerkraut   35
Sautéed Baby Marrows   102
Sautéed Baby Marrows with Cheese   103
Sautéed Carrots and Onions   38
Sautéed Kohlrabi with Pork   91
Sautéed Lettuce   96
Sautéed Mushrooms   108
Sautéed Nopal Leaves   37
Sautéed Quinces and Beef   153
Schnitzels, Bananas and Cheese   15
Scrambled Nopal Leaves   37
Sea-Kale Croquettes   167
Seaweed Soup   169
Silver Beet and Chick Pea Soup   139
Silver Beet—The Spanish Way   23
    Vinaigrette Sauce for   22
Snow Peas with Prawns   140
Sloe and Apple Jelly   169
Sorrel and Chervil Soup   86
Sorrel Puree and Eggs   86

197

Soup—
    Cauliflower and Lettuce 39
    Chicken and Hairy Melon 103
    Cucumber 47
    Garlic 85
    Iced Melon 105
    Jackfruit 90
    Kidney with Cucumber 47
    Leek 94
    Lettuce 96
    Lotus Root or Stem 97
    Mustard Greens 110
    Pomegranate 145
    Seaweed 169
    Sorrel and Chervil 86
    Spanish Almond 115
    Winter Melon 103
    Winter Melon and Ham Broth 103
Spanish Almond Soup 115
Spatchcock and Grapes 66
Spiced Sweet Potatoes 148
Spinach, Florentine 170
Spinach and Mushroom Entrée 170
Split Peas—Pease Pudding 139
Squash, Candied 171
Squash, Sweet for Breakfast 171
Steamed Minced Pork and Salted Cabbage 111
Stewed Rhubarb with Cardamoms 157
Stock, Vegetable 58–9
Strawberries, Berry Cheese 28
Stuffed and Baked Cucumber 47
Stuffed Capsicum 84
Stuffed Globe Artichokes 8
Stuffed Grape Leaves 67
Stuffed Lotus Roots 98
Stuffed Marrow 102
Stuffed Mushrooms 110
Stuffed Olives Dip 121
Stuffed Quinces 153
Sweet Corn Stew 46
Sweet Potato Dessert 148
Sweet Potato Kebabs 148
Sweet Potatoes, Spiced 148
Sweet and Sour Salad Dressing 164
Sweet Squash for Breakfast 171

Tamarind Chutney 174
Tamarind Fried Fish 174
Tamarind Juice 174
Tamarind Syrup 174
Taro with Braised Duck 175
Tartare Sauce Salad Dressing 164
Tiger Lilies with Braised Chicken and Mushrooms 96

Toasted Coconut Crisps 129
Tomato Aspic 175
Tomatoes, Devilled 176
Tomato Eggs 176
Tomato, Sambal Indonesian 176
Tomato Sauce 176
Tropical Fruit Salad with Mango Sauce 166
Turnips Glacé 177
Turnips Pickled 177

Veal and Chestnut Pudding 116
Veal a l'Orange 124
Vegetables—
    Cooking (xii)
    Deep Frying (xiii)
    French Pre-Cooked (xiii)
    Macedoine of 138
    Matching Herbs and Spices 71
    Pan Shaking (xiii)
    Preparation (xii)
    Raw Tenderizing (xii)
    Steam with Butter (xii)
    Stir Frying (xiii)
    Types (xiii)
Vegetable Pear, Braised 137
Vegetable Pear and Cheese Sandwiches 137
Vegetable Pear Meringue 137
Vegetable Pear, Tomatoes and Onions 137
Vegetable Salad, Fruit and 165
Vegetable Stock 58–9
Velouté Sauce 115
Vinaigrette 164
Vinaigrette Sauce for Silver Beet 22
Vineyard Salad Dressing 165

Waldorf Salad 163
Walnut Meringues 118
Walnuts, Pickled 118
Water Chestnuts and Pork Dumplings 43
Water Cress and Egg Tart 180
Watermelon, Mint Syrup for Flavouring 106
Watermelon Glacé 106
Wattle Fritters 2
White or Chinese Cabbage for Cabbage Hearts with Crabmeat Sauce 36
White or Chinese Cabbage Soup 36
Winter Melon and Ham Broth 103
Winter Melon Soup 103
'Winter Vegetable' Salted Cabbage and Steamed Minced Pork 111

Yams, Boiled in Cheese Sauce 181
Yam and Haricots 181
Yam Soufflé 181

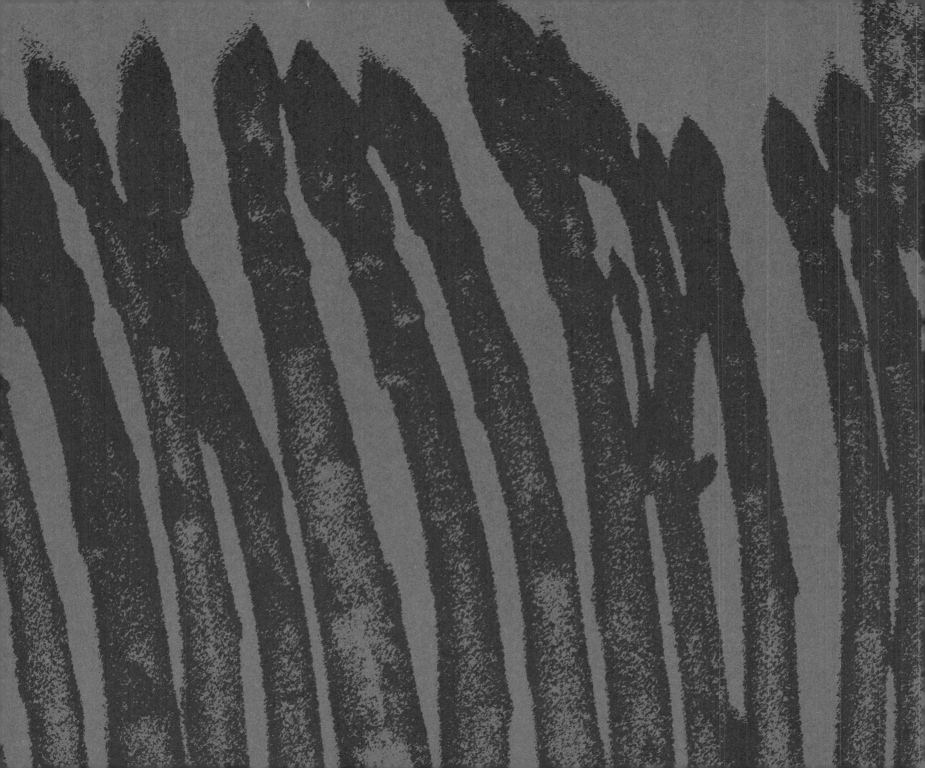